STANDARD REFERENCE LIBRARY
THROUGH-THE-BIBLE COMMENTARY

NEW TESTAMENT VOLUME ONE

The Life and Ministry of Jesus

THE GOSPELS

compiled by Douglas Redford

Standard®
PUBLISHING
Bringing The Word to Life

Cincinnati, Ohio

Library of Congress Cataloging in Publication data:
Redford, Doug, 1953-
  The life and ministry of Jesus : the Gospels / compiled by Douglas Redford.
    p. cm. -- (Standard reference library. New Testament ; v. 1)
  ISBN 0-7847-1900-4 (casebound)
  1. Jesus Christ--Biography. I. Title.
BT301.3.R43 2007
226'.07--dc22   2006029563

Published by Standard Publishing, Cincinnati, Ohio.
www.standardpub.com

Table of Contents

Introduction

FROM OUR HOUSE TO YOURS

At the conclusion of the series of parables recorded in Matthew 13, Jesus offered a striking comparison. He had been offering a variety of comparisons to the kingdom of heaven, challenging his hearers to consider what that kingdom is like. He closed, however, not with a reference to the kingdom but to a particular type of individual: "Therefore every teacher of the law who has been instructed about the kingdom of heaven is like the owner of a house who brings out of his storeroom new treasures as well as old" (Matthew 13:52).

The volume you hold in your hands is an effort to take from a "storeroom" both "new treasures as well as old" and include them into what we at Standard Publishing hope will be a source of treasures to students of the Bible for years to come. The "storeroom" is the *Standard Lesson Commentary*®—a resource that has provided instruction and encouragement to untold numbers of Sunday school teachers and students ever since the first edition appeared for use in 1954. (Standard Publishing had been printing adult Sunday school materials since the 19th century, but not in the format that came to be known as the *Standard Lesson Commentary*®.)

THE PASSION FROM THE BEGINNING

The basis for the lessons in every *Commentary* has been the International Sunday School Lessons. These lessons are arranged in six-year cycles to provide for every teacher and student who uses these lessons a survey of the Bible's significant people and principles. By the end of each cycle, the individual who has taken part in this survey should "graduate" with an enhanced understanding of what the Bible is all about. Of course, no Christian can ever truly "graduate" from the study of God's Word; in fact, a lifetime of study could not exhaust the treasures that one can mine, even from passages as familiar as John 3:16 or the parable of the Good Samaritan. Thus whenever a new cycle begins, the student can prepare to embark on a fresh examination of the Bible's timeless truth.

The strength of the *Standard Lesson Commentary*® over the years has always been its thorough treatment of the lesson Scripture text. Whenever Standard Publishing has conducted a survey to obtain input from users about the

Commentary's strengths and weaknesses, the verse-by-verse study of the Scriptures has been cited as the primary reason people continue to use the *Commentary*. In a world that increasingly denies the existence of any absolute truth, people are hungry for materials that simply explain the truth of what the Bible has to say.

Over the years, new features have been added to the *Commentary*, such as suggested learning activities, Bible helps (such as maps, charts, and time lines), and "Teacher Tips" to help teachers carry out their vital ministry with maximum effectiveness. The heart of every *Commentary*, however, has always been a passion to explain God's Word as clearly as possible to God's people.

THE PROJECT IN PREPARATION

When the project that has produced the volume you are now holding was first discussed, it was apparent that the verse-by-verse treatment of Scripture had to receive top priority. The result is what we have referred to as a "reference library" for teacher, preachers, and other church leaders. For that matter, anyone who desires a source of further insight into God's Word can benefit from the contents. This is a tool that could well be labeled a "best of" the *Standard Lesson Commentary*® over its fifty-plus years of existence. Eventually this project will culminate in a five-volume set of books; three will cover the Old Testament, and two will cover the New Testament. We have begun the series, as you can see, with a volume of lessons on the life of Christ, to be followed by a second volume on the remainder of the New Testament.

It is, of course, impossible in a project such as this to treat every passage in the Bible. (The *Standard Lesson Commentary*® itself has not covered every passage in the Bible in more than 50 years of publication.) What we have done is to select certain key passages that have been covered on different occasions throughout the history of the *Commentary*. Then we have attempted to choose the most insightful, most helpful portions of commentary in order to present to you, the user, a tool that you will find of continual benefit in your own ministry of teaching and preaching the treasures of the Bible.

The format for each chapter has been kept purposefully simple. Under the title of each chapter is a list of the passages to be examined within that chapter. Each passage is then studied under two main headings: *Establishing the Groundwork* and *Examining the Text*. The *Groundwork* section aims to place a passage in its proper context, providing background information about the significant people, places, and events. For example, the texts covered in this volume all deal with the life of Christ. The *Groundwork* portion will explain where in Jesus' life and ministry the passage occurred, and it will also seek to provide a smooth transition between passages so that the flow of thought is maintained.

The *Examining the Text* portion will do what has made the *Standard Lesson Commentary*® the invaluable resource it has become over the years: provide a verse-by-verse explanation of the Biblical text being considered. (The *New International Version* is the text of the Bible that is printed in boldface type.) In some cases, two or more verses will be grouped together (for example, verses that describe something that took place within one of Jesus' parables). But as one could imagine, so much has been written about certain texts over the years the *Commentary* has been produced that many verses have been "mined" quite often—and with new and different insights every time! Such is the nature of the riches to be obtained from God's Word.

THE PEOPLE WHO HAVE CONTRIBUTED

In thinking about the many insights that have been offered on the Bible through the years the *Commentary* has been published, we would be remiss if we did not recognize the contributions of many special people—those who have worked for Standard Publishing in editing the materials and those preachers, Bible college professors, and other Christian leaders who have accepted the assignments to provide the lesson commentary and have met the necessary deadlines. In particular, we should mention the efforts of Orrin Root, who, as editor-in-chief of Standard Publishing's Sunday school materials, oversaw the production of the first *Standard Lesson Commentary*®. Mr. Root went to be with the Lord on May 13, 2003, at the age of 98. Even in his 90s, Mr. Root had continued to accept assignments to write commentary on an entire quarter's worth of material, and he consistently submitted his work on time and with a quality that reflected a steadfast commitment to both Biblical accuracy and grammatical clarity. The 2004-2005 edition of the *Commentary* included his last contribution and marked the thirty-third consecutive edition in which he was writer or co-writer of one full quarter of the verse-by-verse exposition of the Scripture text.

One of Mr. Root's favorite pieces of advice to aspiring writers and editors was this: "Write and edit not only to be understood, but also not to be misunderstood." If the volumes to be produced within this set can adhere to that advice and reflect the quality for which Orrin Root became so highly respected, this effort will have accomplished its goal.

With these thoughts in mind, we present to you the first of this series of studies from our house (at Standard Publishing) to yours. At the same time, we acknowledge that we are not really the "owner" (to use Jesus' word) of this material; we are simply stewards who have been given a trust to be faithful (1 Corinthians 4:2) in how we handle the precious treasures of God's Word. That Word tells us that "man does not live on bread alone but on every word that comes from the mouth of the Lord" (Deuteronomy 8:3). Our prayer is that these treasures will become ever clearer and ever dearer to you.

Chapter 1

"The Word Became Flesh"
Luke 1:1-4; John 1:1-18

LUKE'S TESTIMONY (LUKE 1:1-4)

Establishing the Groundwork

The New Testament writers were insistent on establishing the truth of their message. They wanted people to know that Jesus was real, not a creation of their imaginations. They wanted to confirm that people had seen, heard, and touched him.

In recent generations, certain scholars have considered it fashionable to question the historical reliability of the four biographers of Jesus—Matthew, Mark, Luke, and John. These scholars claim to be engaged in a search for the "historical Jesus," suggesting that the world has been waiting for *them* to discover just who Jesus really was, how he actually lived, and precisely what he taught. Their assumption is that ancient historians lacked the objectivity that is essential to accurate reporting, or that they were moved more by emotional, doctrinal, or legendary motives and sources than by an impartial, investigative technique.

These criticisms are lengthy and involved, but essentially unconvincing. In support of the work of Luke, there are some factors that cannot be ignored. First, he was a well-educated man, accustomed to dealing with facts. As a physician (Paul calls him "our dear friend Luke, the doctor" in Colossians 4:14), Luke recognized the importance of getting all relevant information and getting it accurately. Second, his research was intensive. Investigating everything related to the life story of Jesus, he wrote from the direct testimony of eyewitnesses rather than rely on hearsay. Third, Luke's testimony sprang from the totally unselfish motive of a man who was sure of his convictions and stood by them, not for personal gain, but because he had a vital message to share.

But the most vital factor by far is the work of the inspiration of the Holy Spirit. In Jesus' last message to the apostles before his crucifixion, he promised to send the Counselor to dwell within them. Among the reassurances given was the promise that the Spirit would "remind you of everything I have said to you," and "guide you into all truth" (John 14:26; 16:13). What historian would not want a resource such as these apostles—men who would never forget what they had heard or been told, and who would be guided in the discovery and relating of all pertinent facts? While Luke was not one of the original twelve apostles, he was surely guided in his effort by the same Spirit who guided them and who was responsible for the inspiration of all Scripture (2 Timothy 3:16; 2 Peter 1:20, 21). In view of all these factors, it is not unreasonable for us to believe that Jesus, as he is presented to us by Luke and the other Gospel writers, actually lived on earth, did and said the things reported by these writers, and was indeed who he claimed to be.

Luke is also the author of Acts, as indicated by the fact that both Luke and Acts are addressed to "Theophilus" (Luke 1:3; Acts 1:1). (The "former book" mentioned in Acts 1:1 is Luke's Gospel.) Luke was a close associate of the apostle Paul, as indicated by the various "we" passages in Acts that show Luke's presence with Paul on certain occasions (Acts 16:10-17; 20:5—21:18; 27:1—28:16). Some suggest that Luke may have been one of Paul's converts. In Philemon 24, he is listed among Paul's "fellow workers." In 2 Timothy 4:11 he is listed as one of the last to be with Paul as Paul's martyrdom approached.

The specific verses from Luke included in this study clearly demonstrate with what great care this man prepared for his task of writing a record of the life of his (and our) Lord Jesus.

Examining the Text

I. Received from Eyewitnesses (Luke 1:1, 2)

¹ Many have undertaken to draw up an account of the things that have been fulfilled among us,

While we generally think of four Gospels, Luke records that *many* in his day had *undertaken to draw up an account of the things that* Jesus had done. Just what accounts did he have in mind? There is no way of knowing. Was he referring to the Gospels we have in our Bibles? Some of these may be included. Luke's Gospel is often dated at around AD 60, which would place his writing after Matthew's and Mark's but before John's. Luke surely was also including some accounts that were not inspired and have not been preserved to the present. Apparently many disciples were eager to preserve an account of what had transpired during the earthly life of Jesus. Some of the accounts perhaps were inaccurate because they had been written without careful investigation and without guidance from the Holy Spirit. Luke, of course, does not intend any criticism of the inspired records of the other Gospel writers.

In fact, Luke did not actually criticize the accuracy of any of the other efforts to set forth a record of Christ's life. He may have believed that these records were simply incomplete or perhaps not as orderly as they should have been. He undertook his writing, therefore, not to correct misinformation but to substantiate the things that Christians already knew and believed about Jesus. These early writings disappeared, probably because their content was included in the more systematic and thorough accounts of the four Gospels that have been preserved for us.

The word *fulfilled* occurs frequently in the Gospels to indicate the link between the events of Jesus' life and ministry and the words of Old Testament prophecies. It should cause us to reflect on the fact that these events were no accident; they were part of a divinely orchestrated plan. Near the end of his record, Luke records how the resurrected Christ declared to his followers, "Everything must be fulfilled that is written about me in the Law of Moses, the Prophets and the Psalms" (Luke 24:44).

> [2] *. . . just as they were handed down to us by those who from the first were eyewitnesses and servants of the word.*

Luke was not an eyewitness of any of the events of the earthly life of Jesus, but he received accurate information from those who were. The terms *eyewitnesses and servants* are very interesting in light of Luke's medical background. The first is from the same word from which we get our word *autopsy.* It had to do with the personal examination of a body: in this case, a body of facts. *Servants* is from a word that referred to the assistants who served under the direction of another. In a medical context, it might refer to one who assisted a surgeon or chief physician. Thus the *servants of the word* could be viewed as carrying out their duties under the direction of the "Great Physician," Jesus.

No doubt Luke spoke with as many of those who were directly involved in the events of Jesus' life as possible—all who were still living at the time in which he undertook his writing. For example, it is very likely that Luke conferred with Mary, the mother of Jesus. Of all the Gospel writers, he alone mentions the visit of the angel Gabriel to Mary before the birth of Jesus, the shepherds in the fields near Bethlehem, the manger, and other details connected with the birth and infancy of Jesus. Luke could also have spoken to some of the women who supported Jesus' ministry (Luke 8:2, 3) or to Jesus' brothers (Mark 6:3).

Those who view the stories of Jesus as legends or myths have to reckon with the fact that there was but a brief period of time between when the events took place and when the written works began to appear. There were people alive who could verify the truthfulness of the Gospel accounts. Matthew, Mark, and Luke were written within about thirty years of Jesus' death. It takes much longer than thirty years to create a legend. The Gospel accounts are not accumulations or collections of such legends. They are records written by men inspired of God, two of whom (Matthew and John) were themselves with Jesus and two (Mark and Luke) who most surely conferred with eyewitnesses.

The inspiration of Scripture does not mean that a writer could not use his own personality or that his writing would not reflect his own style. Notice that in Luke's case, the Holy Spirit inspired him to talk to eyewitnesses. The doctrine of inspiration does not require that every word of Scripture be supplied by God directly. Inspiration is the process by which God guarded the words that were written, whether they came by revelation from God, from the author's memory or research, or from another source. Together, revelation and inspiration have produced for us a Bible that is reliable and trustworthy, completely inerrant in the original manuscripts.

II. An Orderly Account (Luke 1:3, 4)

³ Therefore, since I myself have carefully investigated everything from the beginning, it seemed good also to me to write an orderly account for you, most excellent Theophilus,

Luke approached his work with a passion for accuracy. He did not just put together whatever stories or rumors drifted into his mind. Rather, he *carefully investigated everything*; he made strenuous efforts to obtain accurate, authentic information, separating fact from rumor.

From the beginning in this case includes much more than the beginning of Jesus' earthly life. Luke's Gospel actually begins with the appearance of Gabriel to Zechariah, announcing the birth of a son to him and his barren wife Elizabeth. That son, of course, was John, the forerunner of Jesus.

It seemed good also to me to write. What prompted Luke to write what he did? As noted earlier, it appears that Matthew and Mark had written their accounts of Jesus by the time Luke began his; and John later compiled another. Matthew, in his writing, referred to many Old Testament prophecies that were fulfilled in Christ. This would be of great significance in evangelizing the Jews but of lesser concern to Gentiles. Mark wrote a brief, swiftly moving account, stressing the deeds of the Lord—a record that would appeal more to the Romans. Luke wrote in superb literary style, in a manner that would not fail to impress cultured Greeks such as himself. John later provided supplementary material not included by the other three writers.

In addition, Luke mentions compiling an *orderly account.* Although his account is written by and large in chronological fashion, this expression is not a promise that every single detail is related in chronological sequence. It may simply mean that Luke wrote in an orderly, and not a haphazard, manner. Sometimes the order is chronological and sometimes topical, but it is always carefully and deliberately ordered.

In this verse, Luke also mentions the name of the person to whom he has addressed his account: *most excellent Theophilus*. The name *Theophilus* means "friend of God" or "lover of God." Some have therefore suggested that this is a designation of all friends and lovers of God wherever they may be. Theophilus might thus represent all Christians. Others propose that Theophilus was an otherwise unknown Christian who was the recipient of Luke's accounts of Jesus' life (Luke) and the life of the early church (Acts). The expression *most excellent* suggests that he was either a high government official or a person otherwise deserving high honor. It is similar to a title such as "Your Excellency." (The same title is translated this way in Acts 23:26.) Some have suggested that Theophilus was a Roman official somehow connected with Paul's trial in Rome. Those who hold this position believe that Theophilus was involved in Paul's defense in court, and needed an orderly account of the life of Jesus in order to learn more about the Christian message. Still another view is that Theophilus was a benefactor who supported Luke in the production of his writings.

On the other hand, we cannot be absolutely certain that Theophilus was a Christian at the time Luke wrote his Gospel. Luke's intention may have been to write this account in order to win Theophilus to Christ. Those who espouse this position point out that later, when Luke wrote Acts to the same individual, he dropped the title and addressed him simply as "Theophilus" (Acts 1:1). Perhaps the title was omitted because by this point Theophilus was a Christian brother and the title was not necessary.

⁴ . . . so that you may know the certainty of the things you have been taught.

The word *certainty* conveys the idea that the matters about which Luke was writing were matters of fact, not fiction; of history, not myth; of reality, not romance. Whatever Theophilus's spiritual condition may have been, Luke's record would provide an accurate standard by which to measure all that he was hearing about Jesus. Through the centuries millions of people have continued to benefit from Luke's precise, orderly account of the life of Christ.

JOHN'S TESTIMONY (JOHN 1:1-18)

Establishing the Groundwork

The Gospels written by Matthew, Mark, and Luke tell us about John, the son of Zebedee and brother of James, who was called from his fishing business to become an apostle of Jesus (Matthew 4:21, 22; Mark 1:19, 20; Luke 5:8-11). This John also wrote a Gospel account, some thirty years after the others wrote theirs. Nowhere in this Gospel does John mention himself by name; however, by comparing material in this Gospel with that in the other three, we can conclude that the writer was the apostle John. He usually refers to himself as "the disciple whom Jesus loved" (John 13:23; 21:7, 20; cf. 19:26; 20:2), apparently to keep himself in the background of his writing. Along with his brother James, John was among Jesus' first disciples. It is generally assumed that John was directed to Jesus by John the Baptist, whom he and Andrew had followed earlier (John 1:35-40).

Jesus nicknamed James and John *Boanerges,* meaning "sons of thunder" (Mark 3:17), apparently from their highly temperamental personalities (Luke 9:51-55). Nevertheless, John was so completely transformed by his acquaintance with Jesus that he came to be known as the apostle of love—a theme that permeates his writings, particularly his three epistles. Along with Simon Peter (another temperamental fisherman), the sons of Zebedee became Jesus' closest followers, sharing with him significant experiences not shared by the other disciples (Mark 5:37; 9:2; 14:33). John seems to have done his writing—his Gospel, his three brief epistles, and the book of Revelation—later in a long life. Most students date these writings toward the end of the first century.

Many believe, on the basis of his long career, that John was the youngest of the apostles in the time of Jesus. Along with Peter and James the brother of Jesus, John was a leader in the early church (Galatians 2:9). The Scriptures give us little specific information about the closing years of his life. The book of Revelation informs us that John lived for a time in exile on the island of Patmos (Revelation 1:9). Traditions of the early church relate that John became a resident of Ephesus, where he taught and influenced the church for many years.

John's Gospel is different from the other three in several respects. It says nothing of Jesus' birth or early life; it tells more of his ministry in Judea and less of his work in Galilee; it focuses on Jesus' discourses rather than his parables; it includes more of Jesus' one-on-one encounters; and it highlights strong contrasts—life and death, light and darkness, spirit and flesh, truth and falsehood, love and hate. Mentioned among the one-on-one encounters are the following individuals: Nicodemus (3:1-21), the Samaritan woman at the well in Sychar (4:4-42), the woman who had been taken in adultery (8:3-11), the man born blind (9:1-41), and Mary and Martha just prior to the raising of Lazarus (11:17-37).

John's prologue is also unique. Nothing in the other Gospels (or elsewhere in Scripture) compares with the description of God's revelation of himself found in these verses. It begins with an introduction of Jesus as the eternal Word, active in creation, but who then "became flesh and made his dwelling among us" (John 1:14). The prologue is interrupted briefly (in verses 6-8) by a reference to John the Baptist as the man sent from God to announce Jesus' coming.

Examining the Text

I. The Eternal Word (John 1:1-5)
A. The Word and God (vv. 1, 2)

¹ In the beginning was the Word, and the Word was with God, and the Word was God.

The Gospel of John begins with a simplicity that camouflages its sublime and profound message. The opening words of Genesis are used by John deliberately: *In the beginning.* The apostle will soon discuss a new creation or "new birth" (John 3:3), to be accomplished through Jesus Christ. These words, as we will see, introduce the relationship of Jesus to the first creation.

The term *word* was important in Hebrew thought as God's vehicle of creation. He spoke, and things came into being (Psalm 33:6). *Word* also designated his command; the term *Ten Commandments* is literally, in the Hebrew text, "ten words." Prophets often introduced God's messages with "Hear the word of the Lord."

This term was also important to first-century Greeks. *Logos,* which is the Greek term translated as "word," signified thought and reason as well as a unit of speech or writing. It is difficult to determine whether John had one of these specific ideas in mind by his use of this concept. Perhaps he simply chose a term that people had been using for years and with which his readers were familiar in order to show them that the divine Word entered into the arena of our existence in a real person, Jesus Christ. This point will become clearer in verse 14, although John will not specifically mention the name of Jesus Christ until verse 17.

Still another possibility is that John simply wanted to emphasize with his use of *Word* that God is a God who communicates, who reveals, who speaks to his creation. Thus John's interest was not so much in philosophical speculation, but in revelation. By the guidance of the Holy Spirit, John chose the term with which to identify Jesus, and what an appropriate term it was! A word is something that communicates. It carries an idea or ideas from the speaker to the hearer or from the writer to the reader. Jesus was God's living Word, just as the Bible is God's written Word. He brought God's thoughts to us. He revealed God's nature and God's will.

The Word was with God. John now begins to reveal the identity of the Word. This statement highlights two truths: the eternality of Christ and his separate personality. In Genesis, the *beginning* refers to a specific point in time when created matter was called into existence by divine fiat. Here in John, the reference is to eternity, which has no beginning. The human mind is incapable of grasping fully the concept of eternity, which has no beginning. But even if we cannot comprehend it, John's point is clear. Before time or matter was, the Word was with God.

The Greek preposition *with* conveys not only proximity but also the idea of motion toward. Some even suggest that it carries the idea of "face to face." Again, a distinct being is recognized, as indicated in Genesis 1:26: "Let *us* make man in *our* image." The Word was with God—not only in his presence but with him in the sense of agreeing with all his purposes and doings. In his prayer given on the eve of his crucifixion, Jesus speaks of "the glory I had with you before the world began" (John 17:5).

The Word was God. John now climaxes his affirmations about the Word in this single verse. Jesus not only existed from the beginning and was with God, but he *was God*. The Scriptures consistently affirm the deity of him who came to earth as Jesus of Nazareth (John 20:28; Romans 9:5; Colossians 2:9; Hebrews 1:1-4). John does not say that the Word was one of many gods such as the pagans might worship, nor does he say that the Word was like God. Rather, he affirms that the Word was God. Jesus did not begin his existence when he was born to Mary. He is eternal.

² *He was with God in the beginning.*

The repetition here of a portion of verse one gives emphasis, underscoring what has been said as of paramount importance. It is far more than a literary device; it is a profound reaffirmation of a spectacular truth.

During the past two thousand years, the nature of the Word and his relationship to God have been frequently debated. Some theologians have denied the deity of Christ, making him inferior to, or less than, God. Such denials are based on human speculation rather than divine revelation. With finite minds we will never be able to comprehend the eternal mysteries of God, but we can anchor our faith squarely in the Scriptures, refusing to profess wisdom beyond what is written. To deny that the Word is truly God is to undermine God's plan for our redemption. The incarnation (a word that literally means "in flesh") plays a vital part in God's purpose for humanity. If the Word is not God who became man through the incarnation, then we do not have a sinless high priest who is able to sympathize with our weaknesses and through whom we may approach the throne of grace with confidence (Hebrews 4:15, 16).

B. The Word and Creation (v. 3)

³ Through him all things were made; without him nothing was made that has been made.

John now tells us that the Word was involved in the creation of the physical universe. This teaching is also found in verse 10, in Colossians 1:16, and in Hebrews 1:2. Jesus' involvement in creation is further evidence of his deity, since the Old Testament ascribes the creation to God (Genesis 1:1; Exodus 20:11; Psalm 33:6-9). Notice that the teaching in this verse is stated both positively and negatively for emphasis. Positively, we are told that *through* the Word *all things were made*, that is, by his creative activity and power. Negatively, John tells us that not even one thing that *was made* came into being *without* the Word.

It may be that this particular emphasis of John was intended to combat the teaching of a group called the Gnostics, whose teachings were infiltrating the church toward the end of the first century. The Gnostics taught that all matter is evil. Creation, therefore, could not have been the work of God; instead, it must have been produced by an "emanation" from God that was so far removed from him as to have become a hostile, evil force. Thus, all material items are corrupt and evil; and God in his purity would never desire any contact with anything material.

"Not so," John would say. Matter is not evil, but is the creation of God and is very good (Genesis 1:31). All things were created by God, not by an evil emanation, and the Word was his agent in creation. Later in this passage, John will provide another refutation of Gnostic teaching by his declaration that "the Word became flesh" (verse 14).

C. The Word and Light (vv. 4, 5)

⁴ In him was life, and that life was the light of men.

Not only did the Word live, but he also imparted *life* to all other living things. One of the greatest mysteries confronting modern scientists is the origin of life. No scientist has even come close to giving an adequate explanation of this mystery. Yet John gives us that answer very simply: *In him was life.*

Of course, we need not limit this to physical life; indeed, the stated purpose of John's Gospel is "that you may believe that Jesus is the Christ, the Son of God, and that by believing you may have life in his name" (John 20:31). John also includes references to the "eternal life" (John 3:16) and the life "to the full" (John 10:10) that Jesus came to bring. And only John cites Jesus' declaration, "I am the bread of life" (John 6:35).

John also adds that *that life was the light of men*. What does this mean? Several interpretations are possible, and perhaps all of them are included in John's statement. According to the opening verses of Genesis, the whole earth was in darkness until God declared, "Let there be light" (Genesis 1:3). Where did that light come from? It came from the living Word, the agent through which everything was created, as John has already said. We call the sun the source of light, and so it is. But it is not the ultimate source. Where does the sun get its light? Again, from the living Word, the creative Word.

Man has a light of intelligence immeasurably brighter than that of the animals. Where did that brighter light come from? It came from the life in the Word. For ages, men willing to be guided have been guided by the light of God's revelation; and this too comes to them by God's Communicator, the Word, who declared, "I am the light of the world" (John 8:12). Paul develops this theme and links it to God's creative activity in Genesis when he tells the Corinthians, "For God, who said, 'Let light shine out of darkness,' made his light shine in our hearts to give us the light of the knowledge of the glory of God in the face of Christ" (2 Corinthians 4:6). With the Father, Jesus will be the light of that heavenly city where no sun or moon is needed (Revelation 21:23).

It is worth noting that the terms *life* and *light* and also *love* are key words in John's writings, used often and meaningfully. These are three such simple words, yet John, guided by the Holy Spirit, uses them to convey spiritual truths that continue to have an impact on those who allow the love, life, and light of Christ to transform them.

⁵ **The light shines in the darkness, but the darkness has not understood it.**

It is in contrast with *darkness* that *light* demonstrates its merit and its usefulness. When God said, "Let there be light," the darkness was driven back on earth. That is a symbol of the age-long conflict between the light of God and the darkness of sin. In this particular context, the phrase *the light shines in darkness* most likely refers specifically to God's efforts to reach people through the incarnation of his Son, although it may also be seen in a broader sense to apply to the efforts of his Word to do so through the years.

The present tense of the verb *shines* is significant. The light of Christ continues to shine amidst the moral and spiritual darkness of our times, just as it did in the darkness of first-century paganism. If his light is not dispelling the darkness around it, it is because its handlers have kept it hidden! Jesus is the "light of the world," (John 8:12), but so are his followers (Matthew 5:14-16).

The darkness has not understood it. The Greek word rendered as *understood* may be taken in two ways—perhaps best illustrated by the English word "grasp." One may grasp something or someone physically in the sense of "seize, arrest, overpower, or overcome." But we also speak of "grasping" an idea or a concept, which refers to the use of one's mental powers. This is the double meaning of the term used by John in this verse. The enemies of Jesus never "grasped" mentally or spiritually what he was trying to teach them, so they attempted to "grasp" him physically and put him to death. Darkness seemed to triumph at the cross; note the references to darkness or night that John records as the cross drew near (John 12:35, 36, 46; 13:30). But Jesus' enemies could not extinguish the light that he ignited to dispel the darkness of sin. That light will continue to lead individuals to salvation, despite the failures of its followers and the attacks of its foes.

II. The Faithful Witness (John 1:6-13)
A. God's Man for the Work (vv. 6-8)

⁶ *There came a man who was sent from God; his name was John.*

Having introduced the Word and having touched on the impact of the Word's earthly ministry, John now calls attention to the messenger who prepared individuals to receive the Word. That was another *John*, son of Zechariah the priest and his wife Elizabeth. The angel Gabriel had appeared to Zechariah, assigning the name *John* to the child not yet conceived and describing his ministry (Luke 1:5-21). Thus John the Baptist, as we know him, was no self-appointed preacher of righteousness. He was a *man . . . sent from God* with a divine mission, and he faithfully carried out his appointed task. Jesus once described John as "a prophet . . . and more than a prophet." He also declared, "Among those born of women there has not risen anyone greater than John the Baptist" (Matthew 11:7-11).

⁷ *He came as a witness to testify concerning that light, so that through him all men might believe.*

John's entire mission is summed up in this verse. Gabriel told Zechariah that John would "make ready a people prepared for the Lord" (Luke 1:17). The *witness* John could bear was to make the inspired predictions of Jesus' appearance and to identify him when he did appear. "I have seen and I testify that this is the Son of God" (John 1:34).

John's impact was far-reaching: *that through him all men might believe.* John's testimony to his own generation was immediate and direct as far as his voice and life could reach. To the rest of his generation and to all succeeding ages, he has been a mighty factor in bringing people to faith in Christ through the inspired records of the New Testament and through all who have faithfully set forth John's testimony to others. This is in keeping with the stated purpose of the apostle John's Gospel (John 20:30, 31).

> **⁸ He himself was not the light; he came only as a witness to the light.**

Although Jesus called John the Baptist "a lamp that burned and gave light" (John 5:35), John *was not the light.* John himself made it very clear to those who questioned him that he was not the promised Messiah (John 1:20). John's task was to prepare the way for him, to bear *witness* of him.

Our own relationship to Christ is analogous to that of John the Baptist. Our task is to witness to the Light. In so doing, we must take every precaution lest people look to us rather than to him whom we serve. John's humble example reminds us how important this is. We may not have the kind of call or commission from God that John did, but we can use our lives as a testimony for our Lord. John's statement recorded in John 3:30 is one that should become the guiding principle for every follower of Jesus: "He must become greater; I must become less."

B. God's Light for the World (v. 9)

> **⁹ The true light that gives light to every man was coming into the world.**

By saying that Jesus *was coming into the world* John refers to the fact that Jesus was about to enter his public ministry. But what does John mean when he describes Jesus as *the true light that gives light to every man?* Certainly he does not mean that every person born into the world is enlightened by Christ, for in the next two verses he shows that some rejected him. The meaning seems to be that the divine Word is the *true* (that is, genuine, perfect, or real) light who gives spiritual illumination and life to individuals and that this illumination and life come through no other. In other words, not all will be saved, but none will be saved who are not saved by believing in Jesus.

The term *world* is another of John's words that can be subject to more than one meaning. It can designate the universe, the earth, the people on the earth, most people, or the human system that stands opposed to God's purposes. Here it signifies the population of the earth, including all those multitudes yet to be born into the world. The light of life had come to save all by giving his life for "the sins of the whole world" (1 John 2:2). This point is also emphasized in the well-known passage of John 3:16: God loves the entire world so much that he gave his only Son, but each person must choose to allow his light to dispel his or her darkness.

C. The Light Rejected (vv. 10, 11)

¹⁰ He was in the world, and though the world was made through him, the world did not recognize him.

In the middle portion of this verse, John repeats what he stated previously of the Word in verse 3: "Through him all things were made." In a sense, he was in the world through the centuries that followed, "sustaining all things by his powerful word" (Hebrews 1:3) and holding all things together (Colossians 1:17). Yet when the Word, the true light, *was in the world*, its people *did not recognize him.* "No room . . . in the inn" (Luke 2:7) describes how Jesus was treated not only as a baby, but throughout his life.

¹¹ He came to that which was his own, but his own did not receive him.

The words *his own* occur twice in this verse, and the Greek text shows a distinction in the gender of the two. The first occurrence is neuter, while the latter is masculine. The former may be understood as "his own things" or "his own world." Jesus had made it, it belonged to him, he had a right to come, and he was showing his regard for his world by coming to it. The latter phrase means "his own people," or the Jews. For the most part, the Jews did not receive Jesus, or acknowledge him as the "true light" (verse 9)—a fact that Pilate noted when Jesus stood before him (John 18:35).

This brief passage is filled with pathos. Since the time of Abraham, God had been preparing Israel as the nation through whom all peoples on earth would be blessed (Genesis 12:3). They were chosen "out of all the peoples on the face of the earth to be his people, his treasured possession" (Deuteronomy 7:6). In a special sense, Israel belonged to the Lord. They should have known and welcomed the Messiah's coming, but instead, when he came to his own people, they rejected him. Isaiah's words, written to his own generation, were equally applicable to the Jews of Jesus' day: "The ox knows his master, the donkey his owner's manger, but Israel does not know, my people do not understand" (Isaiah 1:3).

D. The Light Received (John 1:12, 13)

12 Yet to all who received him, to those who believed in his name, he gave the right to become children of God—

Not all people rejected the light when he came. In contrast to those who "did not receive" Jesus (verse 11), this verse describes those *who received him*, in terms of what that means and what that provides to the recipient. To receive Jesus involves believing *in his name*. To do this is to recognize and confess by word and deed the sonship, saviorhood, and lordship implied in the name of Jesus. "There is no other name under heaven given to men by which we must be saved" (Acts 4:12).

John the Baptist was among the first and most influential of those who gladly welcomed Jesus as "the Lamb of God, who takes away the sin of the world" (John 1:29). Those who follow in doing so receive the *right to become* what no one can become in any other way—*children* in God's family. All people are children of God by creation, but sin has shattered this relationship and alienated people from God. Now, by the power of the new birth, we may once more enjoy that blessed relationship. Within this family relationship there is a precious fellowship unknown to those who are outside. But in addition, there is a promised inheritance "kept in heaven" (1 Peter 1:4) that none but members of the family can hope to receive.

13 . . . children born not of natural descent, nor of human decision or a husband's will, but born of God.

The family relationship described here comes through a process parallel to, but very different from, the birth that makes us members of human families. That birth is physical and takes place in accordance with the willing participation of the parents. The new birth, or birth from above, was the concept that Nicodemus found puzzling (John 3:3). This new birth has nothing to do with *natural descent*. Human bloodlines have nothing to do with becoming a child of God. The Jews prided themselves on their lineage from Abraham, but John the Baptist informed them that God could raise up children of Abraham from stones if he chose to do so (Matthew 3:9).

The new birth is also not the result of a *human decision*. We know, as Nicodemus did, that a grown man cannot return to the womb and be born again as he was the first time (John 3:4). The person who is reborn looks much as he did before, but he thinks and talks and acts differently. He has new ideals, new motives, and new desires.

In addition, *a husband's will* has no say in the matter of the new birth. The new birth clearly does not depend on the virtues of man to bring it about. The plan resulting in this special relationship with God is not something that originated in the mind of man but in the will *of God*; therefore, man has no basis on which to boast about it.

In his first letter, John often uses the idea of birth to describe the radical new relationship that God desires with humanity (1 John 3:9; 4:7; 5:1, 4, 18). Paul uses the term *adoption* to convey the same idea (Ephesians 1:5). James states that one who is born again is given birth "through the word of truth" (James 1:18), indicating the important part that the Scriptures play in conversion. (See also 1 Peter 1:23.)

III. The Word Made Flesh (John 1:14-18)
A. "Full of Grace and Truth" (vv. 14-16)

14 The Word became flesh and made his dwelling among us. We have seen his glory, the glory of the One and Only, who came from the Father, full of grace and truth.

How simply John expresses this profound truth! All the mystery and power of the incarnation are wrapped up in one brief sentence: *The Word became flesh and made his dwelling among us.* The previous verses of the prologue reach their climax here. This is the event we celebrate at Christmas time and remember much more frequently. The divine being who had always lived with God became a human being and lived among other human beings. In fact, for the first time since Adam and Eve were created, a human being came into existence without a human father. By clothing the divine nature in a human body, God broke through the curtain of flesh and shared in human existence. In the person of Jesus of Nazareth, God entered the world of our experience as we all do, through birth. He grew up through childhood and youth to adulthood, subject to the joys and sorrows, the trials and temptations common to us all. What grace! What love! That he should become like us that we may become like him!

The phrase *made his dwelling* translates a Greek word that conveys the idea of living in tents, hence not permanently in one place. In the days of Moses, God had made his dwelling in the midst of his people in the tabernacle or tent of meeting. God's glory had filled that tent. So in Jesus, the *glory* of God lived and moved among people. His physical presence was for a limited time, but it allowed for the closest acquaintance.

John the writer includes himself among those who saw his glory. Following his record of Jesus' first miracle in Cana of Galilee, John writes of Jesus, "He thus revealed his glory, and his disciples put their faith in him" (John 2:11). Along with Peter and James, John witnessed Jesus' transfiguration, when the glory of Jesus was manifested in visible form (Matthew 17:1-8). With the other disciples, John saw the risen Lord ascend to Heaven (Luke 24:51; Acts 1:9-11). In the opening verse of his first letter, John notes his experience of being able to hear, see, and touch "the Word of life" (1 John 1:1).

There is an innate longing for God within the human soul. This has stirred many to a lifelong search for God, resulting in the development of various religions. But in Jesus the process is reversed. Here we have God in search of man! Here we have the incarnation—God coming to earth to seek those lost in the darkness of sin to bring them to the light of his love, whereby they may be brought to new life as children of God.

John then describes the glory of Jesus as *the glory of the One and Only*. Thus John moves swiftly in this one verse from the humbling of the Word through his coming in the flesh to the majesty of the Word. The phrase *the One and Only* is used by John five times and always in direct reference to Jesus. It indicates that Jesus is the only one of his kind; there is no other like him.

Though the Word dwelling among humanity manifested power and glory, John goes on to say that he was *full of grace and truth*. In Old Testament times, God revealed great grace and much truth; but the most sublime revelation of both was given in his Son. Grace is favor that is not deserved. Such favor was evident in the helpfulness of Jesus as he healed the sick and crippled, gave sight to the blind, and gladdened mourners by raising their loved ones from the dead. It was seen also in his forgiveness of sinners (Matthew 9:2; Luke 7:48-50). As for truth, it was so evident in his teaching that his enemies were unable to argue with him. Passing centuries have only substantiated Jesus' declaration, "I am the way and the *truth* and the life" (John 14:6).

Jesus demonstrated a perfect balance of grace and truth. In him grace was most merciful without being indulgent, and truth was most complete without being cruel. Since he who dwelt for a time among us now dwells within us (Colossians 1:27), we must demonstrate a similar balance in our daily conduct and our dealings with others.

As noted earlier, John's emphasis on the Word becoming flesh may have been an intentional effort to counter the false teachings of the Gnostics, who believed and taught that a good God could not possibly have anything to do with matter or flesh, which in their view was evil. In his first letter, John declares that a person is to be acknowledged as from God or from the antichrist based on whether or not he believes Jesus has come in the flesh (1 John 4:1-3).

¹⁵ John testifies concerning him. He cries out, saying, "This was he of whom I said, 'He who comes after me has surpassed me because he was before me.'"

John the Baptist had been introduced earlier (verses 6-9); now his testimony *concerning* Jesus is quoted. It will be cited again in John 1:29, 30. (The first two verbs in this verse are properly in the present tense (*testifies* and *cries out*), for John's testimony was not meant to be a one-time event; it still speaks to all who will listen. *Cries out* calls to mind John's role as the "voice of one calling in the desert" (Matthew 3:3), much as a herald shouts his message for an entire town to hear.

John referred to Jesus as both *he who comes after me* and the one who *was before me*. In terms of time from an earthly perspective, Jesus did come after John, being about six months younger. (See Luke 1:35, 36, where Gabriel tells Mary that she will give birth to the Son of God and also notes that Elizabeth, John's mother, is in the sixth month of her pregnancy.) John's ministry also began before Jesus' ministry. Yet in terms of honor and of time from an eternal perspective, Jesus was *before*, or preeminent over, John. Such a statement points to Christ's preexistence with the Father, reaffirming what John the apostle has stated in the opening verses of his Gospel.

16 *From the fullness of his grace we have all received one blessing after another.*

This testimony was written by John the apostle long after the close of Jesus' earthly ministry. (As noted previously, John's Gospel is usually dated sometime near the close of the first century.) He and all the other apostles, plus thousands of believers, had drawn from the divine *fullness* of which Paul wrote: "For in Christ all the fullness of the Deity lives in bodily form" (Colossians 2:9). Paul prayed that the Ephesian Christians would be "filled to the measure of all the fullness of God" (Ephesians 3:19). In Christ we receive *one blessing after another*. The Greek phrase may be rendered "grace in place of grace." The grace of God in Christ provides an inexhaustible supply of blessing upon blessing, like waves one after another washing upon the shore. It is grace given in abundance from the very fountain of grace.

B. Superior to Law (vv. 17, 18)

17 *For the law was given through Moses; grace and truth came through Jesus Christ.*

Here a contrast is drawn between the age of Christ and that which preceded it. Verse 16, with its testimony to the incarnate Word as the channel of God's boundless grace, suggested this comparison between the *law . . . given through Moses*, and *grace and truth*, which *came through Jesus Christ*. (This also elaborates on the thought stated at the conclusion of verse 14.)

Both Moses and Jesus were mediators of covenants. The covenant established through Moses was based on a written code, the law. The fact that grace and truth came through Jesus does not mean that grace and truth were absent from the law, however. The law was not without grace; it offered provisional forgiveness to those who repented of their sins and presented the required sacrifices. But Jesus brought the fullness of grace. He "offered for all time one sacrifice for sins" (Hebrews 10:12). Jesus was the reality toward which all of the types of the law (for example, the sacrifices) pointed.

Furthermore, there was nothing untrue in the law, but Jesus offered deeper truth. The law forbade murder and adultery, for example; but Jesus warned against anger and lust, the feelings that lead to the acts of murder and adultery (Matthew 5:21-28). The law included a wide range of prohibitions, but Jesus pointed out that its supreme commandments were those that touch the heart—the command to love God supremely and the command to love one's neighbor as oneself (Matthew 22:34-40).

The Christian age cannot be called lawless, but its distinctive feature is that Christ gave his life to redeem us from the curse of the law (Galatians 3:10-13) and empowers us through the Holy Spirit to live a life pleasing to him. The law of Moses could condemn, but it could not redeem. Law pays off for works performed; grace can never be earned or purchased by any means. Grace comes through Jesus, not through keeping a code. The law said, "Do this and live"; the gospel says, "Live and do this."

18 No one has ever seen God, but God the One and Only, who is at the Father's side, has made him known.

No one has ever seen God. Moses the lawgiver asked to see God, but his request was not granted. Instead, he was hidden in a cleft in the rock and permitted to see only the partial glory of the Lord (Exodus 33:18-23). Earlier Moses, Aaron, two of Aaron's sons, and the seventy elders of Israel "saw the God of Israel. Under his feet was something like a pavement made of sapphire, clear as the sky itself" (Exodus 24:9-11). These individuals would have also seen partial revelations of God, not his full glory, for no one can see God in his fullness and live (Exodus 33:20).

The phrase *the One and Only* was used previously in verse 14 to describe the Word who became flesh. Here John states that Jesus *has made* God *known*. Much more is involved than merely informing the world of the existence of God. Jesus revealed God's nature, his character, his will, and particularly his love for lost humanity and his desire to bring us life and light. "The Son is the radiance of God's glory and the exact representation of his being" (Hebrews

1:3). "Anyone who has seen me has seen the Father," Jesus declared (John 14:9; see also Colossians 1:15; 1 Timothy 6:14-16).

Jesus' unique relationship with God is captured in the phrase *at the Father's side*. In New Testament times, when individuals reclined at a meal the host's closest friend was positioned next to him and was given special honor. He was taken into confidence, and often shared the innermost thoughts and purposes of the host. The apostle John leaned against Jesus at the last supper and was called the disciple "whom Jesus loved" (John 13:23; 21:20). To be at "Abraham's side" was the equivalent of being in paradise (Luke 16:22, 23). No expression could better convey the closeness that Jesus had with the Father in Heaven. It shows his superiority to Moses and all of the prophets who had revealed the will of God before Jesus came.

How to Say It

AUTOPSY. *aw*-top-see.

BETHLEHEM. *Beth*-lih-hem.

BOANERGES. *Bo*-uh-*nur*-geez (strong accent on *nur*).

ELIZABETH. Ih-*lih*-zuh-beth.

EMANATION. em-uh-*nay*-shun.

EPHESUS. *Ef*-uh-sus.

GABRIEL. *Gay*-bree-ul.

GNOSTIC. *Nahss*-tick.

INCARNATION. in-car-*nay*-shun.

INERRANT. in-*air*-unt.

INSPIRATION. in-spuh-*ray*-shun.

LAZARUS. *Laz*-uh-rus.

LOGOS (*Greek*). *law*-goss.

MEDIATOR. *me*-dee-*ay*-ter (strong accent on *me*).

NAZARETH. *Naz*-uh-reth.

NICODEMUS. *Nick*-uh-*dee*-mus (strong accent on *dee*).

PAGANISM. *pay*-guh-*niz*-um (strong accent on *pay*).

PATHOS. *pay*-thahs or *pay*-those (*th* as in *thin*).

PATMOS. *Pat*-muss.

PREEXISTENCE. pre-ig-*zis*-tunts.

SAMARITAN. Suh-*mare*-uh-tun.

SAPPHIRE. *sa*-fire (*sa* as in *sat*).

SYCHAR. *Sigh*-kar.

THEOPHILUS. Thee-*ahf*-ih-luss (*th* as in *thin*).

ZEBEDEE. *Zeb*-eh-dee.

ZECHARIAH. *Zek*-uh-*rye*-uh (strong accent on *rye*).

Chapter 2

Birth and Beginnings (Part 1)
Luke 1:26-38; Matthew 1:18-25; Luke 2:1-20

JESUS' BIRTH FORETOLD (LUKE 1:26-38)

Establishing the Groundwork

What a contrast the event recounted in this text presents to us—an angel comes from the very presence of God to visit a girl from an obscure village! One is an unearthly, spiritual being from another plane of existence; the other is a fiancée of a Galilean carpenter. Yet the girl is the one who is addressed as "highly favored" by God. God is going to bring his own Son into the world through this girl and will unite himself with human flesh.

The angel seems superior in wisdom and in the knowledge of God's purposes. But the girl is beautiful in her realization of her purity, in her natural concern about the angel's startling message, and in her quiet obedience. She must realize that questions, scorn, and scandal lie ahead, but she places her trust in God and makes no objections once the complete message has been delivered. Salvation would come through the Son whom Mary would bear—the marvelous combination of God's holy will and Mary's yielded body and mind.

Examining the Text

I. Mary Receives God's Messenger (Luke 1:26-29)
A. A Prospective Bride (vv. 26, 27)

²⁶ In the sixth month, God sent the angel Gabriel to Nazareth, a town in Galilee,

In the sixth month refers to the sixth month of the pregnancy of Elizabeth, who was to be the mother of John the Baptist. Luke 1:24 makes this clear, as well as the words of *Gabriel* to Mary in verse 36.

The Greek word translated *"angel"* means "messenger," indicating that the principle work of these spiritual beings is to bring God's messages to human beings. (In the Old Testament the Hebrew word that we translate "angel" also means "messenger.") In the early verses of Luke 1, we read that this same angel appeared to the priest, Zechariah, and foretold that he and his wife would have a son who would be a forerunner of the Lord. Among the words Gabriel spoke on that occasion were: "I am Gabriel. I stand in the presence of God, and I have been sent to speak to you and to tell you this good news" (Luke 1:19).

The town of *Nazareth* was located in the hills of southern *Galilee* about fifteen miles west of the Sea of Galilee and twenty miles east of the Mediterranean Sea. In New Testament times, Nazareth was an insignificant village of fewer than two thousand inhabitants. It is unlikely that the world would have selected someone from such a remote place to become the mother of the Messiah. Galilee was lightly regarded by the Jews in Judea, who thought that no prophet could come from there (John 7:41, 52). Nazareth is not mentioned anywhere in the Old Testament. Nathanael expressed the skepticism of many with his words, "Nazareth! Can anything good come from there?" (John 1:46). Yet God's ways are not man's ways.

> ²⁷ . . . to a virgin pledged to be married to a man named Joseph, a descendant of David. The virgin's name was Mary.

As a physician, Luke would have been especially interested in the *virgin* birth. He mentions Mary's virginity twice in this verse, indicating that he was convinced of it and did not question it in any way. At this time, Mary was *pledged to be married to . . . Joseph*. This pledging, or betrothal as it is sometimes called, was a serious legal commitment. Sexual union did not occur until after the wedding ceremony. Both the man and the woman were to keep their pledge to one another, and any sexual intimacy with another was considered adultery.

Joseph, here introduced, is mentioned only twice outside the accounts of Jesus' birth and boyhood (John 1:45; 6:42). The genealogy in Matthew 1:1-17 identifies Joseph as a descendant of David. That Mary was also a descendant of David is seen from the genealogy found in Luke 3:23-38, which is generally considered to be that of Mary. Even if Mary herself were not a descendant of David, Jesus' legal claim to the lineage of David would have been established through Joseph as Jesus' legal father. It was necessary that an actual descendant of David be the Messiah and occupy David's throne (2 Samuel 7:12-16; Psalm 132:11), which Gabriel would later point out in his message to Mary (v. 32).

The Scriptures tell us little about *Mary*. We do not know who her parents were or if they were living when the events in this passage occurred. Nor do we know how old she was when Gabriel appeared to her. One might expect an angel to appear to a priest such as Zechariah in renowned Jerusalem. But for him to appear in Nazareth to a young peasant girl of "humble state" (Luke 1:48) is most remarkable. Mary demonstrates how "God chose the weak things of the world to shame the strong. . . . so that no one may boast before him" (1 Corinthians 1:27, 29).

B. A Perplexed Listener (vv. 28, 29)

²⁸ The angel went to her and said, "Greetings, you who are highly favored! The Lord is with you."

Gabriel appeared to Mary directly as he had to Zechariah. This was not a dream or a vision. In both instances, however, the manifestation of *the angel* was in private, not in public.

Gabriel's greeting included a descriptive phrase about Mary: she was *highly favored*. This expression was much more than just a courteous greeting or a congratulatory word about her engagement to Joseph. Mary had been chosen to give birth to the Messiah and to rear and nurture him during his early years.

Gabriel's assurance *the Lord is with you* prepared Mary not only for what she was about to hear on this day, but for the difficult days that lay ahead. Such comfort was frequently offered to God's servants when they faced a particularly daunting task (Moses in Exodus 3:12; Joshua in Joshua 1:5; Gideon in Judges 6:12; and Jeremiah in Jeremiah 1:8). One should also keep in mind the meaning of the messianic name *Immanuel* ("God with us," Matthew 1:23) and how this became literally true for Mary when she carried within her, as Elizabeth later noted, "my Lord" (Luke 1:43).

²⁹ Mary was greatly troubled at his words and wondered what kind of greeting this might be.

As Luke later tells us, Mary was someone who "pondered" and "treasured" certain matters "in her heart" (2:19, 51). She tended to think issues through carefully, rather than rush to a conclusion. At first, she did not respond verbally to the angel's *greeting*, but in her mind a variety of thoughts must have been present. Any angelic visitation usually produced great anxiety in the person visited (Judges 6:22, 23; Mark 16:5, 6; Luke 1:11, 12).

II. Mary Hears God's Message (Luke 1:30-33)
A. The Great Favor (v. 30)

³⁰ But the angel said to her, "Do not be afraid, Mary, you have found favor with God.

The angel was aware of Mary's apprehension, and he provided comfort to her in three ways. First, the words *do not be afraid* were meant to bring reassurance. These words were often used when heavenly beings spoke to humans (as in Genesis 21:17; Matthew 28:5; and Acts 27:23, 24). In addition to the passages just cited, we see these words spoken in the early chapters of Luke to Zechariah (1:13) and to the shepherds on the night Jesus was born (2:10).

Second, Gabriel called *Mary* by name. This was likely done in a compassionate way that relieved Mary's anxieties. Third, the thought that Mary had *found favor with God* was repeated. This brought further reassurance, for God's messengers, whether angels or prophets, often pronounced judgment on those who were disobedient to God's commands. To hear that she had found favor with God reassured Mary that the angel was not there in judgment.

B. The Glorious Promise (vv. 31-33)

31 "You will be with child and give birth to a son, and you are to give him the name Jesus.

Here is the announcement that the angel was commissioned to give. Each part provided a more specific detail: Mary would *be with child*; the baby would be *a son*; and she would give him a specific *name*. The fact that Joseph is said to give the child his name in Matthew 1:25 is not a contradiction; rather, it may be considered evidence that there was harmony between both the man and the woman in following God's direction. The same spirit of agreement is seen in Zechariah and Elizabeth's naming of John (Luke 1:60, 63).

Even though Jesus' birth was miraculous in that he was conceived in the womb of a virgin, it was in every other respect a normal human pregnancy and birth. The Son of God did not spring from the head of a god or grow from a flower or appear from the water. The accounts in the four Gospels exhibit none of the markings of ancient myths. Jesus entered the world as all human beings have—by birth. His coming to our world was characterized by a wonderful combination of the supernatural and the natural.

The name chosen for the child was *Jesus*, which is the Greek form of the Old Testament name *Joshua*. While this was a very common name, it was particularly appropriate for the Messiah, since it means, "The Lord is salvation." Just as Joshua led the children of Israel into the freedom of the promised land, so the second Joshua, Jesus, will lead his people from the slavery of sin into the freedom of eternal life.

32 "He will be great and will be called the Son of the Most High. The Lord God will give him the throne of his father David,

The phrases describing the promised Son of God continue to build. *He will be great.* What a simple but profound statement! In Luke's day, the adjective *great* had become incorporated into the name by which some "great" rulers were known. Josephus, writing at about the same time as Luke, refers to Antiochus the Great in his *Antiquities of the Jews,* and Alexander the Great seems to have been known by that title as early as the third century BC. Other rulers also attached the adjective to themselves. On the Cyrus Cylinder, for example, Cyrus was called "King of the World, Great King." Whatever greatness these men possessed, however, would pale in comparison with that which would be bestowed upon the promised son of Mary.

Son of the Most High is a phrase that suggests a special association with deity. It is but another way of saying "Son of God," a title Gabriel will use of Mary's child in verse 35. It is noteworthy that Mary's child is called "Son of the Most High," while John is called "a prophet of the Most High" in Luke 1:76. John was a spokesman for God; Jesus was the Son of God.

The third great fact of this verse is that God would *give* to this child *the throne of his father David.* In both of the genealogical tables relating to Jesus, he is shown to have been descended from David (Matthew 1:1; Luke 3:31). Once again, as in verse 27, the significance of David and the Old Testament promises to him are confirmed.

[33] *". . . and he will reign over the house of Jacob forever; his kingdom will never end."*

When David was king of Israel, God promised that his house would rule forever (2 Samuel 7:12-16). However, the Davidic line was interrupted when Jerusalem fell to the Babylonians and the king (Zedekiah) was taken captive and put to death. The Jews looked for a descendant of David who would become king and rule over the people of God. But the prophecy was not to have its fulfillment in a physical kingdom, as some assumed. Jesus, the Messiah-King, would fulfill Daniel's prophecy of a different kind of kingdom that shall never be destroyed (Daniel 2:44; 7:13, 14).

III. Mary Accepts God's Assurance (Luke 1:34-38)
A. Mary's Question (v. 34)

[34] *"How will this be," Mary asked the angel, "since I am a virgin?"*

While many today find the *virgin* birth a difficult truth to accept, we must keep in mind that this was no less true for *Mary*. Note that when Zechariah questioned Gabriel's promise to him of a miraculous birth, he was struck dumb (Luke 1:18-20). He did not believe the angelic announcement and even asked for a sign by which he could believe. Furthermore, he overlooked the example of aged Abraham and Sarah, who, by God's intervention, had been empowered to have a child after Sarah was beyond the age of childbearing. Yet Mary received no such rebuke for her response. It seems that her question indicated less doubt as to the truth of what Gabriel said than a sense of wonder that such a thing could be. Thus her question deserved an answer and did not call forth any kind of reprimand.

B. God's Answer (v. 35)

35 The angel answered, "The Holy Spirit will come upon you, and the power of the Most High will overshadow you. So the holy one to be born will be called the Son of God.

Gabriel answers Mary's "How?" by telling her "Who." His answer highlighted two factors: the creative power of God and the nature of the child who was to be born. As the Spirit of God was active in the original creation (Genesis 1:2), so he would be the agent in Mary's conception. We are not informed how the Holy Spirit accomplished this. If the angel's explanation had been phrased according to our present understanding of genetics, it would have baffled earlier generations and produced confusion rather than wonder. It was not deemed essential for Mary (or for us) to understand completely the ways of God. Her task was, and ours is, simply this: "The righteous will live by faith" (Romans 1:17).

C. Elizabeth's Example (vv. 36, 37)

36 "Even Elizabeth your relative is going to have a child in her old age, and she who was said to be barren is in her sixth month.

Without Mary's asking for it, Gabriel offered a sign to support the promises he had spoken. The news he brought was intensely personal and readily verifiable. This was likely the first Mary had heard of the pregnancy of *Elizabeth*, her *relative*. Elizabeth's experience calls to mind women such as Sarah (Genesis 17:15-17; 21:1-7), the mother of Samson (Judges 13:2, 3, 24), and Hannah (1 Samuel 1:2, 10, 11, 20), all of whom were considered *barren*. (In Sarah's case, *old age* was also a factor.) Yet God overruled their condition and gave them the privilege of becoming mothers.

We can understand why Mary later hurried to visit Elizabeth (Luke 1:39). God had done something "impossible" for both of them!

37 "For nothing is impossible with God."

This statement (or one similar in meaning to it) is made in more than one place in Scripture (Genesis 18:14; Jeremiah 32:17; Matthew 19:26), but here it is especially appropriate. The virgin birth of Jesus is unique. To believe it, one must affirm that God is not limited by the so-called "laws of nature." Since he is the one who put those laws into effect, he can set them aside or override them at any time to accomplish his purposes.

D. Mary's Commitment (v. 38)

38 "I am the Lord's servant," Mary answered. "May it be to me as you have said." Then the angel left her.

It seems as though it were necessary to secure the consent of Mary for the whole process of world redemption to begin. But God was not going to over-power Mary and force her to become the mother of the Son of God. Neither was he to steal upon her, secretly cause her to become pregnant, and *then* tell her what had happened.

Mary's submission to the Lord's will is a model for all Christians. And yet, at this point she could not have been aware of all she would have to face in fulfilling her extraordinary role. She would endure the gossips in Nazareth (who would speculate as to the *real* father of her child), the long trip to Bethlehem, the birth of her child in less than ideal conditions, the threat from jealous King Herod, and another long trip to Egypt and then back to Nazareth. She would watch as Jesus left the family circle to minister to people all over Galilee and Judea. Ultimately—and worst of all—she would watch as her son was crucified.

While Mary could not have anticipated most of this, the Biblical record indicates that she fulfilled all that was asked of her. This is not to say that her understanding of Jesus and his ministry was flawless. There were times when she did not grasp the full significance of who he was or what he had come to do (Luke 2:48-50; John 2:1-4; Mark 3:20, 21, 31, 32). Still, when one considers the awesome responsibility given her, her faithfulness is exemplary.

MATTHEW'S BIRTH NARRATIVE (MATTHEW 1:18-25)

Establishing the Groundwork

More than any other Gospel writer, Matthew linked Old Testament prophecies with Jesus' life. Here are some of the prophecies Matthew included in his record: Isaiah 7:14 (born of a virgin; see Matthew 1:23); Micah 5:2 (place of birth; see Matthew 2:6); Hosea 11:1 (flight to Egypt; see Matthew 2:15); Jeremiah 31:15 (slaughter of infants; see Matthew 2:17, 18); Isaiah 40:3 (coming of John the Baptist; see Matthew 3:1-3); Isaiah 42:1-4 (Jesus' works; see Matthew 12:15-21); Isaiah 6:9, 10 (Jesus' manner of speaking; see Matthew 13:10-15); Isaiah 29:13 (Jesus' opposition; see Matthew 15:7-9); Zechariah 9:9 (the triumphal entry; see Matthew 21:1-5); Psalm 118:22, 23 (rejection by the leaders of the people; see Matthew 21:42); and Zechariah 13:7 (the disciples' desertion of Jesus; see Matthew 26:31).

After presenting the genealogy that establishes Jesus' credentials through the royal line of David, Matthew turns to the details of the birth of Jesus. The drama of the story is unfolded in such a way as to show clearly how God acted in this event to bring Jesus into the world and protect him from the forces of evil that stood against him.

Examining the Text

I. The Situation (Matthew 1:18, 19)
A. Mary's Pregnancy (v. 18)

18 This is how the birth of Jesus Christ came about: His mother Mary was pledged to be married to Joseph, but before they came together, she was found to be with child through the Holy Spirit.

Matthew's Gospel begins with a genealogy of Jesus and a sketch of his *birth* in Bethlehem. Yet this is not a "natural" conception and birth—far from it! Matthew hints at this in Matthew 1:16 when he notes that Joseph is "the husband of Mary, of whom was born Jesus, who is called Christ." A typical genealogical statement might have said that Joseph was the father of Jesus.

In the previous study from Luke 1:26-38, the same phrase that is used here to describe Mary (*pledged to be married to Joseph*) appeared in verse 27. There the seriousness of the betrothal was noted. That Mary was *with child* before she and Joseph *came together* in sexual intimacy would have created a scandalous discovery for Joseph and his family. If, as is likely, Mary had been three months separated from Joseph in Judea while visiting Elizabeth (Luke 1:39, 56), Joseph must have been tempted to conclude that the child had been conceived as a result of intimacy with some other man while Mary was away. And since Mary had apparently not yet informed Joseph of Gabriel's message, he had no reason to believe anything other than that she had been unfaithful to her betrothal pledge. Later, of course, he would learn that Mary's child was conceived *through the Holy Spirit* (v. 20).

B. Joseph's Response (v. 19)

19 Because Joseph her husband was a righteous man and did not want to expose her to public disgrace, he had in mind to divorce her quietly.

Joseph is called Mary's *husband*, a term that emphasizes the serious nature of the betrothal. He is described as *a righteous man*. Joseph was someone who wanted to do what was right, but he was torn between his love for Mary and the undeniable fact that she was pregnant. On the one hand, he wanted to make the situation as easy for her as possible because of his concern for her well-being. But on the other hand, if he proceeded with the marriage, he knew that others would logically (but wrongly) conclude that he was the other guilty party in this out-of-wedlock pregnancy.

Another factor making this situation awkward to handle was that first-century Judaism did not have the legal authorization from Rome to carry out executions for an act that deserved death (as in the case of adultery). Thus other measures were typically used to punish sexual infidelity. Anyone violating the betrothal pledge could be publicly denounced and humiliated, effectively shutting him or her out from any future marriage prospects (at least from any good ones). Furthermore, the violator's family could be assessed damages for bringing shame to the innocent party.

Joseph, seeking to balance a sense of what was right with his compassion for Mary, decided not to *expose her to public disgrace*. Instead, he chose to *divorce her quietly*. Herein lies a testimony to the gracious character of Joseph. It is not difficult to understand why God selected this man to serve as one of the parents who would nurture and guide the young Messiah in his development.

II. The Vision (Matthew 1:20, 21)
A. God's Intervention (v. 20)

20 But after he had considered this, an angel of the Lord appeared to him in a dream and said, "Joseph son of David, do not be afraid to take Mary home as your wife, because what is conceived in her is from the Holy Spirit.

Joseph was not one to act hastily; he had *considered* how best to handle the situation confronting him when *an angel of the Lord appeared to him in a dream*. He was now permitted to see events from God's perspective. (Note that this was the first of four occasions on which an angel communicated to Joseph by means of a dream; the others are mentioned in Matthew 2:13, 19, and 22.)

The description of Joseph as *son of David* connects him to the preceding genealogy, particularly to the identity of Jesus as the "son of David" (Matthew 1:1). As has been noted, predictions in the Old Testament were clear that the Christ would be of the seed of David. Did the angel's form of address cause Joseph to think that his wife's son could possibly be the Christ? If not, what the angel said next certainly could have: her pregnancy was the result of the work of the *Holy Spirit*. Her conception of this child was not a result of any unfaithfulness to Joseph, but of her faithfulness to God.

The command to Joseph to *take Mary home as* his *wife* without *fear* could be a reference to Joseph's concern that he would be breaking God's law to marry a woman who had become pregnant out of wedlock. It is also possible that the fear refers to the social pressures that would result from going ahead with the marriage.

B. God's Promise (v. 21)

21 "She will give birth to a son, and you are to give him the name Jesus, because he will save his people from their sins."

As the legal father, Joseph would name Mary's *son*; but he would not be free to choose the *name*. As noted earlier, the Greek name *Jesus* is a form of the Hebrew name "Joshua," which means "the Lord is salvation."

Of course, no details concerning how Jesus would accomplish this were revealed to Joseph. But the rest of Matthew's Gospel will reveal how the Messiah must redeem Israel by sacrificing his own life as a ransom (20:28) to *save his people from their sins*. Jewish expectations frequently centered on the idea that the Messiah would free Israel from Roman tyranny. However, the notion that the Messiah would die a criminal's death was too much to accept for most of the Jewish faithful.

The full meaning of the phrase *his people* will unfold throughout Matthew's Gospel. These people are those who belong to the Messiah, whether they are from a Jewish or Gentile background; and being a Jew by birth will not mean being counted automatically as among the saved (Matthew 3:9, 10; 8:11, 12). Christians today can give thanks for the fact that Jesus' arms of mercy include people of many ethnic and national backgrounds!

III. The Prophecy (Matthew 1:22, 23)
A. Matthew's Comment (v. 22)

22 All this took place to fulfill what the Lord had said through the prophet:

This is the first of ten times in his Gospel that Matthew called attention to the fact that an event he was reporting was the fulfillment of prophecy. (The other places are 2:15, 17, 23; 4:14; 8:17; 12:17; 13:35; 21:4; and 27:9.) In each of these instances he said, "Now all this happened in order that the word of the prophet might be fulfilled," or words to that effect. This suggests that the people to whom this Gospel account was written were Jewish Christians, who would have been very familiar with the Old Testament and the prophecies it contained.

Several values of predictive prophecy may be noted. First, such prophecies underscore the importance of the events that came to pass in time, showing that those events were part of a plan; second, they enabled God's people to be prepared for those events when they occurred; and third, they give assurance that the events predicted were of God, for the passing of many centuries between prophecy and fulfillment rules out the possibility of human origin for them.

B. Isaiah's Prediction (v. 23)

23. *"The virgin will be with child and will give birth to a son, and they will call him Immanuel"—which means, "God with us."*

This prophetic quotation—more than seven hundred years old!—comes from Isaiah 7:14. The original context is the prophecy spoken by Isaiah to King Ahaz of Judah when he was threatened with attack. To defeat this attack, King Ahaz was thinking about asking for Assyrian help when the Lord commanded him (through Isaiah) to put his trust in the Lord instead. Isaiah told Ahaz to suggest a sign that would confirm that God would keep his promise that Jerusalem would go unharmed if the king would depend on the Lord. When the king refused to do so, Isaiah gave him one anyway—the prophecy that Matthew cites here.

While the issues involved in interpreting this prophecy can be quite complex, there are some simple observations that are worth noting. First, the "sign" that Isaiah gave King Ahaz was to be "in the deepest depths or in the highest heights" (Isaiah 7:11). This implies that the king was supposed to ask for a supernatural event, such as would be the case with the miraculous conception of the Messiah. Also note that Matthew's interpretation of Isaiah 7:14 was given under the inspiration of the Holy Spirit. Whatever other applications to his own time Isaiah may or may not have had in mind when he spoke these words, Matthew assures us that the miraculous birth of Jesus was the fulfillment of Isaiah's prophecy.

The word *Immanuel* was sometimes used as a kind of "battle cry" by the Jews in times of trouble, expressing confidence that God was present with and fighting for the cause of his people. The name "Immanuel" does not seem to have been literally applied to Jesus as a name by which he is called in the Gospels. However, the whole emphasis of the New Testament is focused on the fact that God did become man and came to be "with us" in Jesus. In his teaching and ministry, Jesus would reveal his true nature. It would be very clear that in him God was indeed with mankind.

We may wonder just how the prediction of the birth of a child to a virgin would have represented a sign to King Ahaz over seven hundred years earlier!

We can answer this question by realizing that prophecies in the Old Testament can be understood either as predictions that persuade people immediately (as in Exodus 4:8, 9), or as sweeping statements to serve as future confirmations of something (as in Exodus 3:12).

In the case of King Ahaz, the prophecy of Isaiah 7:14 fits the second of these two, since Ahaz will be long dead by the time Jesus is born. Isaiah in his day saw destruction coming not just to Ahaz in particular, but also for the "house of David" in general (Isaiah 7:17-25), resulting in the loss of the throne. Long after King David's earthly dynasty has ended, it will be Jesus, born to a virgin and born of David's line, who will fulfill the prophet's words.

IV. The Birth (Matthew 1:24, 25)
A. Joseph's Obedience (v. 24)

24 When Joseph woke up, he did what the angel of the Lord had commanded him and took Mary home as his wife.

Joseph obeyed the command of the *angel* and *took Mary home as his wife*. While weddings were generally joyous celebrations in the time of Christ (Matthew 22:1-14; 25:1-13), the wedding of Mary and Joseph was probably very quiet, omitting the customary feast. People of the community, ignorant of the miraculous series of events, doubtless held Mary in contempt. Joseph of course shared her disgrace. But both of them could share the supreme spiritual joy of knowing that Mary was to be the mother of the Messiah, and they could hope that in time the truth would be made known to all and Mary especially would be justified.

B. Jesus' Birth (v. 25)

25 But he had no union with her until she gave birth to a son. And he gave him the name Jesus.

Though Joseph and Mary lived together, they abstained from sexual relations until Jesus was born. The reasonable implication is that they afterward enjoyed the normal relationship of husband and wife. Brothers and sisters of Jesus are mentioned in the New Testament (Matthew 12:46, 47; 13:54-56; John 2:12; 7:2-5; Acts 1:14; 1 Corinthians 9:5; Galatians 1:19), and there is no reason to think they were not the natural children of Joseph and Mary.

The concluding statement of this passage highlights once more the obedience of Joseph to the divinely given directives. He *gave* the child *the name Jesus*, in accordance with the command found in verse 21.

LUKE'S BIRTH NARRATIVE (LUKE 2:1-20)

Establishing the Groundwork

Luke's Gospel is the only account that includes the visit of the shepherds near Bethlehem. One of the unique characteristics of Luke's Gospel is his interest in common people and those whom society regarded as outcasts. Only Luke mentions the parable of the Good Samaritan (10:25-37), the parable of the prodigal son (15:11-32), the story of the rich man and Lazarus the beggar (16:19-31), the cleansing of the ten lepers (17:11-19), and Jesus' meeting with the despised tax collector Zacchaeus (19:1-10). Shepherds were looked upon with disdain by many because they tended to be rather crude. In addition, their work with animals often left them ritually unclean.

Examining the Text

I. Birth of a Child (Luke 2:1-7)
A. An Emperor's Command (vv. 1-3)

¹ In those days Caesar Augustus issued a decree that a census should be taken of the entire Roman world.

The information provided in the beginning of this account fits well with Luke's stated desire to write an "orderly account" concerning "the things that have been fulfilled among us" (Luke 1:1-3). Here he sets the occasion historically for the most spectacular night in human history.

Caesar Augustus was the nephew of the well known Julius Caesar. Upon the assassination of his uncle in 44 BC, Augustus steadily rose to power in Rome. In the year 27 BC the Roman Senate conferred upon him the title "Augustus," and he became the first emperor of the Roman Empire. He was instrumental in punishing Brutus and Cassius, who had taken part in the murder of his uncle. The name "Augustus" means "reverend," or one who is worthy of reverence as a god.

The *census* covered, as noted, the extent of *the entire Roman world*. Such enrollments occurred every fourteen years and had two purposes: to secure the names of citizens who should be assessed the tax, and to list those who were eligible for military service. The Roman army was continually annexing new territory and bringing new subjects under the imperial government. Thus a count had to be taken regularly. Judea was exempt from the military draft, so the census described here was purely for taxation purposes as far as this portion of the empire was concerned.

² (This was the first census that took place while Quirinius was governor of Syria.)

Some say that Jesus could not possibly have been born while Quirinius was governor of Syria, for there are non-Biblical records of his being governor later. However, there is evidence suggesting that Quirinius held the office of governor for two terms, and that the first coincides with the time of Jesus' birth. We must keep in mind that Luke's account was written within a generation of the event itself. If he had been incorrect here, his work would have been discredited immediately. Luke's concern for historical accuracy and careful research has already been noted. He would not have included this detail if he did not have a sound reason for doing so.

³ And everyone went to his own town to register.

The usual Roman practice of conducting a census was to count people where they lived. The Jews, on the other hand, were accustomed to enroll their people by tribes and families. The enrollment usually occurred at the place where the family records were kept, even though in some cases this entailed considerable travel and inconvenience. In this case, however, the emperor's decree was used by God to fulfill a prophecy uttered more than seven hundred years earlier by Micah, stating that the Messiah would be born in Bethlehem (Micah 5:2).

B. A Couple's Journey (vv. 4, 5)

⁴ So Joseph also went up from the town of Nazareth in Galilee to Judea, to Bethlehem the town of David, because he belonged to the house and line of David.

Luke has previously mentioned *Joseph*, describing him as "a descendant of David" (Luke 1:27). We have noted in the previous study of Matthew 1:18-25 his willingness to obey the commands given him by the angel of the Lord. Here he shows himself just as conscientious about obeying civil authority. *Nazareth in Galilee* was 70 miles from *Bethlehem* in *Judea,* but the usual route taken by people from Galilee probably made the trip one of 90 miles or more. Bethlehem was well known primarily because it was the birthplace of *David*. The name itself means "house of bread" in the Hebrew language, making it a fitting birthplace for the Bread of life.

⁵ He went there to register with Mary, who was pledged to be married to him and was expecting a child.

We may wonder why *Mary* accompanied Joseph on this journey while in the advanced stages of her pregnancy. Such a trip was certainly uncomfortable and even dangerous for her. There were no special accommodations made for travelers along the route to Bethlehem. Joseph and Mary either had to stay with someone or sleep in the open when they stopped for the night. Likely their journey was of several days' duration.

Several commentators suggest that Joseph brought Mary along to protect her from the slander she might have been exposed to in Nazareth had she remained there. This kind of thinking would certainly fit with Matthew's observation that he "did not want to expose her to public disgrace" (Matthew 1:19). Others believe that she too had to *register* in Bethlehem because she was also of the house of David.

Mary is described here as *pledged to be married to* Joseph. This seems to suggest that they embarked on the journey to Bethlehem before they had completed their marriage ceremony. But Matthew tells us that Joseph "took Mary home as his wife. But he had no union with her until she gave birth to a son" (Matthew 1:24, 25). It is more likely, then, that they had already had their wedding ceremony and even lived together as husband and wife. Technically, however, they would not have become husband and wife until their union was consummated—after Jesus was born. Matthew addresses the legal issue while Luke is more technical.

C. A Baby's Arrival (vv. 6, 7)

6, 7 While they were there, the time came for the baby to be born, and she gave birth to her firstborn, a son. She wrapped him in cloths and placed him in a manger, because there was no room for them in the inn.

It is commonly assumed that Jesus was born in a stable because of the word *manger*. That word simply describes a feeding place for animals such as sheep and cows. In the time of Jesus, such animals were sometimes kept near a house in a separate space. Thus Mary and Joseph may have been taken to an area that belonged to the *inn*, but was not the portion where guests usually stayed. Possibly any animals in this space at the time belonged to the persons staying at the inn.

Others have proposed that the birth of Jesus happened in a cave, which is also a place where animals were often kept. Wherever Jesus was born, it is clear that the event took place in very humble circumstances. Perhaps being away from the noise and confusion that probably characterized the inn during the time of taxation was, in some respects, to Mary and Joseph's advantage; at least it offered some privacy.

That Jesus is referred to as Mary's *firstborn* implies that she had other children later. Previously other passages have been cited (Matthew 13:55, 56; Mark

6:3) that indicate this to be the case. Some have proposed that since the first-born son enjoyed special privileges, this designation was also used to show that Jesus would be the recipient of special blessings from the heavenly Father.

This verse is also noted for its reference to the *cloths* in which Mary wrapped Jesus, more familiarly called "swaddling clothes." These were the ordinary clothes placed on a newborn. They were folded around a baby to make him or her feel more comfortable, warm, and secure. The way in which they were wrapped made the baby look almost like a small mummy.

Luke says nothing about an innkeeper in Bethlehem, but it seems every Christmas pageant has one. Often he is portrayed as cruel and heartless. If there were such an individual, perhaps he or she should be commended for finding a quiet, out of the way place where Mary could give birth. Ancient inns were often crowded, noisy, even dangerous places. This may have been especially true on this occasion, given the circumstances that had forced many to make an unwanted journey to Bethlehem in compliance with an unpopular emperor's decree.

II. A Day of Grace (Luke 2:8-12)
A. A Gift for All Men (vv. 8-10)

8 And there were shepherds living out in the fields nearby, keeping watch over their flocks at night.

The story now moves to the *fields nearby* Bethlehem, where *shepherds* were *keeping watch over their flocks at night.* Some believe that the birth of Jesus could not have happened anywhere near December 25, because that would be during the rainy season in Palestine; and shepherds would not be out in the field at that time of year. It is possible, however, that these sheep were being raised for use in the temple sacrifices in Jerusalem (since Bethlehem was not far from Jerusalem). In that case, these shepherds may well have needed to be in their fields throughout the year. In truth, we simply do not know what time of year Jesus was born. Let's just praise God that he was born—of that we can be certain!

9 An angel of the Lord appeared to them, and the glory of the Lord shone around them, and they were terrified.

This is the third time that Luke records the appearance of an *angel* in his narrative. On the other two occasions (to Zechariah in 1:11-20 and to Mary in 1:26-38) the angel was Gabriel, but here the angel is not named. And in this case, the shepherds were privileged to see something not revealed to either Zechariah or Mary: *the glory of the Lord.* This glory was a heavenly brilliance known to be a sign of the presence of God (Exodus 13:21, 22; 40:34, 35; 1 Kings 8:10, 11). According to the Jews, this glory (known as the *Shekinah*) was missing from the second temple. Now this glory had appeared to unsuspecting shepherds, and, quite naturally, they were *terrified* by the sight.

10 But the angel said to them, "Do not be afraid. I bring you good news of great joy that will be for all the people.

Since the immediate reaction of the shepherds was fear, it was appropriate for the angel to begin his message with the words, *Do not be afraid*. Gabriel had spoken these same words to Zechariah (Luke 1:13) and to Mary (Luke 1:30). It is noteworthy that this same angelic command was issued on the morning of Jesus' resurrection (Matthew 28:5). Thus the ministry of Jesus to the world was introduced and climaxed with the banishment of fear.

The reason that fear was not necessary was that the angel had come to convey a message of *good news*. The Greek phrase rendered "good news" is closely related to a word that gives us our word *evangelism*. The gospel is God's good news to a fallen world. Its product is *great joy*, and its scope is universal—*all . . . people*. The apostle John tells us that Jesus died for "the sins of the whole world" (1 John 2:2).

B. A Remedy for Our Sin (vv. 11, 12)

11 "Today in the town of David a Savior has been born to you; he is Christ the Lord.

The mention of the town of David (Bethlehem) here and in verse 4, plus the reference to the "house and line of David" in verse 4, testified to the important link between David and Jesus. That link had already been established in Gabriel's message to Mary (Luke 1:32, 33).

Three of the most familiar titles for Jesus are introduced in this passage. While other New Testament books, particularly the epistles, often refer to Jesus as *Savior*, Luke 2:11 is the only verse in the Synoptic Gospels (Matthew, Mark, and Luke) to use this title in reference to Jesus. At the same time, the concept of Jesus as Savior pervades the Synoptics, perhaps most notably in the angel's message to Joseph of how Jesus would "save his people from their sins" (Matthew 1:21). Interestingly, the Romans used this title to honor those who risked their lives to save the Roman state from the attacks of its enemies. Pagans used it of their gods as they sought to be saved from ill health and death. The Jews had used the term to describe those who had fought to save the Israelites from their opponents. Only Jesus is worthy of the title, for "he is able to save completely those who come to God through him" (Hebrews 7:25).

Jesus is also *Christ* (the Greek word for the Hebrew *Messiah,* which means "anointed"), because he is the anointed or chosen one who fulfills Old Testament prophecy. The term *Lord* calls attention to his authority over all things "in heaven and on earth" (Matthew 28:18). The verse is thus a comprehensive statement of who Jesus is and what he came to do.

12 *"This will be a sign to you: You will find a baby wrapped in cloths and lying in a manger."*

Often in the Scriptures the word *sign* means a miracle, but here it is describing that which gives sure direction. The angel did not explicitly command the shepherds to seek out the newborn child, but his words show that he expected them to do so. That the baby would be *wrapped in cloths* was indicative of the common way infants were cared for (as noted in the comments on verse 7). What was uncommon was the final, climactic phrase in the angel's description: the child would be *lying in a manger*—hardly the place where one would expect to find someone who held the exalted titles found in verse 11.

III. A Night of Glory (Luke 2:13-16)
A. A Sound of Praise (vv. 13, 14)

13, 14 *Suddenly a great company of the heavenly host appeared with the angel, praising God and saying, "Glory to God in the highest, and on earth peace to men on whom his favor rests."*

The heavenly messenger was *suddenly* joined by *a great company of the heavenly host.* Perhaps the timing is an indication of the kindness of God toward the shepherds. To begin this encounter with one glorious angel was frightening enough. To have begun with a vast array of angels might have thrown the shepherds into a state of panic.

Our Christmas carols typically depict the angels as "singing" their praises to God. The terms *praising* and *saying* are consistent with this idea, although they do not necessarily indicate a musical expression of praise. However, there is a sense of balance in the way the angels' words are constructed. *Glory* is paralleled by *peace, to God* is paralleled by *to men on whom his favor rests,* and *in the highest* is paralleled by *on earth.* This is the kind of poetic structure that one might expect to find in a song.

This passage illustrates the twofold meaning of the word *glory* in Scripture. There is the "glory of the Lord" (v. 9), which is the radiant light that shone from the angel, as well as the "glory to God," which refers to the praise that was spoken by the angels. God is worthy of having both kinds of glory attributed to him.

The phrase *on earth peace to men on whom his favor rests* is different from the more traditional rendering of "on earth peace, good will toward men." The translation in our printed text is probably a better rendering of the Greek text, emphasizing the kind of individuals who are to receive peace, but both translations express equally the idea that mankind is under God's good will and grace through Jesus Christ.

During the Christmas season, the thought of "peace on earth" is often treated as a highly noble and desirable ideal that is somehow in the power of man to attain. This is a perspective in direct opposition to what the angels declared in the fields near Bethlehem. Jesus came for the very reason that man cannot achieve real peace through his own agenda. Jesus himself declared, "Peace I leave with you; my peace I give you. I do not give to you as the world gives. Do not let your hearts be troubled and do not be afraid" (John 14:27). Without Jesus Christ, peace will always remain in the realm of elusive possibility. With Christ, any person can possess a peace that "transcends all understanding" (Philippians 4:7).

B. A Scene of Promise (vv. 15, 16)

15 When the angels had left them and gone into heaven, the shepherds said to one another, "Let's go to Bethlehem and see this thing that has happened, which the Lord has told us about."

Immediately the *shepherds* determined to travel to *Bethlehem* and investigate the sign given them. They showed admirable discernment in recognizing that what they had witnessed was not a dream or hallucination; it was something *about* which *the Lord* had *told* them. Their enthusiasm is the kind we often associate with people when they first come into contact with Jesus Christ.

The shepherds did not need to worry about losing their sheep while they were away in Bethlehem. The sheep could remain in their pen under the watch of a single shepherd, as was the case each evening when the men took turns sleeping.

16 So they hurried off and found Mary and Joseph, and the baby, who was lying in the manger.

The shepherds *hurried off* because of their intense excitement over the angel's announcement and instructions. Since Bethlehem was a small town, finding the *baby* probably did not take long. It is likely that the shepherds found him while it was still night. We are not told that they worshiped the Christ as did the Magi (Matthew 2:11), but we naturally suppose that their discovery caused the utmost reverence.

III. A Time of Good News (Luke 2:17-20)
A. A Message Worth Retelling (vv. 17, 18)

17 When they had seen him, they spread the word concerning what had been told them about this child,

These shepherds quickly became evangelists, for the basic definition of *evangelist* is one who "proclaims good news to others." The angel had delivered "good news" to the shepherds (v. 10), and they in turn felt compelled to share that good news with others.

Here is an example that should challenge us. The shepherds knew very little about the Messiah. They had not yet witnessed his ministry, his death, or his resurrection. They had not had the opportunity to enjoy the benefits of Jesus' work, to mature within the fellowship of his church, or to read the New Testament Scriptures. But they were ready to witness to what they did know regarding Jesus. We have a great number of advantages over the shepherds, and yet we are often so quiet among non-Christians that one might not even know that we have good news within us. We can learn much from the enthusiasm and forthrightness of these simple shepherds.

18 ...and all who heard it were amazed at what the shepherds said to them.

Is it any wonder that people *were amazed* at this extraordinary account told to them by the *shepherds*? While this initial reaction characterized *all who heard* what the shepherds had to say, many of the hearers may have proceeded to ignore their message, just as they would have normally written off the shepherds themselves because of their rustic, unsophisticated background.

It is not likely that the shepherds revealed the name of the young Messiah or his parents, since there is no indication in the Gospels that Jesus' identity was known prior to his revealing himself at his baptism. What is more likely is that the shepherds simply reported what they had seen and heard in the field and in the stable. This "rumor" that the Messiah had been born in Bethlehem would then serve to stir up a messianic expectation that both John the Baptist and Jesus could later tap into when they began their ministries.

B. A Story Worth Remembering (vv. 19, 20)

19 But Mary treasured up all these things and pondered them in her heart.

In stark contrast to the shepherds, who proclaimed boldly what they had witnessed, Mary *treasured up all these things and pondered them* in the privacy and quietness of *her heart*. It is considered natural for a mother to want to talk about her infant or to show her child proudly to any passerby. Yet, given the danger that this child would often face in the coming months, it was wise that Mary not be too vocal regarding Jesus. This characteristic of Mary provides another illustration of the wisdom of God in choosing her to be the mother of his Son.

> [20] *The shepherds returned, glorifying and praising God for all the things they had heard and seen, which were just as they had been told.*

The *shepherds* had left their flocks to see the child for themselves, but having seen and then witnessed of their experience, they *returned* to their tasks in the fields. What about us and our witness today? Some who follow Jesus answer the call to vocational service in his name. That is, their vocation—what they do to earn a living—is itself related to the spread of the gospel. Most of us, however, serve Christ in more "secular" settings. Just as the shepherds "returned" to their fields, so we return to our occupations each day. In so doing, however, we also return to our "fields," for the places where we work are often fields "ripe for harvest," as Jesus described them (John 4:35). There is great need in these places for the faithful, consistent testimony of dedicated Christians. Wherever we work, whether it be an office, an assembly line, a restaurant, a department store, or a farm, let us be committed to making a difference for Christ.

How to Say It

ALEXANDER. Al-ex-*an*-der.

ANTIOCHUS. An-*tie*-oh-kus.

AUGUSTUS. Aw-*gus*-tus.

BETHLEHEM. *Beth*-lih-hem.

BETROTHAL. be-*troe*-thul.

BRUTUS. *Broo*-tuss.

CAESAR. *See*-zur.

CASSIUS. *Cash*-us or *Cass*-ee-us.

CYRUS. *Sigh*-russ.

ELIZABETH. Ih-*lih*-zuh-beth.

GABRIEL. *Gay*-bree-ul.

GALILEAN. Gal-uh-*lee*-un.

GIDEON. *Gid*-e-un (*g* as in *get*).

HEROD. *Hair*-ud.

IMMANUEL *(Hebrew).* Ih-*man*-you-el.

JOSHUA. *Josh*-yew-uh.

JULIUS. *Jewel*-yus or *Joo*-lee-us.

LAZARUS. *Laz*-uh-rus.

MEDITERRANEAN. *Med*-uh-tuh-*ray*-nee-un (strong accent on ray).

MESSIAH. Meh-*sigh*-uh.

QUIRINIUS. Kwy-*rin*-ee-us.

SHEKINAH *(Hebrew).* Sheh-*kye*-nuh.

SYNOPTIC. Sin-*op*-tick.

ZACCHAEUS. Zack-*key*-us.

ZECHARIAH. *Zek*-uh-*rye*-uh (strong accent on *rye*).

Chapter 3

Birth and Beginnings (Part 2)

Luke 2:21-38; Matthew 2:1-12; Luke 2:39-52

PRESENTATION AT THE TEMPLE (LUKE 2:21-38)

Establishing the Groundwork

Having described the birth of Jesus and the visit by the shepherds, Luke records the circumcision and naming of the child on the eighth day after his birth (Luke 2:21). We are then told about a visit to the temple in Jerusalem by Joseph, Mary, and the baby Jesus. This would have been on the 40th day (Leviticus 12:1-4), but we know nothing about what transpired between these two occasions. We surmise that Joseph surely moved his family to more appropriate quarters than a stable just as soon as possible.

It is interesting to consider where the incident in the passage before us fits in relationship to the visit of the Magi and to the journey of Joseph, Mary, and Jesus into Egypt (Matthew 2:1-15). Probably these events followed the incident in the temple (though we cannot be sure how much time elapsed). It does not seem likely that Joseph and Mary's offering would have been a pair of birds if they had just received the treasures from the Magi. In addition, since Herod and "all Jerusalem" were "disturbed" by the word of a new king (Matthew 2:3), the presentation of Jesus in the temple at that time would have been extremely risky.

Some students question this sequence of events, because Luke says the couple and Jesus "returned to Galilee to . . . Nazareth" after fulfilling the Law's requirements concerning Jesus (Luke 2:39)—not to Bethlehem (where the Magi would find them). But Luke chose not to include the visit of the Magi or the flight to Egypt at all, so it was proper for him simply to mention the return to Nazareth at this point.

Examining the Text

I. Obedience to the Law (Luke 2:21-24)
A. Parents' Actions (vv. 21, 22)

21 On the eighth day, when it was time to circumcise him, he was named Jesus, the name the angel had given him before he had been conceived.

Since the time of Abraham, circumcision had been the sign of God's covenant with his people (Genesis 17:9-14). This ceremony was practiced *on the eighth day* after a male child's birth (Genesis 17:12) and accompanied the naming of the child. Joseph shows himself once again to be a righteous man (Matthew 1:19) not only by keeping the covenant of circumcision but also by obeying the command of *the angel* to name the child *Jesus* (Matthew 1:21; Luke 1:31) instead of some family name such as his own or that of his father.

> ²² *When the time of their purification according to the Law of Moses had been completed, Joseph and Mary took him to Jerusalem to present him to the Lord*

The student of the Bible must never forget that Jesus Christ was born under the *Law of Moses* and that he fulfilled its provisions fully in his life and teachings. The law specified in Leviticus 12 that a woman was to be considered ceremonially unclean for a specified period of time following childbirth. During this time, she was not to participate in public worship services or other activities outside the home. This period of being "unclean" was not intended to be a negative reflection upon women or upon childbearing, but was essentially a time of recuperation.

To mark the end of this time of uncleanness, the couple was expected to take a designated offering to a priest. While this could be done at home in the local synagogue, the ideal location for this act of purification was the temple. Since Jesus had been born in Bethlehem, just a few miles from *Jerusalem*, and Joseph and Mary apparently had decided to remain in the area, it was an easy thing for them to take advantage of their close proximity to the temple.

The law of Moses stipulated a period of uncleanness of forty days following the birth of a boy and eighty days after the birth of a girl (Leviticus 12:4, 5). Therefore, we can date Joseph and Mary's temple visit by knowing that the *time* of Mary's purification *had been completed* forty days after Jesus' birth. The forty-day period included the eight days during which circumcision occurred, as the Leviticus 12 passage shows.

B. Law's Requirements (vv. 23, 24)

²³ . . . *(as it is written in the Law of the Lord, "Every firstborn male is to be consecrated to the Lord"),*

The purification ceremony for the mother took an additional significance when she had given birth to her *firstborn* son. In the last of the ten plagues brought upon Egypt, every firstborn *male* of man and beast died, except in those families whose front door had been smeared with the blood of a slain lamb (Exodus 12:1-7, 13). From that point on, God laid claim to every first-born male among the Israelites (Exodus 13:1, 2, 12, 13).

In the verse before us, God's command to Moses found in Exodus 13:1, 2 is quoted. With livestock, an owner had the option of either killing the firstborn male animal as an offering to God or redeeming the animal through a substitute offering. In the case of children, there was only one option. Every Jewish couple was required to present their firstborn son to the Lord in the presence of a priest and redeem him with a sacrifice pre-scribed by the *Law of the Lord*.

²⁴ *. . . and to offer a sacrifice in keeping with what is said in the Law of the Lord: "a pair of doves or two young pigeons."*

The preferred *sacrifice* for this occasion, according to the *Law of the Lord*, was a yearling lamb and a small pigeon or dove (Leviticus 12:6, 7). However, in cases of poverty, the law permitted the presentation of *a pair of doves or two young pigeons* (Leviticus 12:8). As noted earlier, this offering suggests that the visit of the Magi occurred at some point after this purification ceremony; Joseph and Mary certainly could have afforded a lamb had they previously received the gifts that the Magi brought.

II. Encounter with Simeon (Luke 2:25-35)
A. Simeon's Background (vv. 25, 26)

²⁵ *Now there was a man in Jerusalem called Simeon, who was righteous and devout. He was waiting for the consolation of Israel, and the Holy Spirit was upon him.*

Luke's account shifts its focus, as he proceeds to introduce *a man in Jeru-salem called Simeon.* He seems not to have been a priest or a member of a group such as the Pharisees or Sadducees, or else the fact would probably have been stated. He is described as *righteous and devout*; that is, he was concerned for the welfare of his fellow human being and lived humbly and obediently before God.

In addition, Simeon *was waiting for the consolation of Israel*, which is an-other way of saying that he was anticipating the coming of the Messiah. Condi-tions for God's people at this time in history were bad. Things were bad politi-cally because the Israelites had little to say about their lives and laws, which were dictated by Rome. Things were bad religiously because Jerusalem was controlled by a coalition of scribes, Pharisees, and Sadducees, whose internal differences were forgotten only when they had a common enemy. Otherwise, their hypocrisy, legalism, laxity, and traditionalism on various points were notorious. The people of the day needed exactly the kind of "consolation" that only the Messiah could bring.

Also noted is the fact that *the Holy Spirit was upon* Simeon. This is important since, as the next verse states, the Spirit was the source of a special revelation given to Simeon.

26 *It had been revealed to him by the Holy Spirit that he would not die before he had seen the Lord's Christ.*

We are not told exactly how the information mentioned in this verse was *revealed to* Simeon *by the Holy Spirit.* It may have been in a dream, through an "inner voice" of intuition, or by some audible voice. In any case, Simeon's faithfulness and patience were rewarded with the assurance that *he would not die before he had seen the Lord's Christ.* This phrase seems to indicate that Simeon was an old man nearing death at this point (though it should be acknowledged that no indication of his actual age is ever given in Scripture).

Simeon enjoyed a privilege unparalleled among the saints of old. Hebrews 11 speaks of the Old Testament saints as men and women of faith who looked forward to something far better that God was preparing, but they died without experiencing the fulfillment of his messianic promise (Hebrews 11:39). Simeon was guaranteed that he would live long enough to see the Messiah.

Consider the kinds of people God gave special attention to surrounding the conception and birth of Jesus: a humble peasant couple (Joseph and Mary), older people (Elizabeth and Zechariah, Simeon, and Anna), shepherds (a despised occupation), and Zechariah, a priest (a respected occupation). From the outset God was communicating that Jesus is for all people—a point later proclaimed by Simeon (v. 31).

B. Simeon's Prayer (vv. 27-32)

27 *Moved by the Spirit, he went into the temple courts. When the parents brought in the child Jesus to do for him what the custom of the Law required,*

Joseph and Mary were going to be in the *temple* only briefly, so *the Spirit* directed Simeon to go just then in order to see the holy *child.* It is likely that this meeting occurred in the outer *courts* of the temple or in the court of the women, because Mary would not have been permitted to go beyond the court of the women.

The fact that Luke refers to the *parents* of Jesus does not contradict his own record or Matthew's of Jesus' miraculous conception and virgin birth.

Luke is speaking of Joseph as a parent in the legal sense here, just as he does later in 2:48.

28 . . . Simeon took him in his arms and praised God, saying:

Imagine the shock of having a stranger approach you and ask to hold your child. Luke's simple account does not indicate how much persuasion it took (if any) for *Simeon* to convince Jesus' parents to trust him. But with all of the unusual events that had already occurred surrounding Jesus' birth, Joseph and Mary were apparently open to granting this unusual request. It is one of the marvels of God becoming flesh (John 1:1, 14) that he who had held and directed Simeon all of his long life was now, in the person of his Son, held in Simeon's *arms.*

29 "Sovereign Lord, as you have promised, you now dismiss your servant in peace.

Simeon's words in verses 29-32 have come to be called the *Nunc Dimittis,* which is a Latin phrase for "you now dismiss." Having seen the *promised* Christ, Simeon knew that he could face death with *peace.* This verse also suggests that Simeon was elderly. We'd hardly expect a young man to suggest he was ready for God to "dismiss" him from life.

30, 31 "For my eyes have seen your salvation, which you have prepared in the sight of all people,

Simeon probably would not live to see any of Christ's miracles, but these brief moments in his presence were sufficient for him. His *eyes* looked at this baby and saw *salvation* for *all people.* This is somewhat similar to what Jesus did in his first recorded encounter with Simon Peter. He saw the potential within Simon and gave him the name *Peter,* from the Greek word meaning "rock." We should be challenged by Simeon's example to look beyond the external appearances of the people we meet and imagine the possibilities and potential that could emerge from their lives with the appropriate encouragement and support.

32 ". . . a light for revelation to the Gentiles and for glory to your people Israel."

Simeon exhibited an insight into God's plan of salvation that was uncommon among the Jews. The Jewish people were not an evangelistic people, sending missionaries among the *Gentiles.* Even the early church had difficulties understanding the full import of Jesus' Great Commission.

Simeon, however, spoke like the Old Testament prophets (see, for examples, Isaiah 42:6, 7 and Micah 4:1, 2) who anticipated the salvation of Gentiles as well as Jews. Since the Gentiles had lived for ages in spiritual darkness, without the knowledge of the Lord, the Messiah would bring them *light*. On the other hand, Israel enjoyed a covenant relationship with God that the Gentiles did not have. Some of the Jews had selfishly thought that this covenant was strictly for their benefit. But now they would realize their true *glory* when through them God's salvation would come to all nations just as he had promised when he first established his covenant with Abraham (Genesis 12:1-3).

C. Simeon's Prophecy (vv. 33-35)

33 The child's father and mother marveled at what was said about him.

Being strangers in Jerusalem, Joseph and Mary had been blending in anonymously with the temple crowd. It was highly unusual for a stranger to pick them out of the crowd and know the identity of their son. But what they *marveled* most at were the words of Simeon: the special promise that he would live to see the Messiah, his insight into their son's messianic mission, and his exceptional grasp of the broad extent of God's plan of salvation. All of this constituted still more evidence (added to what they had experienced thus far) that this child was like no other.

34 Then Simeon blessed them and said to Mary, his mother: "This child is destined to cause the falling and rising of many in Israel, and to be a sign that will be spoken against,

Simeon's initial words had been more general and seem to have included any who may have been standing nearby. Now he turned and spoke directly to *Mary*. That Jesus would *cause the falling and rising of many in Israel* indicates how he would become a kind of "watershed." Some would believe in him and find eternal life; others "did not receive him" (John 1:11). Some experienced his "consolation" (v. 25); others rejected it. The "rising" could apply to, for example, the humble fishermen who became Jesus' disciples. The "falling" would apply to those religious leaders who fancied themselves as recipients of the choicest places in the kingdom of Heaven, yet would find themselves cast out because they rejected the King (Matthew 8:12).

Simeon also described Jesus as a *sign* that would be *spoken against*. This too highlighted the rejection that Jesus would ultimately face, leading to his crucifixion. How different was the response of the shepherds to the "sign" given them, for they gladly accepted it as coming from God (Luke 2:12, 15).

35 ". . . so that the thoughts of many hearts will be revealed. And a sword will pierce your own soul too."

Here Simeon introduced the ominous thought that the Messiah's mission would include suffering (represented by the word *sword*). This is the first time such a thought appears in Luke's narrative of the birth of Jesus. The previous verse notes that Simeon's words at this point were directed specifically to Mary. The opposition against Jesus would become so pronounced that it would wound Mary, piercing her very *soul*.

No doubt it was difficult for Mary when the religious and political leaders began their verbal attacks against her son. Most agonizing of all, of course, was the pain she endured in watching him die the humiliating death of crucifixion. The fact that Jesus himself would be pierced is clear from the word *too*. Thus, even at this early stage in the life of Christ, we see the foreshadowing of the cross.

How are *the thoughts of many hearts . . . revealed* through Jesus? The ministry of Jesus would force people to respond either for him or against him. Neutrality would be impossible. Some three decades later, perhaps on the very spot where Simeon stood to utter his prophecy, it would be fulfilled. Some would believe in Jesus; but others, including the religious leaders, would reject him and demand his crucifixion. Even now, whenever we read Jesus' teachings and consider his example, we see his unique insight into the human condition.

III. Anna's Witness (Luke 2:36-38)
A. Anna's Devotion (vv. 36, 37)

³⁶ *There was also a prophetess, Anna, the daughter of Phanuel, of the tribe of Asher. She was very old; she had lived with her husband seven years after her marriage,*

Simeon was not identified as a prophet, yet he, through God's Spirit, prophesied on this day. *Anna*, on the other hand, is described as a *prophetess*. Her name is essentially the same as the Old Testament character Hannah, and it means "grace."

Anna is also described as a member *of the tribe of Asher*. When the promised land had been divided among the twelve tribes, Asher was assigned an area along the Mediterranean coast north of Mount Carmel. Although many of the people of this northern tribe had been carried away by the Assyrians (following the conquest of the northern kingdom by Assyria in 722 BC), the tribe had not completely lost its identity. Luke also mentions that Anna *lived with her husband seven years after her marriage*.

37 *. . . and then was a widow until she was eighty-four. She never left the temple, but worshiped night and day, fasting and praying.*

Following the death of her husband seven years into their marriage, Anna had never remarried. At the time of the incident recorded by Luke, she was *eighty-four* years old. To say that *she never left the temple* could mean that she had made some kind of arrangements for living in a residence on the temple grounds. But since this was not usually done for single women, the phrase more likely means that she made long visits to the temple each day. Whatever the case, it is clear from Luke's description that Anna possessed a spiritual character comparable to that of Simeon.

B. Anna's Declaration (v. 38)

38 *Coming up to them at that very moment, she gave thanks to God and spoke about the child to all who were looking forward to the redemption of Jerusalem.*

As a prophetess (v. 36), Anna most likely spoke words of encouragement and exhortation to the temple pilgrims she encountered regularly. On this occasion, she seems to have arrived just as Simeon was completing his message. Whether she heard the conclusion of his prophecy or whether she spoke independently of him, we are not told. Like Simeon, she *gave thanks to God*. Unlike him, she did not address the child's parents, but *spoke about the child* to others who possessed a strong messianic hope. Like the shepherds earlier in Luke 2, she too was a kind of evangelist.

It is not likely that either Simeon or Anna revealed the names of Jesus and his parents, since later, when Herod attempted to locate Jesus, his only clue for finding him was a birthplace and an approximate age. What these two godly individuals did was initiate a kind of "rumor" like that of the shepherds, which would stir up a messianic expectation. This in turn would prepare people for the preaching of John the Baptist and of Jesus, which would come later.

VISIT OF THE MAGI (MATTHEW 2:1-12)

Establishing the Groundwork

At this point in our study, it may be helpful to review the relationship between Matthew's and Luke's accounts of the birth and infancy of Jesus. In the first chapter of his Gospel, Matthew provides the genealogy of Christ and relates the simple facts about Joseph's initial perplexity concerning God's instructions, then his obedience as he married Mary and tenderly cared for her.

Luke gives details surrounding the birth itself, including the crowded inn, the announcement of the angels to the shepherds near Bethlehem, and the visit of the shepherds.

It seems clear that all of this had taken place approximately six weeks before the arrival of the Magi. For at the end of a forty-day period, as specified in the Law of Moses, Mary and Joseph had traveled to Jerusalem for her purification at the temple and the presentation of Jesus. The fact that Mary and Joseph presented the offering allowed for poorer people to provide suggests that the Magi had not yet come and presented their gifts. Furthermore, the very night the Magi arrived, Joseph and Mary found it necessary to depart in great haste to Egypt. The events in the temple must have occurred before this time.

Examining the Text

I. The New King's Star (Matthew 2:1, 2)
A. Journey of the Magi (v. 1)

¹ After Jesus was born in Bethlehem in Judea, during the time of King Herod, Magi from the east came to Jerusalem

The *King Herod* mentioned in this passage was the ruler known to history as Herod the Great, who ruled Judea as a result of his appointment by the Roman senate in 40 BC. Because Judea was in turmoil at that time, it took three years for Herod and the Romans to conquer this territory. He then continued as king from 37 BC to 4 BC. Jesus was born near the end of that time period.

Frequently the question is raised as to how Jesus could have been born four years "before Christ." The Gregorian Calendar, devised in 1582, was calculated to center on the birth of Christ. Thus, many Christians today assume that AD 1 corresponds to Christ's first year on earth and that his death at age 33 took place in AD 33. However, we now know from other research that these calculations were off by some four to five years. For example, we know that Herod died in March of 4 BC, but Jesus was born while Herod was still living. None of this should be of great concern to us, because calendars are human creations that have been modified frequently throughout history. What matters most is the historical certainty that "the Word became flesh and made his dwelling among us" (John 1:14).

Our word *Magi* is a Latin word that comes from the Greek word used here, *magoi*. The term is used of magicians or sorcerers (Acts 8:9; 13:6, 8) as well as other so-called "wise men" who advised kings and amazed the people. Their specific origin in *the east* is not certain. The ancient Medes and Persians (who lived in what is modern Iran) had their "wise men" who specialized in several scholarly disciplines. Daniel was considered to be one of their wise men in his day (Daniel 2:13), but he is not to be confused with the "enchanters, astrologers and diviners" who typically wore that name (Daniel 5:7). The ancient Babylonians (who lived in what is now Iraq) also had "wise men" who studied astronomy and developed charts for planetary and stellar orbits as well as accurate astral calendars.

As to the Magi mentioned in our text, some believe they were proselyte converts to Judaism; others claim that they were simply scholars interested in knowing more about the Jewish messianic hope, a subject of which people in all of the regions surrounding Jerusalem would have been aware. After all, many Jews had been dispersed throughout the known world centuries earlier by the Assyrians and Babylonians. Also, Jerusalem was located on a major trade route in the Middle Eastern world. Foreign travelers passing through could easily pick up bits and pieces of Jewish thought. Like Daniel, these men knew a different source of wisdom from that followed by the typical pagan wise men.

B. Quest of the Magi (v. 2)

2 . . . and asked, "Where is the one who has been born king of the Jews? We saw his star in the east and have come to worship him."

These Magi had more than just a passing interest in the Jewish Messiah. They had come to *worship* him. They claimed to have seen *his star in the east.* The nature of this star is not explained in the Scriptures, and many theories concerning it abound today. One view is that there was an alignment of certain stars and planets, such as Jupiter, the "king planet," that was interpreted as signaling the birth of a new king. It is also suggested that there may have been an unusual amount of meteoric activity, which became the source of a variety of interpretations. Given the precise movements of the star in conjunction with the Magi's search and Jesus' location, the only plausible explanation is that God created this particular star to guide the Magi to Palestine. He could have created and used one of the astronomical phenomena described above.

It is also possible that the Magi were familiar with a prophecy of the Old Testament uttered by Balaam, who was given prophetic insight concerning a "star" that "will come out of Jacob" and a "scepter" that "will rise out of Israel" (Numbers 24:15-17). Perhaps God provided special guidance to the Magi (similar to what he had provided to the shepherds and to Simeon and Anna) concerning the star and what it signified. (We know from Matthew 2:12 that such guidance was given later to the Magi.)

There may be some significance to the fact that no actual movement is attributed to the star until after the visit of the Magi to Jerusalem (v. 9). Some suggest that the fact that the Magi journeyed to Jerusalem rather than to Bethlehem suggests that the star was not yet guiding them to the whereabouts of the child; the Magi were simply assuming that the *king of the Jews* would be *born* in the capital city of the Jews.

Others propose that while no earlier movement of the star is mentioned, it is possible that the star had been the leading the Magi by taking them along the normal trade route from the East, which would have brought them to Jerusalem. Those who propose this suggest that clouds may have obscured the star for a time, which would account for the Magi's premature assumption that they had arrived at the proper location when they reached Jerusalem and for their joy at seeing the star as they left the city (v. 10).

II. The Old King's Plot (Matthew 2:3-8)
A. Demand of the King (vv. 3, 4)

³ When King Herod heard this he was disturbed, and all Jerusalem with him.

The words of the Magi *disturbed* Herod. Herod harbored a constant insecurity regarding his position as king of Israel. Herod's family was not of Jewish descent; they were Edomites. The Edomites were a people who, even though they could claim Jacob's brother Esau as their ancestor, had been hostile toward Israel for most of their history. Herod practiced the Jewish religion somewhat, but he was not a true Jew. Throughout his reign he feared that people would revolt against him, including members of his own family. Already by this time, Herod had killed several family members, including some of his own sons, because he suspected that they wanted his throne. In fact, shortly after this episode, and only five days before his death, Herod killed one more son out of fear and suspicion. If Herod heard talk of a new "king of the Jews," he would be more than a little disturbed!

Thus it was with good reason that *all Jerusalem* was disturbed along with Herod. The people had learned through bitter experience that when Herod was in a fit of envy and rage, no one within his reach was safe.

⁴ When he had called together all the people's chief priests and teachers of the law, he asked them where the Christ was to be born.

The high priest, those who had previously held the office, and those eligible to the office were referred to as *chief priests*. They, along with the teachers of the law (often called "scribes"), would be most likely to answer Herod's question as to *where the Christ was to be born.* Herod was familiar enough with the Jewish religion to know that their prophetic Scriptures spoke of a Messiah, but he did not know the specific details of those prophecies.

B. Report of the Priests and Scribes (vv. 5, 6)

⁵ *"In Bethlehem in Judea," they replied, "for this is what the prophet has written:*

The chief priests and teachers did not need to consult a concordance for the answer to the king's question. They answered immediately that the promised Messiah was to be born *in Bethlehem in Judea. The prophet* Micah, over seven hundred years before this time, had predicted this (Micah 5:2).

⁶ *". . . 'But you, Bethlehem, in the land of Judah,*
are by no means least among the rulers of Judah;
for out of you will come a ruler
who will be the shepherd of my people Israel.'"

Bethlehem was a small village, both in Old and New Testament times, but it was famous for being the birthplace of David. Now it was to become immortalized as the birthplace of the Son of David, the Messiah. Two functions of the Messiah are noted here: he would be a *ruler,* though not in the manner of a tyrant such as Herod, for he would also be a *shepherd,* carrying on the task that was also associated with David.

Here we see one reason why the church has often used fulfilled prophecies as an important component of "apologetics," or the defense of the Christian faith. Jesus fulfilled all messianic prophecies, even those that spoke of precise details outside of his control, such as the condition of his mother (a virgin) and the place of his birth (Bethlehem).

C. Instructions for the Magi (vv. 7, 8)

⁷ *Then Herod called the Magi secretly and found out from them the exact time the star had appeared.*

The initial inquiries of the *Magi* may have been in public areas such as the temple, where crowds of people could hear their story and be "disturbed," as noted under verse 3. But shortly thereafter they were summoned to a private meeting with *Herod.* The king wanted to know *the exact time the star had appeared* to the Magi.

Herod's subsequent actions reveal the motive behind his interest in the star. Assuming that the star first appeared on the day the new King was born,

Herod calculated the age of the child in order to know the age of the person he should look for as he tried to have the new King killed. His order to kill all male children two years old and younger (v. 16) may indicate that the star had first appeared two years earlier, and thus much earlier than the actual birth of Christ. More likely, Herod was giving his soldiers a "margin for error" to make sure they did not miss the one boy he was after.

> *8 He sent them to Bethlehem and said, "Go and make a careful search for the child. As soon as you find him, report to me, so that I too may go and worship him."*

Herod's scheme was set in motion. If *the child* was being hidden by his family for protection, the location was more likely to be revealed to foreign dignitaries seeking to honor the future King than to armed soldiers scouring through Bethlehem. So Herod sent the unsuspecting Magi out to do his searching for him and then inform him of the results. The king's craftiness and guile were worthy of the devil himself, as he cloaked his real intentions in pious language: *so that I too may go and worship him.*

III. The Magi's Success (Matthew 2:9-12)
A. Appearance of the Star (vv. 9, 10)

> *9 After they had heard the king, they went on their way, and the star they had seen in the east went ahead of them until it stopped over the place where the child was.*

The Magi now had the information they needed to locate where the new King was born, but they still did not know where in that town they would find the right child. However, once they resumed their journey, *the star they had seen in the east* guided them to *the place where the child was.* Such movement by the star clearly suggests God's guidance and not merely a natural phenomenon.

> *10 When they saw the star, they were overjoyed.*

This implies that the Magi had not seen *the star* for a while. As noted previously, some see this as evidence that the star had not led them the entire way and that the last time they had seen it was when they were in their homeland in the East. Others believe that the star may have been obscured for several days by clouds while the Magi were in Jerusalem. Thus the reappearance of the star would have indeed produced great rejoicing on their part, because they recognized that the divine guidance given by the star so clearly confirmed the information that the chief priests and teachers had given from the prophecies.

B. Gifts for the Child (v. 11)

11 On coming to the house, they saw the child with his mother Mary, and they bowed down and worshiped him. Then they opened their treasures and presented him with gifts of gold and of incense and of myrrh.

The shepherds found Jesus lying in a manger, probably in a stable of some sort. But the Magi found him in a *house.* Obviously Joseph had moved his family to more appropriate quarters just as soon as something became available. (Our modern nativity scenes with both shepherds and Magi surrounding the manger are historically inaccurate, but are usually done for the sake of convenience in telling the story.)

The *gifts* that the Magi presented to *the child* were extremely valuable. Many commentators have noted how the gifts highlight specific aspects of Jesus' ministry. *Gold* was certainly a fitting gift for a king. *Incense* (the traditional rendering of "frankincense" literally means "pure incense") refers to an expensive incense derived from the resin of a milky white tree. It was usually burned in a bowl to release a sweet aroma in a room. It was used in the temple worship and points to Jesus' high priestly ministry. *Myrrh* was also made from a tree resin and was quite expensive. It was used to alleviate pain (Mark 15:23) and to prepare a body for burial (John 19:39), thus this gift would call attention to Jesus' death on the cross. Some have observed that such gifts as these may have helped provide for the material needs of Joseph and his family during their journey to and from Egypt.

Consider the actions of the Magi toward Jesus. They presented him with expensive gifts and with acts of worship—and all of this before Jesus had actually done anything for them. He was just a baby, the promise of a King and a Savior. We today can see his work from a different perspective, as already completed. Yet, with this advantage, do we seek him and honor him with the same diligence and eagerness of these men?

C. Departure of the Magi (v. 12)

12 And having been warned in a dream not to go back to Herod, they returned to their country by another route.

This is the first indication of God actually speaking to the Magi. He had been guiding them before, but in a manner that had required them to seek out guidance from "secondary" sources (the star and the Jewish leaders). This time clear instructions were needed. God could not allow the Magi to assist *Herod* unwittingly in his murderous plot; therefore, he spoke through a *dream* to move the Magi away from Herod. At about the same time, he also used a dream to instruct Joseph to flee with his family to Egypt (Matthew 2:13). Thus the child who would someday be slain by "wicked men" (Acts 2:23) was carried to safety from the wicked King Herod.

JESUS ASTONISHES HIS PARENTS AND OTHERS (LUKE 2:39-52)

Establishing the Groundwork

The final passage to be examined in this segment of our study is another portion of Luke's Gospel. While chapter 2 of this Gospel focuses primarily on Jesus' birth and early life, the chapter also reveals much concerning Joseph and Mary.

Just after giving us the birth account, Luke shows us a picture of parents who desire "to do for [Jesus] what the custom of the Law required" (v. 27). Then at the conclusion of the account of the presentation of Jesus in the temple, Luke repeats this emphasis so that the parents' obedience forms a kind of "bookends" around this account (v. 39). Luke also records how the family of the young Jesus was serious in keeping the Passover in Jerusalem; and even though the law of Moses did not require women to attend, Mary's faithful attendance is noted (v. 41). In verse 42, the "custom" of the family's attendance at Passover is once more highlighted. Thus we are permitted a glimpse into the spiritual life of a dedicated family—a family in which the oldest son is actually the Son of God!

Examining the Text

I. To the Feast (Luke 2:39-42)
A. Jesus Grows Up (vv. 39, 40)

39 When Joseph and Mary had done everything required by the Law of the Lord, they returned to Galilee to their own town of Nazareth.

When Luke first introduced *Joseph and Mary* earlier in this chapter, he described their travel from *Nazareth* in *Galilee* to Bethlehem in obedience to the decree of Caesar Augustus (Luke 2:1-5). Now he relates their return to Nazareth following their obedience to the requirements found in *the Law of the Lord*.

40 And the child grew and became strong; he was filled with wisdom, and the grace of God was upon him.

Earlier the "bookends" found in verses 27 and 39 were noted. Luke 2:40 and 2:52 provide yet another set of such bookends, enclosing this account with an emphasis on Jesus' growth, both physical and spiritual. The reference to *wisdom* prepares us to understand the incident that follows.

B. Jesus Observes the Passover (vv. 41, 42)

⁴¹ Every year his parents went to Jerusalem for the Feast of the Passover.

The law of Moses stipulated that "three times a year all your men must appear before the Lord your God at the place he will choose" (Deuteronomy 16:16). The passage goes on to list these three feasts: Unleavened Bread (Passover), Weeks (Pentecost), and Tabernacles (Booths).

In New Testament times it was customary for many Jews to journey to Jerusalem to observe the Passover. The fact that Joseph and Mary made this trip *every year* reveals their sense of duty to God. The Jews had established a requirement (not found in Scripture) that required every Jew who was physically able and lived within 15 miles of Jerusalem to come to the city for the observance. Nazareth was about 70 miles away (or closer to 90 miles, if one traveled by the Jordan Valley route, which was used to avoid Samaritan territory), yet Joseph and Mary attended the Passover every year.

⁴² And the child grew and became strong; he was filled with wisdom, and the grace of God was upon him.

At the age of *twelve*, Jesus was nearing a point in life where Jewish boys were expected to become aware of their spiritual duties. Jewish literature outside the Bible states that the age of 13 was the point at which Jewish boys became obligated to the law of Moses. However, it was customary for Jewish youths to attend the Passover *Feast* as much as two years in advance of the "legal" age.

II. On the Road (Luke 2:43-45)
A. Parents Unaware (vv. 43, 44)

⁴³ After the Feast was over, while his parents were returning home, the boy Jesus stayed behind in Jerusalem, but they were unaware of it.

Galileans traveling to *Jerusalem* at feast times journeyed in large groups, perhaps as an extended family or clan. Such a group could pool its resources; in addition, the size of the group helped protect the members from would-be robbers. Under these circumstances, Jesus' *parents* perhaps assumed that he was traveling with other members of their caravan, including cousins, uncles, and aunts, or neighbors from Galilee. That they were *unaware* of his whereabouts does not show a lack of responsibility on their part; rather, it indicates how exemplary Jesus' obedience had been to this point.

44 Thinking he was in their company, they traveled on for a day. Then they began looking for him among their relatives and friends.

To travel *for a day* means that Joseph and Mary may have covered some fifteen to twenty miles of their journey before realizing their son was missing. As evening fell, they *began looking for* Jesus before making camp for the night.

B. Parents Frantic (v. 45)

45 When they did not find him, they went back to Jerusalem to look for him.

It is easy to imagine the fear and anxiety that Joseph and Mary felt upon realizing that Jesus was not in their group. They probably did not get much sleep that night before returning *to Jerusalem* the next day *to look for him.*

III. In the Temple (Luke 2:46-50)
A. Jesus Astonishes the Scholars (vv. 46, 47)

46 After three days they found him in the temple courts, sitting among the teachers, listening to them and asking them questions.

Most likely the period of *three days* can be understood to include the day's journey away from Jerusalem (v. 44), the day it took to travel back again, and one more day in Jerusalem looking for Jesus. Looking for someone in a Passover crowd could be a daunting task, since Jerusalem's "normal" population of between sixty and one hundred twenty thousand could swell to five times as many during this time.

One wonders whether Joseph and Mary may have had a notion about where to look for Jesus and thus headed straight for the *temple.* Even then, it was no small project to locate him; the temple's complex of *courts* covered more than twenty-five acres!

Jewish literature indicates that during special feast days, priests might come out from the temple sanctuary (where no "ordinary" worshiper could go) to mingle with the people in the various courts of the temple grounds and teach about the law. Perhaps it was in such a gathering that young Jesus stood listening to the teachers and asking them questions. We naturally wonder what specific matters Jesus and these men discussed, but Luke is silent about this.

47 And the child grew and became strong; he was filled with wisdom, and the grace of God was upon him.

The spiritual maturity that Jesus displayed *amazed* the teachers *who heard him.* It was not just that Jesus was able to ask profound questions (v. 46), but that he also provided *answers* to questions—answers that revealed an unusual depth of *understanding* for one so young. This certainly will not be the last time in Luke's Gospel that Jesus causes such astonishment (see Luke 4:22, 32, 36; 5:26; 9:43; 11:14).

B. Jesus Puzzles His Parents (vv. 48-50)

48 When his parents saw him, they were astonished. His mother said to him, "Son, why have you treated us like this? Your father and I have been anxiously searching for you."

The reaction of Jesus' *parents* upon finally locating their son is captured in the word *astonished. His mother* voiced their concern. Probably there had been very few times when Mary and Joseph had been given any anxious moments because of Jesus' conduct. The phrase *your father* conformed to the common usage of the day and should not be taken as indicating that Joseph was the real father of Jesus. The same could be said of the term *his parents.*

49 "Why were you searching for me?" he asked. "Didn't you know I had to be in my Father's house?"

In response to Mary's question, Jesus gave an answer that highlighted his mission as the Son of God and that is quite in keeping with all that Luke has related thus far concerning Jesus in the opening chapters of his Gospel. Jesus' reference to *my Father's house* was probably intentional, stating a contrast with Mary's reference to "your father" in verse 48. The phrase *my Father's house* is not that specific in the Greek text; it is much more general: "the things of my Father." The *King James Version* takes that to be "about my Father's business."

Most likely Jesus did not fully understand at this point in his life all that God the Father had given him to do. But his response does suggest his understanding that he had a divine purpose to fulfill.

50 But they did not understand what he was saying to them.

The words of Jesus presented riddles to Joseph and Mary that they could not solve. Perhaps they wondered whether their role as Jesus' parents would be taking a different direction. And yet, they should not have been too ashamed at their failure to understand Jesus' words. This same refrain would be heard more than once during the ministry of Jesus. Over and over those who witnessed his miracles and heard his words asked themselves what Jesus meant by what he did or said (see Luke 4:22; 9:45; 18:34). In all of these scenes, Luke will draw a sharp contrast between the wisdom of Jesus and the slowness of those around him. What we see before us in Luke 2:40, 47, 52 is an introduction to his superior wisdom.

THE TEMPLE IN JESUS' DAY

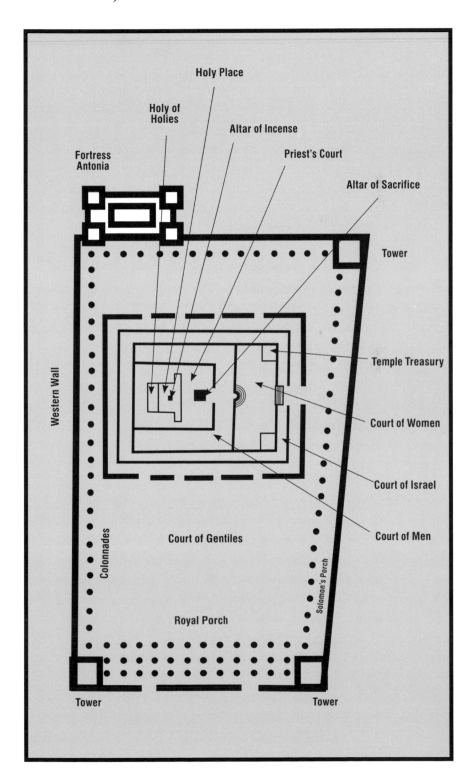

IV. Toward Home (Luke 2:51, 52)
A. Jesus' Obedience (v. 51)

51 Then he went down to Nazareth with them and was obedient to them. But his mother treasured all these things in her heart.

The previous verses may leave the impression that Jesus was a defiant child, or at least was becoming more so. But Luke's comment here cancels that possibility. As he grew toward manhood, Jesus *was obedient to* his parents. He demonstrated a godly example to the entire village of *Nazareth*. Sadly, these very people will be among those who reject Jesus' message in years to come (Matthew 13:53-58).

That Mary *treasured all these things in her heart* is in keeping with what Luke has previously recorded about her (v. 19). The implication seems to be that she did not share the events of this chapter with her neighbors in Nazareth. There was sufficient misunderstanding and difficulty as it was. Jesus himself would seek to make all things plain in his own time.

B. Jesus' Growth (v. 52)

52 And Jesus grew in wisdom and stature, and in favor with God and men.

Luke's brief statement about Jesus' growth carries none of the sensationalism of the fabricated, non-biblical accounts of Jesus' life that surfaced a few years later. Instead, Luke simply states how complete was Jesus' maturity—mentally (*in wisdom*), physically (*stature*), spiritually (*in favor with God*), and socially (*and men*).

How to Say It

ABRAHAM. *Ay*-bruh-ham.

ANNA. *An*-nuh.

APOLOGETICS. uh-*paw*-luh-*jet*-iks (strong accent on *jet*).

ASHER. *Ash*-er.

ASSYRIA. Uh-*sear*-ee-uh.

BETHLEHEM. *Beth*-lih-hem.

CIRCUMCISION. *sir*-come-*sih*-zhun (strong accent on *sir*).

CONSOLATION. kon-soe-*lay*-shun.

COVENANT. *kuv*-un-unt.

CRUCIFIXION. kroo-suh-*fix*-yun.

EDOMITES. *Ee*-dum-ites.

EGYPT. *Ee*-jipt.

ELIZABETH. Ih-*lih*-zuh-beth.

ESAU. *Ee*-saw.

FRANKINCENSE. *frank*-in-sense.

GALILEANS. Gal-uh-*lee*-unz.

GALILEE. *Gal*-uh-lee.

GREGORIAN. Grih-g*or*-ee-un.

HANNAH. *Han*-uh.

HEROD. *Hair*-ud.

INCENSE. *in*-sense.

ISRAELITES. *Iz*-ray-el-ites.

JACOB. *Jay*-kub.

JERUSALEM. Juh-*roo*-suh-lem.

JUDAISM. *Joo*-duh-izz-um or *Joo*-day-izz-um.

JUPITER. *Joo*-puh-ter.

MAGI. *May*-jye or *Madge*-eye.

MAGOI (*Greek*). *mahg*-oy.

MEDES. Meeds.

MEDITERRANEAN. *Med*-uh-tuh-*ray*-nee-un (strong accent on *ray*).

MESSIAH. Meh-*sigh*-uh.

MESSIANIC. Mess-ee-*an*-ick.

MICAH. *My*-kuh.

MIRACULOUS. mere-*rack*-you-lus.

MYRRH. mur.

NAZARETH. *Naz*-uh-reth.

NUNC DIMITTIS *(Latin).* Nunk Dih-*mit*-us.

PALESTINE. *Pal*-us-tine.

PASSOVER. *Pass*-oh-ver.

PENTECOST. *Pent*-ih-kost.

PERSIANS. *Per*-zhunz.

PHANUEL. Fuh-*nyoo*-el.

PHARISEES. *Fair*-ih-seez.

PROPHECIES. *prah*-fuh-seez.

PROPHETESS. prah-fuh-tess.

PURIFICATION. *pyoor*-if-ih-*kay*-shun (strong accent on *kay*).

SADDUCEES. *Sad*-you-seez.

SAMARITAN. Suh-*mare*-uh-tun.

SIMEON. *Sim*-ee-un.

SYNAGOGUE. *sin*-uh-gog.

TABERNACLES. *ta*-ber-*na*-kulz (strong accent on *ta*).

ZECHARIAH. *Zek*-uh-*rye*-uh (strong accent on *rye*).

Chapter 4

John the Forerunner
Matthew 3:1-12; Luke 3:10-14; John 1:19-34

CONTENT OF JOHN'S PREACHING
(MATTHEW 3:1-12; LUKE 3:10-14)

Establishing the Groundwork

The Gospel of Luke records John's birth and adds that he "lived in the desert until he appeared publicly to Israel" (Luke 1:80). Luke also includes the angel Gabriel's announcement to Zechariah that John would be dedicated to God's service from birth. "He is never to take wine or other fermented drink, and he will be filled with the Holy Spirit even from birth" (Luke 1:15). Later, Zechariah was filled with the Holy Spirit and prophesied that his son would be called "a prophet of the Most High" and would "go on before the Lord to prepare the way for him" (Luke 1:76).

When Mark begins his Gospel, he introduces the ministry of John the Baptist and follows with the account of the baptism of Jesus by John (Mark 1:2-11). Perhaps he does this because Jesus' baptism is the event that marked the active beginning of his public ministry. Matthew and Luke include brief accounts of Jesus' infancy and one event that occurred when he was 12; but Mark focuses especially on Jesus' works, so his baptism is the logical place to begin.

The second chapter of Matthew's Gospel contains the record of the visit of the Magi and of Joseph and Mary's flight to Egypt with the young child Jesus to escape King Herod's murderous intentions. Nearly 30 years of Jesus' life are passed over in silence between the end of chapter 2 and the beginning of chapter 3. There Matthew records John the Baptist's striking entrance upon the scene and his startling announcement.

Examining the Text

I. John's Ministry (Matthew 3:1-6)
A. Forceful Preaching (vv. 1, 2)

[1] In those days John the Baptist came, preaching in the Desert of Judea

The phrase *in those days* points back to the last verse of Matthew 2, and refers to the days when Jesus was still living in Nazareth. Luke is more specific than Matthew in designating *those days* to be "in the fifteenth year of the reign of Tiberius Caesar" (Luke 3:1). This would be late AD 26 or early AD 27. John's parents, Zechariah and Elizabeth, lived in "a town in the hill country of Judea" (Luke 1:39). Perhaps in his boyhood John became familiar with the area designated as the *Desert of Judea*, from which he would launch his ministry.

In the Synoptic Gospels (Matthew, Mark, and Luke), John is identified as *the Baptist*, or, more literally, "the Baptizer." When and by whom John first received this title is not known. Apparently the name was given due to John's most distinguishing action, the practice of immersing people in water as a sign of their change of heart toward God and his moral requirements.

The area known as the Desert of Judea is mainly west of the Dead Sea, but it extends up the Jordan Valley about four miles. Probably John began to preach southeast of Jericho where a ford across the Jordan gave John access to multitudes of travelers and merchants who might pause and listen. Those who heard him quickly spread throughout the nation the exciting news of this strange preacher and his thrilling announcement. The capital city of Jerusalem, only some 20 miles away, was shaken by the news, and so was the entire country.

² . . . *and saying, "Repent, for the kingdom of heaven is near."*

We can be certain that John's sermons were considerably longer than this one sentence. This statement captures the essence of John's preaching. The word *repent* describes, literally, a "change of mind." But it is not just a change in the way we think; it is also a change in the way we act. It is a turning *from* Satan and evil and a turning *toward* God and righteousness. The people listening to John needed to repent because God was about to do something marvelous in their time. That which had been predicted in both the law and the prophets and for which the Jews were waiting with great anticipation—the coming of the Messiah and the establishment of his *kingdom*—was *near*. If people were indifferent regarding obedience to the truth they had already been given, they would not be prepared to receive the revelation that the King would bring.

What is referred to in Matthew as the *kingdom of heaven* is often described in the other Gospels as "the kingdom of God." These are parallel phrases, as can be seen by comparing Matthew 13 and Mark 4. In neither case is the focus on a place (a kingdom located in Heaven or a territory on earth), but on a relationship. We are in a "kingdom relationship" with Heaven when God is our King and we are his servants.

It is in this sense that John could preach that the kingdom of Heaven was near. The Magi had asked, "Where is the one who has been born king of the Jews?" (Matthew 2:2). Now that King was about to begin his ministry. Then, after his resurrection, when "all authority" was given to him (Matthew 28:18), Jesus would begin to summon all people through the gospel to enter into a kingdom relationship with him by accepting him as their Lord and King.

B. Prophetic Fulfillment (v. 3)

³ This is he who was spoken of through the prophet Isaiah:
"A voice of one calling in the desert,
'Prepare the way for the Lord,
make straight paths for him.'"

Matthew refers to the prophecy in *Isaiah* 40:3. There the prophet called on God's people to *prepare the way* for God to come and rescue them from captivity in Babylon. Just as God had indeed delivered Israel from physical captivity in the sixth century BC, he would now rescue from the power of sin and death all who would accept the Deliverer he was sending.

The imagery of preparing the way and making *straight paths* is that of what might be termed an "advance team" preparing for a visit from a royal dignitary. Roads were smoothed out, straightened, and/or leveled in order to welcome the esteemed visitor. Such language was used to illustrate the need for leveling the hills of pride in the hearts of people and straightening out their manner of living to be in harmony with God's will. John was the "advance team" for Jesus, and those who heeded John's preaching gave ready hearing to Jesus' preaching. Those who scorned and rejected John's message became the enemies of Jesus.

C. Personal Characteristics (v. 4)

⁴ John's clothes were made of camel's hair, and he had a leather belt around his waist. His food was locusts and wild honey.

The description of both John's clothing and the food he ate indicates that his lifestyle was extremely simple. He devoted himself to his mission, not to seeking personal comfort.

Camel's hair was woven into a rough, heavy coat that gave protection from the weather and a covering for sleep at night. His *leather belt* held his robe together and also allowed him to gather up the bottom of his robe so he could move freely when he traveled through rocky terrain or waded into the Jordan River.

Locusts were a brown, grasshopper-like insect about three inches in length. They are still eaten by the bedouin tribes in the deserts of the Near East. Usually they are roasted. Locusts, along with *wild honey*, could be readily secured in the desert.

John's link with the ministry of the prophets is seen not only in the fulfillment of the prophecy in Isaiah 40:3, but in his similarities to the prophet Elijah. It was predicted by Gabriel that he would proceed "in the spirit and power of Elijah" (Luke 1:17). The backgrounds of both Elijah and John were obscure. Both were religious leaders of their day. Both upset female members of royal families—Jezebel and Herodias (respectively). Both spent time in the wilderness. Both preached about contemporary ethical issues. Both were bold. Both wore strange clothing. Both called for repentance. And both went through a period of time in which they questioned the validity of their ministry.

D. People's Response (vv. 5, 6)

⁵ People went out to him from Jerusalem and all Judea and the whole region of the Jordan.

The ministry of John was extremely well received. Though the religious leaders despised him, the multitudes loved him (note how a similar observation could be made of Jesus). So great was their regard for John that the Pharisees hesitated to make public statements critical of John for fear of agitating the crowds (Matthew 21:23-27). John's preaching appealed both to those from the capital city of *Jerusalem* and to those throughout *Judea and the whole region of the Jordan*, which would have included smaller communities of common laborers such as shepherds and farmers.

⁶ Confessing their sins, they were baptized by him in the Jordan River.

As previously noted, John must have received the nickname of "the Baptizer" because of the baptism that he required of those who responded to his preaching. Such a practice must have been rare or even non-existent in John's day for the title to have much meaning. First-century Judaism did devise a "proselyte baptism" to initiate Gentile converts into the Jewish faith, and the Jewish sect known as the Essenes used water baptism to symbolize their desire for spiritual cleansing. But there is no clear evidence that these pre-dated John's baptism. John's baptism was unique, both in its form and its purpose, and was intended to prepare the people spiritually for the arrival of the Messiah and the kingdom of Heaven.

The baptism of John was like Christian baptism in its outward form (immersion), but not in its meaning. John's baptism was not linked to the gift of the Holy Spirit (Acts 2:38). His audience was not told that they would be buried with Christ (Romans 6:3-6) or be clothed with Christ (Galatians 3:27). John offered a baptism "with water for repentance" (Matthew 3:11) that anticipated the coming of the Messiah and his salvation (Acts 19:4). This is how the link between John's baptism and forgiveness of sins (Mark 1:4; Luke 3:3) should be understood. His baptism looked forward to the time when forgiveness of sins could be offered as a result of Jesus' death and resurrection, just as the sacrifices under the law of Moses had looked forward to Christ's perfect sacrifice.

Note that believers in Jesus who had been baptized with John's baptism were challenged with the gospel to finish what they had started and to be "baptized into the name of the Lord Jesus" (Acts 19:1-5). John's baptism looked *forward* to the One who would fulfill the prophecies uttered by God's prophets under the Old Covenant. Christian baptism looks *back* to the actual fulfillment of those prophecies, specifically to the death, burial, and resurrection of Jesus (Romans 6:1-4).

Note also that John's baptism of Jesus had nothing to do with the forgiveness of sins, for Jesus had no sin. Jesus submitted to baptism, in his words, "to fulfill all righteousness" (Matthew 3:15).

II. John's Message (Matthew 3:7-12; Luke 3:10-14)
A. Challenge to Leaders (Matthew 3:7-10)

⁷ But when he saw many of the Pharisees and Sadducees coming to where he was baptizing, he said to them: "You brood of vipers! Who warned you to flee from the coming wrath?

Not all the responses to John's preaching were positive. The *Pharisees and Sadducees* were two religious parties among the Jewish people. They are not mentioned in the Old Testament because they arose during the approximately 400 years between the events recorded in Malachi (the last book of the Old Testament and the last of the Old Testament prophets) and those recorded in Matthew.

The name *Pharisees* comes from a Hebrew word meaning "separated." Members of this party were very careful to keep themselves separated from anything and anyone regarded as legally unclean. They had elevated the traditions of the Jewish rabbis to such an extent that they were regarded as being equal in authority to the written law of God. Toward the conclusion of his earthly ministry, Jesus exposed this group for the hypocrites that they were (Matthew 23:1-36).

The Sadducees were less rigid in their observance of the law and much more tolerant of contacts with the non-Jewish world. They openly cooperated with the pagan Romans who ruled Palestine at this time. They rejected the authority of oral rabbinic tradition. Whereas the Pharisees believed in the resurrection of the dead and the existence of angels and spirits, the Sadducees denied both (Acts 23:8). It is said that "nothing makes better friends than a common enemy," and for the Pharisees and Sadducees to join forces as they did to investigate John (and later Jesus) says something about the kind of threat they saw in him (as well as in Jesus).

The fact that these two groups were *coming to where he was baptizing* does not mean that they were coming to be baptized (see Luke 7:29, 30). They opposed John's ministry because he operated outside their oversight and disrupted the religious status quo. As they approached, John sounded like one of the ancient prophets as he challenged their hypocrisy and denounced them as a *brood of vipers*—an image that recalled the activity of the serpent in the Garden of Eden. It is one thing to tell an acknowledged sinner that he is on the outside of God's will; it is quite another to tell a person who thinks he is an insider that he is an outsider. But John was unafraid and unthreatened by those in high positions. Later, in verse 12, John would have more to say about God's *coming wrath* that unrepentant individuals such as these religious leaders faced.

⁸ *"Produce fruit in keeping with repentance.*

Just as "faith without deeds is dead" (James 2:26), so likewise *repentance* that does not bear *fruit* is nothing more than empty words. Biblical repentance is more than remorse at getting caught or regret at how badly a situation turned out. It is an honest acknowledgment of having done wrong and a genuine desire to live in a manner that demonstrates a true change of heart.

⁹ *"And do not think you can say to yourselves, 'We have Abraham as our father.' I tell you that out of these stones God can raise up children for Abraham.*

Many of John's hearers, and certainly the Pharisees and Sadducees, were intensely proud of their Jewish heritage. The mere fact that they were descendants of *Abraham,* and thus the chosen people of God, led them to believe that they had nothing to fear from the wrath of God. The general feeling among those in John's audience was that when the Messiah came and established his kingdom, all the Jews would be part of it. In contrast to this way of thinking, John made it clear that no one is born into God's favor, that behavior counts more than birthright in his sight. As both Jesus and Paul will stress, the true children of Abraham are those who have Abraham's faith and deeds (John 8:31-41; Romans 4:16).

To the leaders in particular, John pointed out that if they persisted in their disobedience, God could easily replace them. This had been demonstrated in the history of God's people. The corrupt leaders of an earlier time had been destroyed in the Babylonian captivity, but God had preserved a remnant and provided new leaders.

[10] *"The ax is already at the root of the trees, and every tree that does not produce good fruit will be cut down and thrown into the fire.*

Earlier John had introduced the metaphor of fruit *trees* (v. 8), and here he returned to it. *The ax is already at the root of the trees*; that is, the time of divine judgment is at hand. Unless there is a change of heart within those who until now have refused to repent, destruction is certain. The *fire* of God's wrath, mentioned in verse 7, refers to the judgment of Hell and is described as "unquenchable" in verse 12.

B. Coming of the Messiah (vv. 11, 12)

[11] *"I baptize you with water for repentance. But after me will come one who is more powerful than I, whose sandals I am not fit to carry. He will baptize you with the Holy Spirit and with fire.*

Here John drew a contrast between his baptism and that of the *one* who would *come* after him. John's baptism was *with water*, which may also be translated "in water." John's baptism was also *for repentance*. It was an act that publicly marked a person's turning away from sin and toward God and his ways.

However, the one coming after John would *baptize . . . with the Holy Spirit and with fire*. When Jesus was about to ascend into Heaven, he repeated the first part of this promise to his apostles: "For John baptized with water, but in a few days you will be baptized with the Holy Spirit" (Acts 1:5). This was fulfilled ten days later on the Day of Pentecost (Acts 2:1-4). Some suggest that the baptism with the Holy Spirit and fire were the same event, noting that "what seemed to be tongues of fire" rested on the apostles at the beginning of Acts 2. Jesus, however, made no mention of a baptism with fire in his statement in Acts 1:5. In addition, the fire mentioned by John in the verse before us clearly refers to the fire of judgment, as the next verse indicates. It seems, therefore, that John was describing two different events: the baptism of the Holy Spirit on the Day of Pentecost and the baptism of fire for the wicked on the Day of Judgment (Matthew 25:41; Revelation 21:8).

Others suggest that the promise concerning the Holy Spirit seems to include a broader group than just those who would later become apostles. Under this interpretation, Jesus, after his death and resurrection, would baptize in the power of the Holy Spirit all who would trust and obey him. The fulfillment of this promise began with the apostles in a special way at Pentecost, but was expanded to include all subsequent baptized believers (1 Corinthians 6:11; 12:13). However, Peter's reference to the outpouring of the Holy Spirit on Cornelius and his family "as he had come on us at the beginning" (Acts 11:15) suggests that what happened to the apostles had not been repeated until then. This baptism of the Holy Spirit was apparently a special event and not for every believer.

John described the one who would follow him as *more powerful than I, whose sandals I am not fit to carry*. John operated with a clear understanding of his relationship to Jesus. Desiring no glory for himself, all that he did was for the advancement of the Messiah's ministry. He knew that his was a temporary role; he later declared, "He must become greater; I must become less" (John 3:30). Taking the *sandals* off another in preparation to wash that person's feet was considered the most lowly and least desirable act of a domestic servant. John considered himself farther removed from the Messiah than the lowest slave was from his master. That's humility!

> *12 "His winnowing fork is in his hand, and he will clear his threshing floor, gathering his wheat into the barn and burning up the chaff with unquenchable fire."*

After *wheat* was gathered at the harvest, it was taken to the *threshing floor*, where the grain was separated from the straw, usually by having oxen trample it or drag something resembling a sled over it to break the grain out of the husks that surrounded it. The straw could then be easily removed, but the grain was still mixed with *chaff* (the husks and the small, broken pieces of straw). So the grain, including the chaff, was then scooped up with a *winnowing fork* and tossed into the air. The wind separated the light chaff from the heavier grain. The grain was then stored for later use, and the chaff was scooped up and burned.

John's picture of wheat and chaff clearly pictures what will occur on the Day of Judgment when the saints will be separated from the sinners. Jesus gave a similar description of the judgment using the figure of sheep and goats (Matthew 25:31-46).

C. Counsel to the People (Luke 3:10-14)

> *10 "What should we do then?" the crowd asked.*

In this section from Luke's Gospel, we see examples of those among John's audience who wanted to "produce fruit in keeping with repentance" (Matthew 3:8). Some in the crowd responded to his appeal in a way strikingly similar to the response to Peter's sermon on the Day of Pentecost (Acts 2:37): *What should we do then?*

¹¹ John answered, "The man with two tunics should share with him who has none, and the one who has food should do the same."

John suggested a very practical application of his message: he urged compassion on the needy. In John's day, most people had no need of *two tunics* (a tunic was worn by both men and women under one's outer garment or robe). John also encouraged the sharing of *food* with any who needed it. If this spirit of kindness characterized disciples of John, how much more should it be the trademark of followers of Jesus! That Jesus wants this spirit to be our trademark is clear from his teaching about final judgment in Matthew 25:31-46.

¹² Tax collectors also came to be baptized. "Teacher," they asked, "what should we do?"

Different occupations offer different temptations and different needs for expressions of repentance. *Tax collectors* have never been popular, but in Jesus' day they were especially despised as thieves and traitors. They were viewed as traitors because of their cooperation with the Romans. They were regarded as thieves because many of them were! The Roman system of tax collection encouraged them to use strong-arm tactics and take more than was required of the citizens, allowing them to pocket the surplus. (Recall that Jesus made a significant difference in the lives of two tax collectors—Matthew and Zacchaeus.) These men addressed John respectfully as *Teacher.*

¹³ "Don't collect any more than you are required to," he told them.

John commanded the tax collectors not to *collect any more than* what was *required* by law. Note that Zacchaeus, following his encounter with Jesus, was so concerned about his own practices that he gave half of his wealth to the poor and offered to those whom he had wronged four times the amount they had been cheated (Luke 19:8).

¹⁴ Then some soldiers asked him, "And what should we do?"
He replied, "Don't extort money and don't accuse people falsely—be content with your pay."

Even *soldiers* were attracted to John's message. We do not know what kind of soldiers these were. Limited numbers of them were available to guard the king, to monitor the temple, and to escort tax collectors. Soldiers also served as a kind of police force; perhaps some had been assigned to keep order in the crowds that had come to hear John. John urged these men to be ethical in all their dealings with the public. They were not to *extort money* or *accuse people falsely*. They must be satisfied with what they earned and not take money "on the side."

Notice that John did not recommend that either tax collectors or soldiers resign from their positions. He told them to demonstrate integrity in everything they did. Notice also that the repentance demanded of all the inquirers who came to John dealt with money and property in relation to people. God would always have his children use their money and property for the benefit of people—never the other way around!

CONFLICT WITH RELIGIOUS LEADERS (JOHN 1:19-34)

Establishing the Background

John 1:18, which concludes the "prologue" of the Gospel of John, says that the eternal Word, who "became flesh" (v. 14), was the One who revealed God to humanity. That Word was then made known through the testimony of John the Baptist (whom the apostle John had introduced in John 1:6-8). John 1:19-34 records John's testimony concerning who he was not, who he was, and who Jesus was.

Examining the Text

I. John the Announcer (John 1:19-23)
A. Identification Demanded (v. 19)

¹⁹ *Now this was John's testimony when the Jews of Jerusalem sent priests and Levites to ask him who he was.*

As used in this Gospel, the term *the Jews* often refers particularly to the Jewish leaders who were hostile to Jesus (see John 7:1; 9:22; 18:12-14). The Jewish leaders *of Jerusalem* would include members of the Sanhedrin, a body of seventy men, including the chief priests, elders, and scribes (the high priest served as president). This group served as the guardians of the nation's faith, overseeing the religious practices and activities among the Jewish people. John the Baptist had made such an impression that he could not be ignored by these leaders. Some among them may have shared the feelings of those who responded positively to John's message, but others were interested in him only because he posed a threat to their vested interests.

The delegation sent by the Sanhedrin included *priests and Levites*. Priests conducted worship and offered sacrifices in the temple. Levites usually assisted the priests in their ministry but occasionally assisted in teaching (Nehemiah

8:7-9). Later we are told that members of the Pharisees, which was the party most interested in matters of Scriptural interpretation and religious practice, were also represented in this committee of inquiry (v. 24). The group began with a very simple question of John; they wanted to know *who he was*.

B. Messiahship Denied (vv. 20-22)

20 He did not fail to confess, but confessed freely, "I am not the Christ."

John the Baptist was aware of the rumors circulating that he might be *the Christ* (see Luke 3:15). Had John been a lesser man or more concerned with his own "image," he might have used such rumors as an opportunity for personal glorification. With the public following that he had gathered, he could have claimed he was the Messiah, thus heading a great revival movement that would have challenged the religious leaders in Jerusalem.

The structure of his response emphasizes the *I*. The anticipated Christ was not he, but someone immeasurably greater.

21 They asked him, "Then who are you? Are you Elijah?"
He said, "I am not."
"Are you the Prophet?"
He answered, "No."

Since John had so quickly assured his questioners that he was not the Christ, the investigating committee now raised other questions. *Are you Elijah?* The Old Testament had closed with the prediction that God would send Elijah "before that great and dreadful day of the Lord comes" (Malachi 4:5). Once more John's answer was *I am not*, but in his answer he was rejecting the commonly held view that Elijah would come back to earth in the flesh. Before the birth of John the Baptist, the angel Gabriel had told his father, Zechariah, that he would go "before the Lord, in the spirit and power of Elijah" (Luke 1:17). Jesus himself stated that John was the fulfillment of the prophecy concerning Elijah (Matthew 11:7-10; 17:10-13). Thus the prophecy was to be interpreted figuratively, not literally as those who questioned John were thinking.

The question concerning *the Prophet* most likely refers to a statement made by Moses in Deuteronomy 18:15: "The Lord your God will raise up for you a prophet like me from among your own brothers. You must listen to him." Again, John responded negatively; he was not that Prophet—Jesus was (see Acts 3:18-23). At the same time, Jesus' testimony concerning John should be noted: "What did you go out to see? A prophet? Yes, I tell you, and more than a prophet" (Matthew 11:9). But John was not "the Prophet" in the way in which this delegation meant the term.

Notice how John's replies to his questioners became increasingly brief as the questions continued. The last one was answered with a simple *No*.

²² Finally they said, "Who are you? Give us an answer to take back to those who sent us. What do you say about yourself?"

The members of this delegation were in an embarrassing and increasingly frustrating situation. They had been sent to obtain information, and all they had received thus far was disappointment in their expectations and denial of their allegations. All they had learned to this point was who John was not. So they returned to their original question (v. 19): *Who are you?* They also acknowledged that they were not acting independently; they needed *an answer to take back to those who sent* them.

C. Purpose Declared (v. 23)

²³ John replied in the words of Isaiah the prophet, "I am the voice of one calling in the desert, 'Make straight the way for the Lord.'"

In a previous study, we noted Matthew's citation of *Isaiah* 40:3 as being fulfilled through the ministry of John the Baptist (Matthew 3:1-3). Here we have John's own quotation of the prophecy. The picture is that of a herald for a king. Before modern means of communication, heralds were very important persons, making public pronouncements in the name of or on behalf of a king. And when a herald announced that the king planned to visit a particular territory within his realm, the roads would be prepared so that there would be no obstacles in the way. "This," John declared, "is who I am; I am the herald of a king, and my king is the Lord."

II. John the Baptizer (John 1:24-28)
A. Posing the Question (vv. 24, 25)

²⁴, ²⁵ Now some Pharisees who had been sent questioned him, "Why then do you baptize if you are not the Christ, nor Elijah, nor the Prophet?"

As was noted previously, the *Pharisees* were eager guardians of the law of Moses and the traditions of the elders. They seem to have been rather persistent in their interrogation of John. Apparently they figured that the *Christ*, or even a returning prophet, would have recognizable authority to introduce a new religious practice (such as John's baptism seemed to be) or even to require a ceremonial cleansing of those who were already faithful Jews. But what right did an ordinary person such as John, who had already denied that he was the Christ, *Elijah*, and *the Prophet*, have to do this?

This issue resurfaced amidst discussions that transpired during the final week of Jesus' life. Did John's practice of baptism have divine authority, or was it a human invention (Matthew 21:23-27)?

B. Pointing to Jesus (vv. 26, 27)

26 "I baptize with water," John replied, "but among you stands one you do not know.

John did not answer the Pharisees' question directly, but took it as an opportunity to announce the presence of the promised Messiah. He did acknowledge that he baptized *with water*, but there was a larger issue. The Pharisees needed to become acquainted with the greater One whom John had come to introduce. His authority for baptizing was based on his role as the forerunner for the Messiah. A dramatic change in the way God would deal with humanity was on the horizon. It was proper that a change of such magnitude should be announced in a striking manner.

Jesus had been *among* the people who had come to John to be baptized, and he would be among the crowds again the following day (v. 29). Until now, however, they had no idea of his real identity.

27 "He is the one who comes after me, the thongs of whose sandals I am not worthy to untie."

John uses language similar to that found in Matthew 3:11. It was ordinarily the duty of a servant to loosen the *sandals* of arriving guests. But John considered even this lowly task too noble for him to perform. He saw himself as lower than a common household servant in his relation to Christ.

How did the inquirers who came to investigate John the Baptist respond to this great announcement? How sincere was their desire to meet this One of whom John spoke? Did they clamor to hear more? Apparently not. They concluded that there was nothing more to be gained from speaking with John; the interview was finished. We can only wonder what the group reported to the Sanhedrin when they returned to Jerusalem.

C. Placing the Event (v. 28)

28 This all happened at Bethany on the other side of the Jordan, where John was baptizing.

Since the *Bethany* mentioned here was located *on the other side*, or the east side, *of the Jordan* River, it should not be confused with the Bethany near Jerusalem where Mary, Martha, and Lazarus lived. Apparently it was one of several places along the Jordan Valley where *John* was preaching and *baptizing* (John 3:23).

III. John the Witness (John 1:29-34)
A. "Here He Is!" (vv. 29, 30)

²⁹ The next day John saw Jesus coming toward him and said, "Look, the Lamb of God, who takes away the sin of the world!

The next day refers to the day after the delegation from Jerusalem had interrogated John. Note the timing of Jesus' *coming*; enough of the same audience remained for John to address them with a reference to previous comments. At the same time, the committee from Jerusalem was gone. Having dealt with their questions, John could now freely and enthusiastically point to the promised One.

A further observation concerning timing is that it had been about six weeks since Jesus had come from Nazareth and persuaded John to baptize him. Immediately following that, Jesus had been alone in the wilderness, fasting and enduring temptation (Matthew 3:13—4:11). Now John was able to say, "Look! This is the One I have been talking about!"

John's reference to the *Lamb of God* opens up a treasure trove of meaning. In faith Abraham had assured Isaac that "God himself will provide the *lamb* for the burnt offering" (Genesis 22:8). A *lamb* had been a part of the annual Passover observance for each family in Israel as the nation celebrated its deliverance from bondage in Egypt (Exodus 12:1-11). The sacrifice of a *lamb* was part of the daily ritual for the Israelites, morning and evening, in the tabernacle (Exodus 29:38, 39). Isaiah spoke of the sacrificial *lamb* in his prophecy of the Suffering Servant (Isaiah 53:7). The final book of the Bible, Revelation, pictures the glorified Lamb, standing though looking as if it had been slain, and recognized in Heaven as the only one worthy to open the sealed scroll (Revelation 5). John the Baptist's language at this point was also appropriate, in that the Passover was soon to be observed (John 2:13).

Something more than the Passover was implied in John's introduction of Jesus as the Lamb of God, *who takes away the sin of the world*. The blood of the Passover lamb protected from immediate physical death; God's Lamb would remove sin entirely by bearing in his own body the suffering that rightly belonged to humanity (1 Peter 2:24; 1 John 2:2). It is most significant that John affirmed that the Lamb's redemptive work would not be limited to the Jews, some of whom had expressed to John great pride in their heritage (Matthew 3:9), but was for the entire world.

30 "This is the one I meant when I said, 'A man who comes after me has surpassed me because he was before me.'

John reminded his audience of his statement of the previous day (vv. 26, 27). At that time, he had referred to Jesus in a veiled manner. Now he made that identification positive. Jesus, the living Word (John 1:14), was unquestionably and immeasurably *before* John, by virtue of both his pre-incarnation existence in eternity and his standing as God's Son on earth.

B. "He Is the Reason I Baptize" (v. 31)

31 "I myself did not know him, but the reason I came baptizing with water was that he might be revealed to Israel."

John was always aware of Jesus as a person. Their mothers were related and had spent time together during their pregnancies, no doubt talking about the sons who were to be born of them (Luke 1:36, 39, 56). John was six months older than Jesus (Luke 1:36), and he had been preaching and baptizing for some time before Jesus came to him for baptism. Until that moment, John *did not know him* in the sense of knowing that Jesus was the Messiah; but he was well enough acquainted with him to know that it was more fitting for him to be baptized by Jesus than the opposite (Matthew 3:13, 14).

C. "This Is How I Know Him" (vv. 32, 33)

32, 33 Then John gave this testimony: "I saw the Spirit come down from heaven as a dove and remain on him. I would not have known him, except that the one who sent me to baptize with water told me, 'The man on whom you see the Spirit come down and remain is he who will baptize with the Holy Spirit.'

God, who had appointed John to be the forerunner of the Christ, revealed to him that the Christ would be identified as the one *on whom you see the Spirit come down and remain*. This sign occurred when Jesus was baptized (Matthew 3:16, 17; Mark 1:9-11; Luke 3:21, 22). The Spirit came down *as a dove*. This visible sign was confirmed by spoken testimony from the Father.

John was also told of how the Christ would *baptize with the Holy Spirit*. (Comments on this phrase were included under the study of Matthew 3:11.)

D. "Now I Tell You" (v. 34)

34 "I have seen and I testify that this is the Son of God."

Here is the climax of John's testimony regarding Jesus. He had heard this testimony from Heaven, and he delighted in fulfilling his ministry as the voice announcing *the Son of God*. Two days later (John 1:35, 43) Nathanael, having been brought to Jesus by Philip, hailed him as "the Son of God" (John 1:49).

The Jews who had interrogated John had suggested high titles that might be linked to him. He rejected them all, reserving all such titles for Jesus alone. But then he attributed to Jesus a title higher than any they had mentioned. Some time later in Jesus' ministry, the people who had heard and observed Jesus suggested again some of those earlier titles as worthy of him (Matthew 16:13, 14). On that occasion, Simon Peter used the title declared by John when he confessed, "You are the Christ, the Son of the living God" (Matthew 16:16). For the apostle John, the sonship of Jesus became the theme of his Gospel as stated in John 20:31: "These [miraculous signs] are written that you may believe that Jesus is the Christ, the Son of God, and that by believing you may have life in his name."

It is a high privilege for any of us to join with John the Baptist, Peter, and John the apostle in affirming that Jesus is the Son of God. It is a high purpose for which we have been born—and born again.

How to Say It

ABRAHAM. *Ay*-bruh-ham.

BABYLONIAN. Bab-ih-*low*-nee-un.

BEDOUIN. *Bed*-uh-wun.

BETHANY. *Beth*-uh-nee.

ELIJAH. Ee-*lye*-juh.

ELIZABETH. Ih-*lih*-zuh-beth.

ESSENES. *Eh*-seenz.

GABRIEL. *Gay*-bree-ul.

HEROD. *Hair*-ud.

HERODIAS. Heh-*roe*-dee-us.

ISAAC. *Eye*-zuk.

JERICHO. *Jair*-ih-co.

JERUSALEM. Juh-*roo*-suh-lem.

JEZEBEL. *Jez*-uh-bel.

JUDAISM. *Joo*-duh-izz-um or *Joo*-day-izz-um.

JUDEA. Joo-*dee*-uh.

LAZARUS. *Laz*-uh-rus.

LEVITES. *Lee*-vites.

MAGI. *May*-jye or *Madge*-eye.

MALACHI. *Mal*-uh-kye.

MESSIAH. Meh-*sigh*-uh.

NATHANAEL. Nuh-*than*-yull (*th* as in *thin*).

NAZARETH. *Naz*-uh-reth.

PALESTINE. *Pal*-us-tine.

PENTECOST. *Pent*-ih-kost.

PHARISEES. *Fair*-ih-seez.

PHILIP. *Fil*-ip.

PROSELYTE. *prahss*-uh-light.

RABBINIC. ruh-*bin*-ick.

SADDUCEES. *Sad*-you-seez.

SANHEDRIN. San-huh-drun or San-*heed*-run.

SYNOPTIC. Sin-*op*-tick.

TABERNACLE. *ta*-ber-*na*-kul (strong accent on *ta*).

TIBERIUS CAESAR. Tie-*beer*-ee-us *See*-zur.

ZACCHAEUS. Zack-*key*-us.

ZECHARIAH. *Zek*-uh-*rye*-uh (strong accent on *rye*).

Chronology of the Life of Jesus

		• BIRTH IN BETHLEHEM •
30 YEARS	Luke 3:23	Youth at Nazareth
		• BAPTISM •
	Matthew 4:2	40 DAYS—TEMPTATION
SEVERAL MONTHS		3 days—Winning first disciples
	John 2:1	Wedding feast at Cana
	John 2:12	"Not many days"—Residence at Capernaum
	• John 2:13 •	• FIRST PASSOVER •
		Cleansing the Temple
		EARLY JUDEAN MINISTRY
	John 4:35	December
		Jesus at Jacob's Well
ONE YEAR		"four months till harvest"
	Matthew 4:12	Beginning of Galilean Ministry
		Ministry at Capernaum
	Matthew 4:23	FIRST CAMPAIGN THROUGHOUT GALILEE
	• John 5:1 •	• SECOND PASSOVER •
		Healing the Lame Man at the Pool of Bethesda
	Matthew 5–7	SERMON ON THE MOUNT
ONE YEAR	Luke 8:1-3	SECOND CAMPAIGN THROUGH GALILEE
		THIRD CAMPAIGN
	Matthew 9:35–11:1	The Apostles sent forth
	• John 6:4 •	• THIRD PASSOVER •
		Feeding of the 5000
		Climax and Close of Galilean Ministry
		Decapolis Ministry
	John 7:2	FEAST OF TABERNACLES
		Sermons and Growing Controversy
ONE YEAR		September
	John 10:22	FEAST OF DEDICATION
		Sermon on the Good Shepherd
		December
		PEREAN MINISTRY
	• Matthew 26:2 •	• FOURTH PASSOVER •
		Crucifixion
43 DAYS		3 days—Resurrection
		40 Days
		• ASCENSION •

Adapted from R.C. Foster, *Life of Christ*, 1971.

Chapter 5

Beginning of Jesus' Ministry
Matthew 3:13-17; 4:1-11;
John 1:35-42; 2:1-11; 3:1-17; 4:7-10, 19-26

JESUS' BAPTISM (MATTHEW 3:13-17)

Establishing the Groundwork

When Jesus was about 30 years of age, he was ready to undertake his ministry. This he did in no ordinary way. He demonstrated his complete dedication to the will of God by walking from Nazareth to the territory near the Jordan River where John the Baptist was conducting his ministry. Jesus did not have a personal need for repentance or the forgiveness of sins, for he was sinless. He desired to be baptized, in his words, "to fulfill all righteousness" (Matthew 3:15). No doubt part of this involved setting an example for us, just as he did in all other aspects of his life.

Examining the Text

I. Arrival at the Jordan (Matthew 3:13-15)
A. John's Protest (vv. 13, 14)

¹³ Then Jesus came from Galilee to the Jordan to be baptized by John.

The distance from Jesus' home in Nazareth of *Galilee* to the scene of John's ministry was approximately seventy miles. John was preaching in the Desert of Judea (Matthew 3:1) and baptizing in the *Jordan* River. Most likely he conducted his ministry near a ford over the Jordan in the four miles of the wilderness through which that river flows just before it empties into the Dead Sea.

According to Luke's Gospel, "crowds" were coming to be baptized by John (Luke 3:7). Most likely Jesus was part of such a crowd when he came to be baptized, for Luke later tells us, "When all the people were being baptized, Jesus was baptized too" (Luke 3:21). We are not told in the Scriptures whether any from the crowds were still present at Jesus' baptism or whether only Jesus and John the Baptist were present at that point. We know that John was forewarned about the significance of the baptism (John 1:33, 34).

14 But John tried to deter him, saying, "I need to be baptized by you, and do you come to me?"

Although John had not yet received the sign that would identify the Messiah, he recognized something special in Jesus' character, and in proper humility he confessed that it was more appropriate for Jesus to baptize him. Since the mothers of John and Jesus were related (Luke 1:36), quite possibly the families met together in Jerusalem at some of the annual feasts or gathered on other occasions. One would think that John knew of Jesus' miraculous birth as much as he knew of his own. Perhaps when Jesus came to him to be baptized, John was virtually certain of Jesus' true nature; but he would not know positively until the Holy Spirit descended upon Jesus after his baptism.

B. Jesus' Plea (v. 15)

15 Jesus replied, "Let it be so now; it is proper for us to do this to fulfill all righteousness." Then John consented.

The answer of Jesus left no room for doubt or further discussion. His baptism was to be performed *now*. The reason Jesus gave was *to fulfill all righteousness*. For Jesus to be baptized was the "right thing" before God. This was the will of the Father, to which Jesus was always subject (John 5:30). Perhaps he saw it as "right" that he should express before God his own readiness for the kingdom of Heaven (Matthew 3:2) and his willingness to assume God's appointed role for him in that kingdom as the Messiah who must suffer and die for the sins of the world (John 1:29).

II. Act of Obedience (Matthew 3:16, 17)
A. What Was Seen (v. 16)

16 As soon as Jesus was baptized, he went up out of the water. At that moment heaven was opened, and he saw the Spirit of God descending like a dove and lighting on him.

The circumstances surrounding the baptism of Jesus make it clear that the action was immersion: *he went up out of the water* (note the similar phrase in Acts 8:39). At that moment *heaven was opened*, and *the Spirit of God* descended *like a dove*. As noted earlier, at least Jesus and John witnessed this event; perhaps others present also saw the dove but did not comprehend the meaning of its *lighting on* Jesus. The descent of the Spirit marked the beginning of Jesus' Spirit-empowered ministry. Immediately after this, Jesus was "led by the Spirit into the desert" (Matthew 4:1) and defeated the devil and his temptations. From that time on, Jesus worked miracles by the power of the Spirit (Matthew 12:28).

B. What Was Heard (v. 17)

[17] And a voice from heaven said, "This is my Son, whom I love; with him I am well pleased."

Once again, it is not clear whether only Jesus and John heard the *voice from heaven*. Perhaps any bystanders on this occasion heard something but did not understand the message given. (For similar occurrences, see John 12:28, 29 and Acts 22:6-9.)

On two other occasions later in his ministry, Jesus heard the voice of God. One occurred at the transfiguration (Matthew 17:5), the other during the last week of his ministry (John 12:23-29). All three came at crucial times. The first came just as he was about to enter his ministry. The second came when his popularity was at its peak, and the third came during the final week as he prepared to die on the cross.

JESUS' TEMPTATION (MATTHEW 4:1-11)

Establishing the Groundwork

It was in the desert that John the Baptist had begun his proclamation of the imminent coming of the Christ and the critical need for all to prepare for his appearance. Likewise, the climactic struggle with the enemy of God and of all that is good took place in the desert. The area was wild and desolate, nearly barren, and usually forsaken by humanity. Mark offers the somewhat ominous detail that Jesus "was with the wild animals" (Mark 1:13).

Examining the Text

I. Trusting God's Word (Matthew 4:1-4)
A. Not Motivated by Feelings (vv.1-3)

[1] Then Jesus was led by the Spirit into the desert to be tempted by the devil.

Jesus had just been baptized. The *Spirit* of God had come to him, and God's voice from Heaven had proclaimed him to be God's Son. One might think that Jesus would be immune to temptation at such a time of exaltation, but it was not so. The first decisive leading of the Holy Spirit after his descent upon Jesus was to lead him into bitter combat with *the devil*. As a part of his preparation for his ministry to those enslaved by the devil (see Hebrews 2:14, 15), Jesus had to pass through the fires of temptation; and this is where the Spirit led him.

² After fasting forty days and forty nights, he was hungry.

The fact that Jesus spent *forty days and forty nights* in the desert *fasting* likely indicates that he was spending a significant amount of time each day in prayer and meditation. The issue for Jesus that would have been serious enough to warrant such intense prayer and fasting was the messianic ministry that now lay before him. Fasting was typically done for short periods of time, from one day to a week. To say that Jesus *was hungry* following his days of fasting is quite an understatement.

No mention is made of Jesus' doing without water during the 40 days. It seems likely that he obtained water from oases or trickling streams that existed in the desert.

³ The tempter came to him and said, "If you are the Son of God, tell these stones to become bread."

We are not told in what form *the tempter came to* Jesus. The devil can appear as "an angel of light" (2 Corinthians 11:14) or as "a roaring lion" (1 Peter 5:8). Since he presented himself as sympathetic to Jesus' needs, one may assume that he resembled in some way an angel of light. Each temptation the devil placed before Jesus was carefully aimed at his present situation, striking where he was most vulnerable and in a manner that actually could have seemed reasonable and thus all the more tempting.

Satan's first temptation focused on Jesus' physical weakness and hunger. Satan also took care to package his temptation in the most appealing manner possible. *If you are the Son of God*, he began. It may appear that he was telling Jesus, "I don't really believe you are the Son of God. Prove it to me." But it is more likely that he meant, "If you are the Son of God (and we both know you are), then do this." Jesus had heard the voice from Heaven say, "This is my Son, whom I love" (Matthew 3:17), and he knew that he was "led by the Spirit" (4:1); but he had yet to do anything truly messianic or supernatural. So far he had simply been alone in the desert for 40 days. Perhaps the devil was suggesting that Jesus attempt a miracle with the stones just to take advantage of his special status as the Son of God. Or he may have proposed that Jesus use his powers to preserve his life so that he would be able to carry out his messianic calling.

Whatever the intent of Satan's words, they constituted a subtle attempt to get Jesus to give up trusting in God for his needs and to take some initiative on his own. But since the Holy Spirit had directed him into the wilderness, the Holy Spirit was the one who should tell him what to do next. To move ahead of the Spirit would have been a sin.

B. Relying on God (v. 4)

⁴ Jesus answered, "It is written: 'Man does not live on bread alone, but on every word that comes from the mouth of God.'"

Jesus responded to the devil's clever ploy with a quotation from Deuteronomy 8:3. Jesus could identify with the full context of this passage, which describes how the children of Israel wandered for 40 years in another wilderness, living each day by the manna that came from Heaven. Moses cautioned them that their greater desire should always be for the Word of God. It has often been noted that by his use of Scripture when tempted, Jesus gave us an excellent example for dealing with our own temptations.

II. Serving God's Will (Matthew 4:5-7)
A. Not Acting With Presumption (vv. 5, 6)

⁵ Then the devil took him to the holy city and had him stand on the highest point of the temple.

The holy city was Jerusalem. *The highest point of the temple* probably would have been at the top of one of the several towers built onto the roof of the temple complex to give it a look of grandeur.

The text does not indicate how *the devil took* Jesus from the wilderness near the Jordan to this new location. He may have challenged Jesus to travel to Jerusalem and meet him at a designated place, but for Jesus to accept such a challenge seems almost the same as yielding to temptation. Thus it is more likely that he used supernatural powers and transported Jesus there immediately. Some believe that this was a "mental" temptation that does not imply actually being present in Jerusalem. And while nothing in the account specifically suggests this, the next temptation strongly suggests that Satan used mental images rather than literal views, since there is no mountain from which "all the kingdoms of the world" (v. 8) can be seen at once.

The order of the second and third temptations in Matthew's account are the reverse of that found in Luke 4:5-12. One may assume that one of the Gospel writers, perhaps Luke, was following a chronological order, while the other was telling the events according to the emphasis he wanted to make (perhaps desiring to end with what he considered the most pivotal of the three temptations). Matthew's climactic "Away from me, Satan!" (v. 10) certainly fits that understanding.

⁶ "If you are the Son of God," he said, "throw yourself down. For it is written:

"'He will command his angels concerning you,
and they will lift you up in their hands,
so that you will not strike your foot against a stone.'"

With this second temptation, the devil completely reversed his strategy. Earlier he had expressed a hypocritical fear that Jesus was about to die. Now he took the position that it was impossible for Jesus to die, no matter what he did. Satan also followed up on what Jesus had said about living by God's Word alone by quoting a portion of that Word (Psalm 91:11, 12). If Jesus would throw himself down from the temple pinnacle, Satan implied that Jesus would be demonstrating that he trusted God's promise to keep him from harm. Wouldn't that be an example of living by the word God had spoken?

As Jesus looked ahead to his ministry, he knew what it held for him—three years of slow, patient teaching and preaching, with often disappointing results, to reach what would become a handful of followers. And then at the end stood a cross. By suggesting that Jesus perform such a spectacular stunt as this, Satan offered an easy way out. In one bold stroke Jesus could astound the people in Jerusalem and gain a quick (and sizable) following. What an impressive way for him to begin his messianic ministry!

B. Humble Before God (v. 7)

7 Jesus answered him, "It is also written: 'Do not put the Lord your God to the test.'"

Returning once again to the book of Deuteronomy, Jesus quoted a verse that effectively called the devil's bluff: *Do not put the Lord your God to the test* (Deuteronomy 6:16). To do as Satan suggested would not have demonstrated trust in God, nor would it have been living by the word that God had spoken. In reality it would have shown doubt and distrust. No one, including the Messiah, should presume to tell God what to do. Jesus did not need proof that God would keep his word and send angels to save him from harm. For Jesus, it took more complete trust in God not to throw himself down from the temple than to do so.

In the future, Jesus will indeed descend to the earth on the clouds of Heaven even as he ascended there (Acts 1:11), but that coming will be based on the spiritual ministry and the saving death of his first coming. It will not be for mere display, but to bring the final summons of judgment.

III. Seeking God's Glory (Matthew 4:8-11)
A. Not Thinking of Self (vv. 8, 9)

⁸ Again, the devil took him to a very high mountain and showed him all the kingdoms of the world and their splendor.

The location and identity of this *very high mountain* are unknown. Of course, it is not possible to see *all the kingdoms of the world* from a single mountain, no matter how high it may be. As a result, some believe that *the devil* showed Jesus these kingdoms in some kind of a vision, particularly because of Luke's statement that the devil showed Jesus "in an instant all the kingdoms of the world" (Luke 4:5).

⁹ "All this I will give you," he said, "if you will bow down and worship me."

The subtlety that characterized the first two temptations was now abandoned by the devil in the third. He came directly to the point: all of what he had just showed Jesus could be his—*if you will bow down and worship me*.

As Jesus considered the kingdoms of the world and their splendor, perhaps he also considered the lonely road to Jerusalem that he must one day travel to die for the sins of the world. And even after he offered such a sacrifice, a large part of the world would still reject him as King. Satan proposed an easier way: Jesus could have the world, and he could bypass the horrible suffering of the cross.

B. Focused on God (v. 10)

¹⁰ Jesus said to him, "Away from me, Satan! For it is written: 'Worship the Lord your God, and serve him only.'"

Jesus recognized Satan's lie for what it was. Jesus would not have gained the kingdoms of the world by bowing to Satan; rather, the devil would have seized both the kingdoms of the world and power over Jesus. In this response, Jesus was as direct with his enemy as the enemy had been with him. Drawing a third time from Deuteronomy (6:13), Jesus refused to give to the devil what belonged only to *the Lord*. For Jesus, there was no room for compromise with the plan laid out for him by his Father.

C. Strengthened by Angels (v. 11)

¹⁰ Then the devil left him, and angels came and attended him.

After his third defeat, *the devil* retreated—but only to watch for another opportune moment to tempt Jesus (Luke 4:13). Now that Jesus had proven himself entirely faithful, God was pleased to fulfill the promise of Psalm 91:11, 12 and to send *angels* to assist Jesus—probably both physically and spiritually—in the recovery of his strength. Mark also notes the presence of angels, though he gives no details about the temptations (Mark 1:13).

JESUS' ENCOUNTER WITH JOHN THE BAPTIST'S DISCIPLES (JOHN 1:35-42)

Establishing the Groundwork

This passage introduces us to some of the men who eventually became disciples of Jesus. At least two of them began as disciples of John the Baptist. This text immediately follows John's declaration of Jesus as the Lamb of God and his testimony of how Jesus' baptism indicated that he was the Son of God (John 1:29-34). Reacting to that testimony, two men sought out Jesus, became his disciples, and came to know for themselves the validity of John's witness.

This remains the New Testament model for evangelism: as one person who knows Christ testifies to another, others also become his followers.

Examining the Text

I. Andrew and John Meet Jesus (John 1:35-39)
A. John the Baptist's Testimony (vv. 35, 36)

35 The next day John was there again with two of his disciples.

The apostle John selects three particularly busy days near the close of the period when Jesus was being tempted in the desert to tell his readers what was occurring in the ministry of *John* the Baptist. The first of these days involved John's being interrogated by the delegation of Jewish leaders from Jerusalem (John 1:19-28). The day after this took place, Jesus came to where John was preaching (vv. 29-34), having completed his 40 days of being tempted. *The next day* mentioned in this verse was the third day in the apostle John's account.

On this day John was present along with *two of his disciples.* From verse 40 we learn that one of these disciples was Andrew, Simon Peter's brother. The other, though his name is never given, was most likely the apostle John, the writer of this book. Never, in this Gospel, does the writer refer to himself by name; usually he designates himself as "the disciple whom Jesus loved" (John 13:23; 19:26; 20:2; 21:7, 20).

36 When he saw Jesus passing by, he said, "Look, the Lamb of God!"

The day before, John had identified *Jesus* by the title of *Lamb of God.* Now he used this title in the hearing of these two disciples.

B. Andrew and John's Response (vv. 37-39)

37 When the two disciples heard him say this, they followed Jesus.

Since John had made it clear that he was only the herald of the Christ, his directing of the *disciples'* attention to *Jesus* could be understood as an invitation to them to seek him out.

38 Turning around, Jesus saw them following and asked, "What do you want?"

They said, "Rabbi" (which means Teacher), "where are you staying?"

With the question *What do you want?* Jesus was not asking for information but was initiating a conversation. In reply the two disciples addressed Jesus as *Rabbi.* This was a title of highest respect among the Jews, used with the meaning of "master" or "teacher." Their addressing Jesus in this manner was a clear indication of their interest in receiving instruction from him.

39 "Come," he replied, "and you will see."

So they went and saw where he was staying, and spent that day with him. It was about the tenth hour.

We are not told *where* Jesus *was staying.* Having just come from the temptations in the wilderness, he may have been camping out in the hills nearby.

With his reference to *the tenth hour,* John most likely was using the Roman method of counting time. This was the same as ours, meaning that the tenth hour would have been 10:00 AM. The two disciples would thus have been able to spend several hours in conversation with Jesus and still have time for Andrew to go find his brother Simon and bring him to Jesus on the same day.

II. Peter Meets Jesus (John 1:40-42)
A. Andrew's Testimony (vv. 40, 41)

40 Andrew, Simon Peter's brother, was one of the two who heard what John had said and who had followed Jesus.

It may seem strange that *Andrew* is identified as *Simon Peter's brother.* When John wrote his Gospel, however (around AD 90-95), the name of Peter was widely known; but many reading this account might not readily identify Andrew.

41 The first thing Andrew did was to find his brother Simon and tell him, "We have found the Messiah" (that is, the Christ).

Although Andrew did not become one of the better-known apostles of Jesus, his contribution to the kingdom of God is incalculable as a result of his bringing his brother Simon to Jesus with the simple testimony, *We have found the Messiah.*

B. A New Name for Simon (v. 42)

⁴² And he brought him to Jesus.
Jesus looked at him and said, "You are Simon son of John. You will be
called Cephas" (which, when translated, is Peter).

It seems to have required no argument or urging on Andrew's part to
persuade *Simon* to return with him to Jesus, who promptly gave Simon a new
name. The name *Cephas* is Aramaic and means "stone." The Greek equivalent
is *Peter* (from the word *petros*), and it was by this name that the apostle would
become known.

Of course, at this point in his life Peter was anything but "rock solid"; the
Gospels show him to be impetuous, brash, sometimes bold, sometimes fearful.
But Jesus could look into Peter's heart and see what it was possible for him to
become and what he would become.

JESUS' FIRST MIRACLE (JOHN 2:1-11)

Establishing the Groundwork

This portion of Scripture records Jesus' first miracle, which occurred at a
wedding at Cana in Galilee. At a first-century wedding, the guests did not see
the happy couple stand together and promise to love, cherish, and protect each
other "till death do us part." The equivalent of such promises occurred at the
"betrothal," when a man and a woman became engaged. The "marriage" was
more similar to what we call a wedding reception—simply a glad celebration
and a time to rejoice with the happy couple and wish them well in their life
together. In some cases the festivities would go on for a week. It is not hard
to imagine that such an extended party might easily consume more food and
drink than the host had provided, producing the kind of crisis described in the
following account.

Examining the Text

I. Embarrassing Situation (John 2:1-5)
A. The Occasion (vv. 1, 2)

¹ On the third day a wedding took place at Cana in Galilee. Jesus' mother
was there,

Most likely *the third day* refers to the third day since Jesus had left the
region of Judea, where John the Baptist was, to go to Galilee (John 1:43). The

exact location of *Cana in Galilee* is not known. Some believe it was situated about nine miles north of Nazareth. *Jesus' mother was there*, probably because Mary was a relative or close friend of either the bride or the groom, or possibly both if Nazareth was not far from Cana. It seems she was also assisting in some way with the wedding feast. No mention is made of Joseph, which may indicate that by this time he had died.

² . . . and Jesus and his disciples had also been invited to the wedding.

Jesus had been away from home for nearly two months. During that time, he had been baptized by John the Baptist; he had spent 40 days in the desert while being tempted; and he had returned to the Jordan and recruited his first *disciples* from among the disciples of John. This group would have included Peter and Andrew (John 1:40-42), John (the "other disciple" in John 1:35-40), and Philip and Nathanael (John 1:43-51). Some suggest that John's brother James was a part of the group as well, making a total of six disciples.

B. The Need (v. 3)

³ When the wine was gone, Jesus' mother said to him, "They have no more wine."

As noted previously, a wedding celebration at that time could last for several days. The reason why *the wine was gone* is not given, nor is it important. The fact that there was no more was terribly embarrassing for the host.

Why did *Jesus' mother* approach him about this dilemma? Perhaps she came expecting a miracle, although Jesus had never done a miracle before, as verse 11 indicates. Yet Mary knew that her son was also God's Son, destined to rule forever (Luke 1:31-33). Now he was approximately thirty years old (Luke 3:23). He had been baptized. He had gathered a few disciples. All of these events might have been taken to indicate that Jesus was about to assert himself and begin the promised rule. Was Mary hoping he would do so by working a miracle to produce more wine? At the very least, she seemed to recognize that Jesus had the power to do something to address the present crisis.

C. The Plan (vv. 4, 5)

⁴ "Dear woman, why do you involve me?" Jesus replied. "My time has not yet come."

Although Mary had not specifically asked Jesus to do anything, the subtle suggestion and appeal were present. The question *why do you involve me?* is literally rendered as "What to me and to you?" Jesus' words seem to say that the shortage of wine was none of his business or of Mary's.

Jesus then added, *My time has not yet come.* References to Jesus' "hour" or "time" occur elsewhere in John's Gospel (7:6, 8, 30; 8:20). It is clear from later usage of this language in John that Jesus' "time" described his crucifixion (12:23, 27; 13:1; 16:32; 17:1). Mary was mistaken if she thought this was the time for Jesus to fulfill his mission as the Son of God. Jesus was respectfully but firmly telling Mary that she must not undertake to dictate his course of conduct in such important matters as the working of miracles.

⁵ His mother said to the servants, "Do whatever he tells you."

Mary's reply shows that she was not offended by Jesus' words. She simply told the *servants* present to *do whatever* Jesus told them to do. The fact that Mary gave orders to the servants suggests that she was a close friend or even a relative of the host.

II. Miracle (John 2:6-10)
A. The Material (vv. 6, 7)

⁶ Nearby stood six stone water jars, the kind used by the Jews for ceremonial washing, each holding from twenty to thirty gallons.

For the benefit of his non-Jewish readers, John provided the information that the *six stone water jars* were necessary to hold the *water used by the Jews for ceremonial washing.* The jars were evidently placed in the courtyard so that the guests might wash their feet and hands. The washing of hands before eating was of particular importance to the Jews (Matthew 15:1, 2). The water would be dipped from the jars and then poured over the feet and hands as servants assisted.

⁷ Jesus said to the servants, "Fill the jars with water"; so they filled them to the brim.

The *servants* immediately responded to Jesus' order to *fill the jars with water.* With the jars *filled . . . to the brim,* there was no way that Jesus could have tricked the servants by adding a little wine on the top.

B. The Product (v. 8)

⁸ Then he told them, "Now draw some out and take it to the master of the banquet."
They did so,

One can only wonder what thoughts must have gone through the minds of these servants. Since the host needed more wine, it would have been more than humiliating to take him a container of water; it might even cost them their position and livelihood. Yet they obeyed, perhaps because of Mary's earlier orders, but also because there was something about the presence of Jesus that commanded obedience. Imagine their shock when they drew wine out of the jars into which they had just poured water!

C. The Result (vv. 9, 10)

⁹ . . . and the master of the banquet tasted the water that had been turned into wine. He did not realize where it had come from, though the servants who had drawn the water knew. Then he called the bridegroom aside

The *master*, or host, *of the banquet tasted the water that had been turned into wine*, and immediately he knew there was a difference between this wine and the wine he had drunk before. Since he did not know the source of the wine, his comments were unbiased. Although the *servants* knew the origin of the wine, they did not divulge that information at this point. For them to try to explain where the wine came from would only have subjected them to ridicule.

¹⁰ . . . and said, "Everyone brings out the choice wine first and then the cheaper wine after the guests have had too much to drink; but you have saved the best till now."

The master of the banquet cited the common practice of serving *the choice wine first,* while the *guests'* sense of taste was keener, and then serving *the cheaper wine* when the guests' sense of taste had become dulled. There is no evidence from the text that anyone was drunk on this occasion; certainly the master of the banquet was not, for with his first sip he knew the wine produced by Jesus was *the best* he had tasted on this occasion.

III. Epilogue (John 2:11)
A. The Beginning of Miracles (v. 11a)

¹¹ᵃ This, the first of his miraculous signs, Jesus performed at Cana in Galilee. He thus revealed his glory,

Of the four Gospel writers, only John records this miracle *at Cana.* He also tells us that it was *the first of* Jesus' *miraculous signs. Sign* is John's favorite word for Jesus' miracles; it emphasizes the purpose of his miracles as pointing a person to faith in him as the Son of God. This is in keeping with the stated purpose of John's Gospel, as found in John 20:30, 31.

Jesus' miracles *revealed his glory*, highlighting those attributes of Jesus that are worthy of honor and praise. This idea is in keeping with a theme in the prologue of John's Gospel, where he states that "the Word became flesh and . . . we have seen his glory" (John 1:14).

B. The Belief of the Disciples (v. 11b)

11b . . . and his disciples put their faith in him.

Thus this sign had the effect on the *disciples* that John desired his record of Jesus' signs to have. As they continued traveling with Jesus, hearing him speak and witnessing further miraculous signs, their faith would continue to grow.

JESUS AND NICODEMUS (JOHN 3:1-17)

Establishing the Groundwork

Following the record of Jesus' first miracle in Cana of Galilee, the second chapter of John's Gospel tells of Jesus' attendance at the Passover in Jerusalem. There Jesus saw the way in which some were using the temple as a marketplace, and he drove them out. While in Jerusalem, Jesus worked a number of miracles and many people "believed in his name" (John 2:23). They were so shallow in their belief, however, that Jesus did not proceed any further in revealing himself to them (John 2:24, 25).

One observer among the Jews was so taken by what he had witnessed that he determined to learn more from Jesus himself about his teaching. He seemed especially interested in what Jesus had to say about the kingdom of God. That observer was Nicodemus.

Examining the Text

I. Need for the New Birth (John 3:1-3)
A. Inquiry (vv. 1, 2)

¹ Now there was a man of the Pharisees named Nicodemus, a member of the Jewish ruling council.

In a previous study, we saw that certain *Pharisees* had interrogated John the Baptist about his identity and his baptism (John 1:24-27). They would clash frequently with Jesus about his nonconformity to their regulations and traditions, particularly regarding the Sabbath. A Pharisee tended to take great pride in what he saw as his own guaranteed position in the kingdom of God.

That *Nicodemus* was *a member of the Jewish ruling council* means that he was a member of the Sanhedrin. (See the earlier comments on the Sanhedrin in the discussion of John 1:19 in chapter 4.) Two and a half years later, Nicodemus was still on the council and spoke up in a meeting of the Sanhedrin to defend Jesus (John 7:50-52).

> *² He came to Jesus at night and said, "Rabbi, we know you are a teacher who has come from God. For no one could perform the miraculous signs you are doing if God were not with him."*

Why Nicodemus *came to Jesus at night* we are not told. Perhaps a meeting at night afforded him a private audience with Jesus that the daytime did not allow. Some suggest that his action betrayed a fear of the other members of the Sanhedrin (who were no doubt still furious with Jesus over his recent actions in the temple).

The term of address used by Nicodemus toward Jesus is striking: *Rabbi*. This was a title reserved for the most honored teachers among the Jews. The fact that Nicodemus would apply it to Jesus, who was not a product of the prestigious rabbinical schools, tells us something of the high esteem in which he held Jesus.

Evidently Nicodemus had discussed Jesus' miracles and teaching with some of his peers. His assertion *we know* indicates that he was not alone in his beliefs about Jesus. (Perhaps he intended to report this conversation to his peers.)

B. Confrontation (v. 3)

> *³ In reply Jesus declared, "I tell you the truth, no one can see the kingdom of God unless he is born again."*

Jesus' reply to Nicodemus's words of tribute may seem abrupt and totally unrelated to what Nicodemus had just said, but it is very much related to a statement found at the end of the second chapter of John: "[Jesus] did not need man's testimony about man, for he knew what was in a man" (John 2:25). Jesus knew the real concerns of Nicodemus and got right to the point with him.

The phrase *I tell you the truth* is sometimes rendered as "verily, verily"; the literal Greek words are "amen, amen." Jesus often used this language to preface a statement of a truth of utmost importance. Here the truth was that *no one can see the kingdom of God unless he is born again*. The Greek word translated "again" can also mean "from above." Perhaps Jesus had both meanings in mind. Judging from Nicodemus's reaction in the next verse, he took the meaning as "again."

II. Receiving the New Birth (John 3:4-11)
A. Water and Spirit (vv. 4-7)

⁴ "How can a man be born when he is old?" Nicodemus asked. "Surely he cannot enter a second time into his mother's womb to be born!"

With his very first statement, Jesus had changed Nicodemus's "We know" (v. 2) to "I don't understand." Nicodemus had taken Jesus' language literally, which occurred on other occasions. (See the example cited earlier from John 2:18-21.)

⁵ Jesus answered, "I tell you the truth, no one can enter the kingdom of God unless he is born of water and the Spirit.

In response to Nicodemus's question, Jesus made it clear that he was not referring to a second physical birth. The birth he had in mind was *of water and the Spirit. Water* and *Spirit* had been dramatically linked in the baptism of Jesus, when the Spirit's visible presence testified to God's acceptance of Jesus' baptism in water (Matthew 3:13-17). The same linking appears in the events of Pentecost, inaugurated by the Spirit (Acts 2:1-4) and completed with the promise that the Spirit would be given in response to believer's baptism into Christ (Acts 2:37-41).

Some may claim that Nicodemus would not have grasped a reference to baptism at this point. But how many of the other propositions Jesus stated to Nicodemus did he understand? He certainly did not comprehend the concept of being "born again." Later Jesus offered an unmistakable reference to his death on the cross (John 3:14), which Nicodemus surely would not have understood either. Clearly Jesus was stretching the thinking of this man who was known as "Israel's teacher" (v. 10).

⁶ "Flesh gives birth to flesh, but the Spirit gives birth to spirit.

Here was Jesus' answer to Nicodemus's question regarding the repetition of physical birth. Physical *birth* and bodily life are God-given and they are good, but they are material and temporal; they are not spiritual and eternal. The latter qualities must come from another source. "Flesh and blood cannot inherit the kingdom of God" (1 Corinthians 15:50).

⁷ "You should not be surprised at my saying, 'You must be born again.'

For the third time Jesus referred to the need for a second birth. Here the pronoun *you* in *you must be born again* is plural, indicating that the new birth is necessary not only for Nicodemus, but for everyone.

B. Wind and Spirit (v. 8)

⁸ "The wind blows wherever it pleases. You hear its sound, but you cannot tell where it comes from or where it is going. So it is with everyone born of the Spirit."

Since the words *wind* and *Spirit* are both translations of the same Greek word (*pneuma*), this passage presents a fascinating play on words. We should not be surprised that we cannot grasp all the intricacies of spiritual truth as well as we would like. We cannot fully understand the movements of natural phenomena such as the wind. However, since we hear its sound and see its impact, we do not doubt that it is real. In the same way, we cannot observe the Spirit at work or actually see the processes of faith, repentance, and forgiveness of sins taking place, but we can see the Spirit's influence in the transformed lives of *everyone born of the Spirit.*

C. Question and Answer (vv. 9-11)

⁹, ¹⁰ "How can this be?" Nicodemus asked.
"You are Israel's teacher," said Jesus, "and do you not understand these things?

Once again Nicodemus verbalized his doubts. In the Greek text the definite article appears before the word *teacher* ("you are *the* teacher of Israel"), calling attention to Nicodemus's standing as a highly respected scholar. Nicodemus should not have found Jesus' teaching so surprising; after all, the prophet Ezekiel had announced God's promise of "a new heart and . . . a new spirit" (Ezekiel 36:26, 27).

¹¹ "I tell you the truth, we speak of what we know, and we testify to what we have seen, but still you people do not accept our testimony.

This is the third time Jesus used the phrase *I tell you the truth* with Nicodemus (see verses 3 and 5). The words *we speak* may be an indication that Jesus did not act alone, but in company with his Father and the Holy Spirit. Another possibility is that we referred to Jesus' disciples or to the Old Testament prophets (including the ministry of John the Baptist).

Notice that Jesus changed from you (Nicodemus) *to you people* (his fellow Pharisees and rulers). These were the people who, for the most part, rejected John the Baptist's *testimony*, and they rejected Jesus as well (Luke 7:29, 30).

III. Understanding the New Birth (John 3:12-17)
A. Life, Not Death (vv. 12-15)

12 "I have spoken to you of earthly things and you do not believe; how then will you believe if I speak of heavenly things?

Jesus had spoken, as he did in his parables, of common and familiar subjects—birth, wind, and water. These *earthly things* receive their permanent value from heavenly and spiritual concepts, such as love, mercy, faith, truth, and goodness. A fuller understanding of such *heavenly things* as these would have to await Nicodemus's further observation of Jesus' ministry, particularly the kind of death Jesus would die as foretold by him in verse 14.

13 "No one has ever gone into heaven except the one who came from heaven—the Son of Man.

John and the other Gospel writers did not use quotation marks to indicate words spoken by a certain person at a certain time. So we do not know whether Jesus spoke these and the following words (through verse 21) to Nicodemus that night or whether John himself added them as additional explanation. In either case, they are inspired words of Scripture and provide further insights into what is needed for entrance into God's kingdom. Jesus may well have spoken these words to give Nicodemus some "heavenly things" (v. 12) to ponder. The translators of the *New International Version* and most other newer versions of the Bible believe that he did, as they enclose the entire passage in quotation marks.

No one has ever gone into heaven to learn about that place (Proverbs 30:4). But Jesus knows about Heaven because he *came from* there. Thus he has the authority to speak about things that only he has seen and that cannot be known by any human being unless Jesus reveals them.

14, 15 "Just as Moses lifted up the snake in the desert, so the Son of Man must be lifted up, that everyone who believes in him may have eternal life.

Numbers 21:4-9 recounts the incident in which God punished the Israelites *in the desert* for their thankless complaints by sending serpents whose bite proved fatal. Penitent prayer from *Moses* followed, and God commanded Moses to set up a bronze *snake* on a pole, directing those bitten by the serpents to look upon it and live.

Jesus used this part of Israel's history to point to his own crucifixion, which brings salvation from the venom of sin to those who look in obedient faith on the uplifted Christ. Jesus later said, "But I, when I am lifted up from the earth, will draw all men to myself" (John 12:32). The next verse then states, "He said this to show the kind of death he was going to die."

B. Salvation, Not Condemnation (vv. 16, 17)

16 "For God so loved the world that he gave his one and only Son, that whoever believes in him shall not perish but have eternal life.

This verse, often called the "Golden Text of the Bible," may be considered the ultimate statement of the "heavenly things" that Jesus wanted Nicodemus (and wants *the world*) to ponder. In it every word is stretched to the full capacity of its meaning: *God . . . loved . . . the world . . . whoever believes . . . perish . . . eternal life.* We cannot grasp this truth on the run. We have to linger and let its truth soak in. And each of us must take the time to substitute his or her own name in place of the word *whoever.*

17 "For God did not send his Son into the world to condemn the world, but to save the world through him."

Many in Jesus' day believed that when the Messiah came, he would *condemn* Gentile nations and set Israel over them. But God's Son came *into the world . . . to save the world.* The world was already condemned by its wickedness (vv. 18, 19). Eventually Jesus will return both to judge and to condemn those who reject the gospel. But he came the first time "to seek and to save what was lost" (Luke 19:10).

JESUS AND THE SAMARITAN WOMAN (JOHN 4:7-10, 19-26)

Establishing the Groundwork

Following Jesus' conversation with Nicodemus, Jesus continued his ministry in Judea for approximately eight months, growing so much in popularity that his followers came to outnumber those of John the Baptist. When Jesus heard of the Pharisees' awareness of this growing support, he decided to leave Judea and return to Galilee (John 4:1-3). For this trip, Jesus chose to go through Samaria rather than around it, as was the usual practice. This journey through Samaria provided the occasion for Jesus' meeting the woman at the well of Sychar, also known as "Jacob's well" (John 4:6).

Examining the Text

I. Unexpected Conversation (John 4:7-9)
A. Startling Request (vv. 7, 8)

7 When a Samaritan woman came to draw water, Jesus said to her, "Will you give me a drink?"

John 4:6 supplies us with the time this encounter with the *Samaritan woman* took place: "It was about the sixth hour" (which would be noon according to the Jewish reckoning of time). This is not an insignificant detail. Women usually came to a well *to draw water* when it was cooler (morning or evening). This gave them an opportunity to socialize and chat. Perhaps this woman had been shunned or demeaned by the other women because of her immoral past (to which Jesus alluded in John 4:17, 18). This forced her to come to the well in the heat of the day—alone.

For Jesus to address this woman as he did was quite out of the ordinary. Jewish men of this period usually did not address women in public. When Jesus' disciples later returned to him after buying food, they were amazed that he was talking with a woman (John 4:27).

8 (His disciples had gone into the town to buy food.)

The rift between Jews and Samaritans (explained in comments under the next verse) did not prevent their doing business on commercial levels, but it might limit what food a Jew would buy in a Samaritan market.

B. Ancient Animosity (v. 9)

9 The Samaritan woman said to him, "You are a Jew and I am a Samaritan woman. How can you ask me for a drink?" (For Jews do not associate with Samaritans.)

The *Samaritan woman* did not refuse Jesus' request, but she seemed in no hurry to grant it. She knew she had "two strikes" against her: her ethnic identity and her gender. There was a third "strike" (her immoral background) that she did not realize Jesus knew. The statement that *Jews do not associate with Samaritans* may have been spoken by this woman, but more likely it was added by the apostle John for the benefit of his non-Jewish readers. The woman probably recognized Jesus as a Jew by either his clothing or his accent.

Tensions between the Jews and the Samaritans can be traced to events that occurred some seven hundred years earlier. In 722 BC, when the Assyrians conquered the northern kingdom of Israel and its capital of Samaria, they scattered its people to other parts of the empire, replacing them with foreigners. The people who resulted from this mixture of populations came to be called Samaritans.

Eventually the Samaritans established their own religious practices, based on the five books of Law (Genesis through Deuteronomy). They built their own temple on Mount Gerizim, at the foot of which the village of Sychar was located. That temple was destroyed by the Jews during the period between the

Old and New Testaments, adding to the hostility between the two groups. The site continued to be considered holy ground by the Samaritans.

By the time of Christ, mutual resentment between Jews and Samaritans had intensified. Jesus, however, refused to be a part of it, taking notable occasions (such as this one) to show that God's love and mercy included Samaritans.

II. Unexpected Solution (John 4:10, 19-26)
A. Deepest Thirst (v. 10)

10 Jesus answered her, "If you knew the gift of God and who it is that asks you for a drink, you would have asked him and he would have given you living water."

Jesus' answer ignored the woman's question and raised a much deeper issue, much as his response to Nicodemus's opening remarks went directly to what Nicodemus had on his mind (John 3:1-3). The woman's need was greater than Jesus' need; it was spiritual, and it would be met by *the gift of God* rather than by her ability.

Living water should be understood as a fresh, flowing stream (as from a spring or an artesian well), in contrast to the standing and stagnant water in a pond or cistern. The water that Jesus offers is as necessary to spiritual life as water is to physical life.

B. Profound Truth (vv. 19-22)

19 "Sir," the woman said, "I can see that you are a prophet.

The dialogue recorded in verses 16-18 led the Samaritan woman to conclude that Jesus was a *prophet*. He had just told her things about herself that a stranger could not have known without having some kind of special insight. Jesus knew about her five previous marriages and that she was now living with a man who was not her husband.

20 "Our fathers worshiped on this mountain, but you Jews claim that the place where we must worship is in Jerusalem."

This mountain would have been Mount Gerizim, which the Samaritans considered especially sacred (see the comments on verse 9). Those whom the Samaritans considered their *fathers* (for example, Abraham and Jacob) had erected altars to God at Shechem, which was near Mount Gerizim (Genesis 12:6, 7; 33:18-20). The *Jews*, however, worshiped at the temple in *Jerusalem*.

Perhaps the woman, knowing that her past was no longer hidden, tried to move the conversation with Jesus in another direction. Or perhaps she was seeking a solution to this dilemma from one whom she had just confessed to be a prophet.

> [21] *Jesus declared, "Believe me, woman, a time is coming when you will worship the Father neither on this mountain nor in Jerusalem.*

Once more, Jesus did not allow himself to be drawn into discussing some aspect of the Jew/Samaritan controversy. In essence, he said that it was time to quit focusing on the place of worship and start honoring the person (*the Father*) who is the object of worship. With the coming of the Christian age, sacred sites have lost their meaning (except for historical purposes). The church is not a building; it is made of "living stones"—a designation for Christians (Ephesians 2:19-22; 1 Peter 2:4-6). Anywhere those "stones" are meeting becomes sacred because of the people, not the place.

> [22] *"You Samaritans worship what you do not know; we worship what we do know, for salvation is from the Jews.*

Jesus had just emphasized that the worship of God could not be restricted to a particular place, but he would not say that just anyone's doctrines were correct. God entered into a covenant with *the Jews* and promised that the Messiah would come through them. The Samaritans could not possibly have known *what* they were worshiping, for they rejected the majority of the writings of the Old Testament. They could not have known all that God had predicted through his prophets regarding the coming Messiah and the *salvation* he would bring.

C. True Worshipers (vv. 23, 24)

> [23, 24] *"Yet a time is coming and has now come when the true worshipers will worship the Father in spirit and truth, for they are the kind of worshipers the Father seeks. God is spirit, and his worshipers must worship in spirit and in truth."*

Here Jesus elaborated on the nature of true, God-pleasing worship: it is not a matter of place, but of the attitude of the person worshiping. At the most foundational level, worship means ascribing worth to God. We can do this properly only when our worship is *in spirit* (is centered on nothing but God) and *in truth* (is faithful to God's Word). We must worship God as he has revealed himself in Scripture, not as we may think he ought to be.

D. Divine Savior (vv. 25, 26)

25 The woman said, "I know that Messiah" (called Christ) "is coming. When he comes, he will explain everything to us."

At this point, it appears that the woman realized that this conversation had taken an unexpected turn and that she was facing issues "over her head." She attempted to steer the conversation in another direction with a reference to the *Messiah*. Like the Jews, the Samaritans held that God would one day raise up a great prophet like Moses (Deuteronomy 18:15, which was part of the Old Testament that the Samaritans accepted as authoritative). They believed that when he came, he would *explain* the mysteries that had troubled humanity for generations.

26 Then Jesus declared, "I who speak to you am he."

The woman had already acknowledged Jesus as a prophet (v. 19), but she could scarcely have been prepared for this announcement: the Messiah whom she claimed was "coming" (v. 25) had arrived and was in her presence! She proceeded to go back to town and tell everyone there of her discovery, becoming an immediate evangelist (vv. 28-30).

Observe the progression in this woman's understanding: she first thought of Jesus as a common Jew, then someone to be respected, then a prophet, and finally the Messiah. Eventually, after Jesus had stayed in that area two days (v. 40), the townspeople became convinced for themselves: "we know that this man really is the Savior of the world" (v. 42).

We may question why Jesus so plainly revealed himself as the Messiah here in Samaria, yet later in Galilee attempted to keep this information restricted. The reason had to do with the spiritual condition and understanding of his audience. In Galilee many of his followers had become highly excited by his ministry but saw the Messiah primarily as a political leader who would free Israel from Roman rule. The knowledge that Jesus was the Messiah could very well have sparked a violent revolt against Rome. With no such explosive tendencies present in Samaria, Jesus could make a more candid declaration of his identity.

How to Say It

ABRAHAM. *Ay*-bruh-ham.

ANDREW. *An*-drew.

ARAMAIC. *Air*-uh-*may*-ik (strong accent on *may*).

CANA. *Kay*-nuh.

CEPHAS. *See*-fus.

GALILEE. *Gal*-uh-lee.

GENTILE. *Jen*-tile.

GERIZIM. *Gair*-ih-zeem or Guh-*rye*-zim.

JACOB. *Jay*-kub.

JERUSALEM. Juh-*roo*-suh-lem.

JUDEA. Joo-*dee*-uh.

MESSIAH. Meh-*sigh*-uh.

MESSIANIC. mess-ee-*an*-ick.

NATHANAEL. Nuh-*than*-yull (*th* as in *thin*).

NAZARETH. *Naz*-uh-reth.

NICODEMUS. *Nick*-uh-*dee*-mus (strong accent on *dee*).

PENTECOST. *Pent*-ih-kost.

PETROS (*Greek*). *peh*-trawss.

PHARISEE. *Fair*-ih-see.

PHILIP. *Fil*-ip.

PINNACLE. *pih*-nih-kul.

PNEUMA (*Greek*). *nyoo*-mah.

RABBI. *Rab*-eye.

RABBINICAL. ruh-*bin*-ick-ul.

SABBATH. *Sa*-buth *(Sa* as in *sat).*

SAMARIA. Suh-*mare*-ee-uh.

SAMARITAN. Suh-*mare*-uh-tun.

SANHEDRIN. *San*-huh-drun or San-*heed*-run.

SHECHEM. *Shee*-kem or *Shek*-em.

SIMON. *Sigh*-mun.

SYCHAR. *Sigh*-kar.

TRANSFIGURATION. tranz-*fih*-gyuh-*ray*-shun
(strong accent on *ray*).

VERILY. *vair*-uh-lee.

Chapter 6

Jesus' Galilean Ministry (Part 1)

Luke 4:16-30; Matthew 4:18-22; Mark 2:1-12;
Matthew 9:9-13; 5:1-20, 38-48

JESUS RETURNS TO NAZARETH (LUKE 4:16-30)

Establishing the Groundwork

Immediately preceding the incident described in this text, Luke tells us about Jesus' ministry in Galilee before he returned to his hometown of Nazareth. (This occurred in Jesus' first year of public ministry—sometimes referred to as his "year of inauguration.") In this brief summary, we learn that Jesus had taught in many of the synagogues in Galilee. He did this "in the power of the Spirit" (Luke 4:14), which may indicate only that he was directed by the Holy Spirit in his teaching. It may, however, suggest that his teachings were accompanied by miracles, which Luke 4:23-27 also suggests. This would account for the fact that Jesus' fame had spread so quickly throughout the territory. Such events undoubtedly contributed to the excitement when Jesus returned to Nazareth.

Examining the Text

I. A Gospel Mission (Luke 4:16-21)
A. Announced in the Synagogue (vv. 16, 17)

16 He went to Nazareth, where he had been brought up, and on the Sabbath day he went into the synagogue, as was his custom. And he stood up to read.

Nazareth, the hometown of Joseph and Mary (Luke 1:26, 27), became their home again after their sojourn in Egypt to escape the murderous jealousy of King Herod against the infant "king of the Jews" (Matthew 2:13-15, 19-23).

It was Jesus' *custom* to attend worship services in a Jewish synagogue every *Sabbath day* (Saturday). The synagogue arose in Judaism during the approximately four hundred years that passed between the end of the Old Testament and the beginning of the New Testament. (It is not mentioned anywhere in the Old Testament.) The synagogue was primarily a place of religious instruction. Jewish tradition stated that a synagogue could be established in any town where there were at least ten married Jewish men. Thus even a small town such as Nazareth could include a synagogue.

On this occasion, Jesus *stood up to read*. It was a common synagogue practice in first-century Judaism to show respect to visiting teachers by inviting them to read Scripture aloud and then give their exposition of the passage read. Anyone who read was expected to stand while doing so.

¹⁷ The scroll of the prophet Isaiah was handed to him. Unrolling it, he found the place where it is written:

A person called an "attendant" (v. 20) took care of the synagogue's property and especially the scrolls of sacred Scripture from which the readings were taken. The *scroll* that Jesus was given was that of the Old Testament *prophet Isaiah*. Jesus then unrolled the scroll to the passage he desired to read (Isaiah 61:1, 2). Scrolls at that time were not marked with chapters or verses as our Bibles are; the reader had to be familiar enough with the contents to be able to find the passage he wanted (or was asked) to read.

B. Foretold in Prophecy (vv. 18, 19)

¹⁸ "The Spirit of the Lord is on me,
because he has anointed me
to preach good news to the poor.
He has sent me to proclaim freedom for the prisoners
and recovery of sight for the blind,
to release the oppressed,

The prophecy that Jesus chose to read was clearly a reference to the Messiah, which means *anointed* one. The Messiah of Jewish expectation was not merely one who was anointed with oil, but was anointed with the *Spirit of the Lord*.

Having identified the source of power for the Messiah, Isaiah then set forth a summary of God's agenda for the Messiah. It was not exactly what first-century Jews were hoping for. They wanted a deliverer who would destroy the hated Romans and reestablish the political empire that David and Solomon once ruled. Isaiah's picture was quite different.

The Messiah's first task would be *to preach good news to the poor*. These words remind us of the first of the "Beatitudes": "Blessed are the poor in spirit, for theirs is the kingdom of heaven" (Matthew 5:3). Once we recognize our spiritual poverty, we can make ourselves dependent on God for salvation. In addition, those who are materially poor can take heart from a Savior who was placed in a manger at birth and had "no place to lay his head" (Luke 9:58).

The idea of *freedom for the prisoners* would have generated great hope in Old Testament times. Originally Isaiah's words were intended to give hope to those who would become captives in Babylon. But their second application had a more far-reaching import. They brought good news not only to those who were held captive by the Babylonians, but to all people everywhere who were held captive by sin. The same could be said of the phrase *to release the oppressed*.

Recovery of sight for the blind also has a twofold meaning. Certainly Jesus gave sight to physically blind eyes (Mark 10:46-52; John 9:1-7), but he also removed the blindness caused by sin (John 9:39-41). The audience that Jesus addressed in Nazareth this day certainly needed that kind of healing.

The fact that many of these phrases describing Jesus' ministry can have a physical and a spiritual application should remind us that Jesus' *good news* made a difference in people's lives in more than one way. We too need a view of ministry that is broad enough to respond to both physical and spiritual needs.

[19] *". . . to proclaim the year of the Lord's favor."*

Here the word *year* is not describing a calendar year. It refers instead to the era when all of the above actions would take place—in other words, the messianic age. The background for this term may well be the Old Testament Year of Jubilee (Leviticus 25:8-55). At that time, which was to occur once every fifty years, slaves were freed, debts were canceled, and ancestral property that had been sold during the previous fifty years (because of poverty) was returned to the family who originally owned it. Whereas Isaiah first uttered these words to promise Israel deliverance from captivity in Babylon and repossession of her "property" in the Promised Land, Jesus used it to announce deliverance from sin and its consequences.

It has been noted that Jesus went no farther in quoting the passage from Isaiah 61; that is, he said nothing at this time about proclaiming "the day of vengeance of our God" (Isaiah 61:2). This may well have been because his first coming was primarily "not . . . to condemn the world, but to save the world" (John 3:17). At his second coming he will carry out judgment and "vengeance" (2 Thessalonians 1:6-10).

C. Fulfilled by Jesus (vv. 20, 21)

[20] *Then he rolled up the scroll, gave it back to the attendant and sat down. The eyes of everyone in the synagogue were fastened on him,*

Jesus followed the usual practice for speaking in a synagogue. Out of respect for the Word of God, a speaker would stand while reading aloud the Scripture text (v. 16), but then it was customary to sit down while speaking and teaching (see Matthew 5:1, 2; 13:2). On this occasion of Jesus' first sermon in his hometown, *the eyes of everyone . . . were fastened on him* as they listened intently to see what he would say regarding his ministry of preaching and healing, which had caused such a stir throughout Galilee (Luke 4:14). No doubt they hoped he would perform a miracle in their midst.

²¹ . . . and he began by saying to them, "Today this scripture is fulfilled in your hearing."

Even though the people were in an expectant mood, they were hardly prepared for Jesus' next words. The *scripture* he had just read was being *fulfilled* at that very moment. The coming of the Messiah was no longer something yet to occur; it had happened. He was in their midst!

II. A Skeptical Response (Luke 4:22-27)
A. The Crowd's Reaction (v. 22)

²² All spoke well of him and were amazed at the gracious words that came from his lips. "Isn't this Joseph's son?" they asked.

This verse indicates that what Jesus said in verse 21 did not comprise all that he said before the crowd responded. The initial reaction appears to have been mixed. On the one hand, the people seemed to enjoy Jesus' style and delivery and to relish the messianic possibilities within his *gracious words*. On the other hand, they found it hard even to imagine that one of their own—from their insignificant town—could actually turn out to be someone who would fulfill a prophecy about the Messiah.

In the previous chapter, it was noted that the lack of any mention of Joseph in John 2 might indicate that he had died. Here Joseph is mentioned, but even if he were deceased, that would not be unusual in Nazareth. The people of that town would have known Joseph personally and would not have hesitated to mention his name in connection with his son, even if the father were dead.

B. Jesus' Defense (vv. 23-27)

²³ Jesus said to them, "Surely you will quote this proverb to me: 'Physician, heal yourself! Do here in your hometown what we have heard that you did in Capernaum.'

Those gathered in the synagogue were probably aware of Jesus' first miracle in Cana (John 2:1-11), which was just a few miles from Nazareth, and of his second miracle—the healing of a royal official's son from *Capernaum*, although Jesus had declared the son healed while in Cana (John 4:43-54). Jesus' remark here leads us to believe that there had been other miracles done at Capernaum. Jesus anticipated that those in Nazareth would want to see some of this miracle-working power for themselves.

[24] *"I tell you the truth,"* he continued, *"no prophet is accepted in his hometown.*

Jesus recognized that "familiarity breeds contempt." There was an arrogance among the residents of Nazareth that said, "Who does this man think he is?" They were convinced that they were just as good as "Joseph's son" and were not willing to accept the claims that he was making.

[25, 26] *"I assure you that there were many widows in Israel in Elijah's time, when the sky was shut for three and a half years and there was a severe famine throughout the land. Yet Elijah was not sent to any of them, but to a widow in Zarephath in the region of Sidon.*

What a dramatic turn! Whereas Jesus began with "gracious words" (v. 22), the skeptical reaction of the audience prompted him to speak words of rebuke.

The prophet *Elijah* pronounced a drought on Israel that lasted for *three and a half years* (1 Kings 17:1; James 5:17). This resulted in a *severe famine throughout the land*. But Elijah did not provide supernatural relief in Israel, in large part because they were under God's discipline for embracing the worship of the false god Baal. Instead, Elijah provided food for a *widow* in *Zarephath* who shared with him the last of her food supply (1 Kings 17:7-16). Zarephath was located in *Sidon* (a place that was not only beyond the borders of Israel, but was also in the center of the land where Baal was worshiped).

[27] *"And there were many in Israel with leprosy in the time of Elisha the prophet, yet not one of them was cleansed—only Naaman the Syrian."*

Like his predecessor Elijah, *Elisha* worked in an environment of hostility, experiencing rejection by both the king of *Israel* and the people. Thus his miracle-working power was allowed to bless someone outside of Israel—*Naaman the Syrian*, whose account is told in 2 Kings 5:1-19.

Jesus' point in citing these two examples from Israel's history was to show that blessings of God are often withheld from those who reject the preaching of God's servants. Nazareth was being warned in no uncertain terms that it was headed down a similar path of disaster.

III. A Determined Spirit (Luke 4:28-30)
A. Facing Hostility (vv.28, 29)

[28] *All the people in the synagogue were furious when they heard this.*

Jesus' claim to fulfill prophecy had raised doubts in the minds of many in the *synagogue*. His rebuke for their lack of faith in him must have stung deeply. But the crowning insult came with his implication that non-Jews were candidates for God's favor as much as they, his chosen people!

²⁹ *They got up, drove him out of the town, and took him to the brow of the hill on which the town was built, in order to throw him down the cliff.*

The public ministry of Jesus had just begun, and already people—the people in his hometown—were trying to kill him! Their plan to *throw him down the cliff* may have been the preliminary step to a stoning. It was common practice among the Jews to cast a person to be stoned down into an area below the crowd, where they could then throw stones from above.

B. Pressing Forward (v. 30)

³⁰ *But he walked right through the crowd and went on his way.*

Luke does not explain specifically how Jesus survived this threat, whether by use of supernatural power or by a piercing look that challenged their intimidation. Regardless of how he escaped, he was in no way dissuaded from the mission he had announced in the synagogue. Jesus *went on his way* and proceeded to carry out the agenda prophesied in Isaiah 61, undaunted by this or any other opposition he would encounter.

JESUS CALLS HIS FIRST DISCIPLES (MATTHEW 4:18-22)

Establishing the Groundwork

Following his controversial visit to Nazareth, Jesus "went down to Capernaum" (Luke 4:31), a fishing town on the northwest shore of the Sea of Galilee. Jesus had earlier made Capernaum the headquarters of his Galilean ministry (Matthew 4:13; Mark 2:1; John 2:12). Matthew notes that in working from Capernaum, Jesus fulfilled a prophecy found in Isaiah 9:1, 2 (Matthew 4:13-16). Jesus also began to proclaim the same message that characterized John the Baptist's preaching: "Repent, for the kingdom of heaven is near" (Matthew 4:17). In addition, he began to seek out men who would assist him in his ministry and become his disciples.

Examining the Text

I. The Calling of Peter and Andrew (Matthew 4:18-20)
A. Preparing to Catch Fish (v. 18)

¹⁸ *As Jesus was walking beside the Sea of Galilee, he saw two brothers, Simon called Peter and his brother Andrew. They were casting a net into the lake, for they were fishermen.*

In the earlier study of John 1:19-34, we noted Jesus' initial encounter with *Simon*, to whom Jesus gave the name *Peter* (the Greek translation of the Aramaic *Cephas,* which means "rock"), and *his brother Andrew*. This had taken place in Judea in the area where John the Baptist was preaching. Andrew was one of John's disciples and had brought Simon to Jesus (John 1:40-42).

Here we learn of Peter and Andrew's occupation as *fishermen* in Galilee. *Casting a net* was the most common means of fishing in New Testament times.

B. Preparing to Catch Men (vv. 19, 20)

19 "Come, follow me," Jesus said, "and I will make you fishers of men."

Luke 5:1-11 tells us more details of this event, which culminated in Jesus' invitation to *follow* him and become engaged in a new and more exciting kind of fishing. Again, it should be kept in mind that Peter and Andrew had already become acquainted with Jesus through his earlier Judean ministry. They may well have been with Jesus when he performed his first miracle in Cana, and may have spent additional time with him on some other occasions. But they would always go back to their homes and their work. Now Jesus was inviting them to make a complete break with everything they were accustomed to—to leave business, friends, and family and to follow him.

20 At once they left their nets and followed him.

Without hesitation, *at once*, Peter and Andrew gave up their livelihood and *followed* Jesus.

II. The Calling of James and John (Matthew 4:21, 22)
A. With Their Father (v. 21)

21 Going on from there, he saw two other brothers, James son of Zebedee and his brother John. They were in a boat with their father Zebedee, preparing their nets. Jesus called them,

Peter and Andrew were partners in the fishing business with *two other brothers*, *James* and *John*, and *their father Zebedee* (Luke 5:10). Once again, the groundwork for this calling of James and John had likely been laid by Jesus' preaching and teaching during his early Judean ministry.

B. With Jesus (v. 22)

22 . . . and immediately they left the boat and their father and followed him.

The reaction of James and John to Jesus' call was similar to that of Peter and Andrew: *immediately they . . . followed him*. We should not imagine that the two sets of brothers left the family business in a predicament by their sudden departure. We are told that Zebedee had hired help to assist him (Mark 1:20). Zebedee's wife was one of several women from Galilee who supported Jesus' ministry (most likely in a financial way) and stood by the cross as he died (Matthew 27:55, 56).

JESUS HEALS A PARALYTIC IN CAPERNAUM (MARK 2:1-12)

Establishing the Groundwork

In the previous study, we noted that the fishing town of Capernaum had become the headquarters for Jesus' Galilean ministry. The miracles of healing that he began to perform after the calling of his first disciples quickly attracted the attention of the public, and Jesus soon had a large following. In fact, it was so large that for a time Jesus could not conduct a public ministry effectively (Mark 1:45).

Jesus' popularity soon began to attract the attention of some other people—the Jewish religious leaders. His rapidly growing popularity made him suspect among the scribes and Pharisees, who considered themselves the custodians of orthodoxy. In their thinking, anyone who gained such popularity had to be doing something unorthodox. One cannot escape the feeling that there was some measure of jealousy involved in their suspicions.

Eventually it became necessary for Jesus to assert his divine authority in his critics' presence and confront them directly. The incident recorded in Mark 2:1-12 records such a confrontation in the aftermath of one of Jesus' most dramatic miracles.

Examining the Text

I. People Gather (Mark 2:1, 2)
A. Jesus' Arrival (v. 1)

¹ A few days later, when Jesus again entered Capernaum, the people heard that he had come home.

The final verse in Mark 1 tells us that Jesus had to withdraw for a time into "lonely places" because of the furor surrounding his miracles in Galilee (Mark 1:45). Now he again *entered Capernaum*, which had become in a sense his new home, or at least the headquarters of his ministry in Galilee. Some suggest that he may have been staying in the home of Peter and Andrew. Earlier Jesus had healed Peter's mother-in-law (Mark 1:29-31).

B. Jesus' Preaching (v. 2)

2 So many gathered that there was no room left, not even outside the door, and he preached the word to them.

A typical house of this time and location usually consisted of a rectangular, one-story building surrounded by a large, walled courtyard. The house in Capernaum on this day was crowded to capacity, causing an overflow into the courtyard. Jesus seized this opportunity and *preached the word* to this crowd, continuing his announcement that "the kingdom of God is near" (Mark 1:15).

II. Paralytic Enters (Mark 2:3-5)
A. Drama (vv. 3, 4)

3 Some men came, bringing to him a paralytic, carried by four of them.

Verse 4 indicates that a mat was used on this occasion to carry this *paralytic*, and it may have been where he spent most of his time. We do not know whether the *four* men who carried him were relatives or friends of the paralytic. Obviously they were aware of Jesus' miracle-working power, and they saw in him some hope for this man.

4 Since they could not get him to Jesus because of the crowd, they made an opening in the roof above Jesus and, after digging through it, lowered the mat the paralyzed man was lying on.

At first the *crowd* described in verse 2 kept the four men from getting their friend to Jesus, but that did not discourage them. Most houses in Palestine at this time were of one story with a staircase or ladder outside to provide access to a flat roof made of crossbeams with branches laid across them and covered with mud, which was then hardened by the sun. The resulting surface was quite durable, hard enough to walk on. It could be used for storage or as a place for people to sit and relax.

By digging a hole through this surface, the four men were able to provide a means to get the paralytic to Jesus, in spite of the crowd in the house. The noise of this activity along with the falling debris undoubtedly caught the attention of the people below.

B. Declaration (v. 5)

⁵ When Jesus saw their faith, he said to the paralytic, "Son, your sins are forgiven."

The *faith* of the *paralytic* and his friends was clear to Jesus. But instead of saying, "Get up and walk" (which might have been expected), he said, *Son, your sins are forgiven.* Jesus was not necessarily suggesting that the man's affliction was the result of his sin, although this belief was popularly held in Jesus' day (John 9:1, 2), and the paralytic himself may have believed it. It seems that Jesus intended to begin to reveal some of the divine authority that he possessed as the Son of God.

III. People React (Mark 2:6-12)
A. The Angry Ones (vv. 6-9)

⁶, ⁷ Now some teachers of the law were sitting there, thinking to themselves, "Why does this fellow talk like that? He's blaspheming! Who can forgive sins but God alone?"

As one might imagine, such a declaration as Jesus had made in verse 5 was bound to cause controversy. First noted is the response of the *teachers of the law,* the "Bible scholars" of their day. Mark has already mentioned them in his Gospel, noting the contrast people saw between their teaching and that of Jesus (Mark 1:22). Immediately these men recognized a problem with Jesus' declaration of forgiveness of sins. They did not voice their concerns at this point, but in their thoughts they accused Jesus of *blaspheming,* since forgiveness of sins was something *God alone* could pronounce. They also knew that the law of Moses made blasphemy a capital offense (Leviticus 24:14-16).

Of course, these teachers were absolutely correct in thinking that only God can *forgive sins.* They failed to consider the possibility of Jesus' divinity, a fact acknowledged by an evil spirit whom Jesus had cast out earlier in Capernaum (Mark 1:23-26).

⁸ Immediately Jesus knew in his spirit that this was what they were thinking in their hearts, and he said to them, "Why are you thinking these things?

Jesus met the teachers' unstated question with a spoken question of his own. Like so many of Jesus' questions, this one stirred the hearer to serious self-examination. (Other examples are found in Matthew 6:25, 26; Mark 3:33; 8:36, 37.)

⁹ "Which is easier: to say to the paralytic, 'Your sins are forgiven,' or to say, 'Get up, take your mat and walk'?

Jesus must have startled these teachers by reading their thoughts and raising the specific issue that had troubled them: his claim to declare the paralytic's sins forgiven. But Jesus went on to propose a test of his ability to do this. It was just as easy to *say* to someone *Your sins are forgiven* as it was to say *Take your mat and walk*. But there was no visible way to test whether someone's sins had actually been forgiven. On the other hand, if one claimed the power to heal, that claim could be checked out by clear, visible evidence, such as telling a paralytic to get up and walk.

B. The Active One (vv. 10-12a)

¹⁰ "But that you may know that the Son of Man has authority on earth to forgive sins. . . ." He said to the paralytic,

Jesus did not wait for a response to his question. Instead, he proceeded to provide clear, visible evidence of his power to do what he had earlier claimed to do: *to forgive sins.* Here Mark records Jesus' first use of the expression *Son of Man*. This term highlighted Jesus' identification with man but also carried significant messianic implications (as seen in Daniel 7:13, 14). Mark 8:29-31 shows the close relationship between the terms *Son of Man* and *Christ*.

¹¹ "I tell you, get up, take your mat and go home."

With these few words, Jesus settled the issue of whether or not he had the authority to forgive sins. Jesus' power to do something that was plainly seen but dependent on divine authority (heal the paralytic) showed his divine authority to do something in the realm of the unseen (forgive sins).

¹²ᵃ He got up, took his mat and walked out in full view of them all.

To put it simply, the paralytic believed and obeyed. As there could be no certain evidence of the man's forgiveness without his healing, there could be no evidence of his faith without his obedience.

C. The Amazed Ones (v. 12b)

¹²ᵇ This amazed everyone and they praised God, saying, "We have never seen anything like this!"

The reaction of being *amazed*, or astonished, at Jesus' mighty works is often recorded by Mark (1:22, 27; 5:42; 6:2, 51; 7:37; 9:15; 10:24, 26, 32; 11:18). One may ask why Jesus would have told someone he healed earlier to keep quiet about it (Mark 1:43, 44), only to perform a miracle in such a public setting as this crowded house. It seems that he was beginning to lay the groundwork for the confrontation with the religious leaders that he knew was inevitable. The teachers of the law left this scene unable to refute Jesus' powerful argument but undoubtedly angry and frustrated at their inability to do so. The people present *praised God*, but probably did not grasp the full implications of what they had just witnessed.

THE CALLING OF MATTHEW (MATTHEW 9:9-13)

Establishing the Groundwork

With admirable brevity, Matthew tells of his own enlistment among the followers of Jesus. The other Gospel writers who record this incident (Mark and Luke) provide no additional information, other than to mention Matthew's other name of Levi. The calling of Matthew may have occurred some weeks or perhaps months after the calling of the four fishermen. Matthew 9:9 indicates that it took place not long after the healing of the paralytic in Capernaum.

Examining the Text

I. Receptive Follower (Matthew 9:9, 10)
A. A Desire to Follow Jesus (v. 9)

⁹ As Jesus went on from there, he saw a man named Matthew sitting at the tax collector's booth. "Follow me," he told him, and Matthew got up and followed him.

Jesus had gone *from there*, referring to the house in Capernaum where the paralytic had been healed (Matthew 9:1-8). *He saw a man named Matthew* at his *tax collector's booth*, the location of which is not known. Apparently it was somewhere near the shore of the Sea of Galilee (Mark 2:13, 14). The extreme contempt in which tax collectors like Matthew were held was noted earlier in the study of Luke 3:10-14 in chapter 4.

Like the fishermen, Matthew responded immediately to the call to *follow* Jesus. It is possible, especially if his place of business was located near the Sea of Galilee, that Matthew had already heard Jesus teach or witnessed some of his miracles. Now he was being asked, as the fishermen had been asked, to leave his profession behind and begin a new life. One should consider how Matthew's work as a tax collector developed in him a greater level of writing and recording skills that later served him well in writing one of the four Gospels.

B. A Desire to Reach Others (v. 10)

¹⁰ While Jesus was having dinner at Matthew's house, many tax collectors and "sinners" came and ate with him and his disciples.

Apparently Matthew hosted a kind of *dinner* party so that he could introduce some of his friends to Jesus. The place was filled with various outcasts of Jewish society—perhaps the only friends a tax collector could claim as his own, being an outcast himself. These people would have included others who made their living in a disreputable manner, such as prostitutes (Matthew 21:31, 32). Matthew's joy at being accepted by Jesus knew no bounds, and he wanted others who faced constant scorn to have a taste of that acceptance.

II. Resentful Pharisees (Matthew 9:11-13)
A. Question Asked (v. 11)

¹¹ When the Pharisees saw this, they asked his disciples, "Why does your teacher eat with tax collectors and 'sinners'?"

It seems that a rich man's feast (like Matthew's) was not such a private affair as a dinner party usually is among us. Only the invited guests were seated at the table, but the table might be set on a porch overlooking a courtyard where others could come in and watch the proceedings.

In this case, *the Pharisees*, whose influence over religious matters was quite powerful, voiced a complaint. One wonders why they spoke with Jesus' *disciples* instead of asking their question of Jesus himself. It may be simply that Jesus was busy spending time with Matthew or with some of the guests, so the Pharisees had no opportunity to address Jesus with their question. But perhaps, instead, the Pharisees sought to plant seeds of doubt in the minds of those who had become more involved with Jesus and his ministry. Whatever their motive, they could not understand how any preacher who wanted to be taken seriously could participate in a gathering of people who were at odds with the high moral code of the Mosaic law. Their criticism of Jesus implied that he had compromised his convictions and was condoning the lifestyles of these people by eating with them.

B. Question Answered (v. 12)

¹² On hearing this, Jesus said, "It is not the healthy who need a doctor, but the sick.

Though the question was asked of the disciples, *Jesus* heard it and had a ready answer. (Of course, even if he had not heard them, Jesus would have known what was on their minds just as he had known what the teachers of the law in the house in Capernaum had been thinking; Mark 2:6-8.) A *doctor* would be useless if he refused to treat the *sick*. He goes to the sick because they need him. In the same way, Jesus came to treat those who were spiritually sick because of sin.

C. Lesson Given (v. 13)

13 "But go and learn what this means: 'I desire mercy, not sacrifice.' For I have not come to call the righteous, but sinners."

Jesus, the Master Teacher, suggested a homework assignment for those who questioned his association with *sinners*: learn the meaning of what God said when he declared through his prophet Hosea, *I desire mercy, not sacrifice* (Hosea 6:6). The prophet Hosea had criticized the people of God for their hypocrisy. They had correctly practiced the religious rituals and sacrifices of the law of Moses, but they had not applied the meaning of it to their relationships with people.

A heart truly devoted to God must demonstrate *mercy* to all sinners. Even though we may be repulsed by the lifestyles of certain individuals, the love of God should draw us near to them. We must recognize that God could have been repulsed by our sins as well and could have left us to perish in them.

EXCERPTS FROM THE SERMON ON THE MOUNT (MATTHEW 5:1-20, 38-48)

Establishing the Groundwork

In his record of Jesus' life, Matthew does not always arrange events in chronological order. His arrangement tends to be topical in nature, often grouping together certain teachings or miracles of Jesus. Although what we call Jesus' "Sermon on the Mount" is found early in Matthew's Gospel, it was actually delivered during the first half of the second year of Jesus' ministry, and probably soon after he had chosen twelve men out of the larger group of disciples to become his "apostles" (Luke 6:12-16). Jesus' sermon was a part of the teaching they received, though it was also given to the larger group of disciples and to a large crowd of other listeners. This second year is often termed Jesus' "year of popularity." Great crowds were gathering wherever he went.

The Sermon on the Mount has been called the constitution of the new covenant. It describes the standard of conduct for those who would be citizens of the kingdom of Heaven that for more than a year Jesus had been declaring was near (Matthew 4:17).

Examining the Text

I. The Setting (Matthew 5:1, 2)
A. People and Place (v. 1a)

1a Now when he saw the crowds, he went up on a mountainside and sat down.

On this occasion, Jesus *went up on a mountainside*, which could describe any one of many possible locations in the hills of Galilee. Tradition places the location at a site slightly north and on the west side of the Sea of Galilee. Jesus *sat down*, assuming the accepted posture of teachers in synagogues or schools (Luke 4:20).

B. Teacher and Students (vv. 1b, 2)

1b, 2 His disciples came to him, and he began to teach them, saying:

The elevated location perhaps weeded out the people who were merely curious from the sincerely interested, and it provided a natural amphitheater for those who were willing to make the climb. The term *disciples* would have included both those who had been earlier chosen as apostles, as well as other followers who were serious about hearing the Master. According to Luke's account, Jesus chose his twelve apostles (Luke 6:12-16), then gave the Sermon on the Mount (assuming that the "Sermon on the Plain" passage in Luke 6:17-49 is parallel to the passage in Matthew 5–7).

II. The Disciple's Character (Matthew 5:3-12)
A. The Poor in Spirit (v. 3)

3 "Blessed are the poor in spirit,
for theirs is the kingdom of heaven.

Some translations use a word such as *happy* to explain the meaning of *blessed*, but what Jesus is talking about goes much deeper than happiness. It carries with it the idea of an inner fortitude that enables one to live through the storms of life. As Jesus will point out at the conclusion of this sermon, those who build their lives on a foundation of obedience to his teachings will have what it takes to withstand life's storms (Matthew 7:24-27).

Observe how Jesus' description of "blessed" people runs counter to the way the world suggests we travel in search of fulfillment or "blessedness." The *poor in spirit* are those who have come to realize their own spiritual bankruptcy and inadequacy, and therefore acknowledge their need to depend totally on the Lord and his grace for salvation.

B. The Mourners (v. 4)

⁴ "Blessed are those who mourn,
for they will be comforted.

Of all the Beatitudes, this one seems to be the most paradoxical. How can people be happy if they *mourn*? The concept of mourning is often found in the Old Testament when people are expressing sorrow for sin (as in Ezra 10:6; Psalms 32:3-5; 119:136), and that would seem to be its primary meaning here. One should keep in mind that this mourning applies not only to personal sin but to the sins of others, much as Jesus wept over the sin and approaching destruction of Jerusalem (Luke 19:41-44).

C. The Meek (v. 5)

⁵ "Blessed are the meek,
for they will inherit the earth.

To some, the idea of being *meek* implies weakness. But Jesus was not commending people for being feeble or spineless. The Greek word rendered "meek" was used in New Testament times to describe a trained elephant, a tamed stallion, or a reliable watchdog. These animals have strength, but their strength has been brought under control to serve purposes beyond themselves. Spiritually, meekness expresses the quality of courage that is exemplified when one is under great tension and pressure, yet refuses either to give way to anger or to cower under the weight of circumstances. It is a controlled strength that is best seen in times of adversity and difficulty.

In what way will the meek *inherit the earth*? Perhaps we should think of inheriting the earth as much more than just the enjoyment of material goods and wealth. There is also the sense of fulfillment and contentment that comes when one uses the resources of earth as the Creator intended them to be used. This is a blessing that those who use the earth's resources selfishly can never call their own. And when this earth is replaced by a new one, the meek will enjoy that one even more (2 Peter 3:10-13).

D. The Hungry (v. 6)

⁶ "Blessed are those who hunger and thirst for righteousness,
for they will be filled.

The words *hunger and thirst* signify an eager longing, a desire that can never be satisfied without that which is craved. They do not represent simply an uneasy feeling, but a genuine need and an urgent wish. The attitude is like that of the Psalmist's longing for God as expressed in Psalm 42:1, 2.

How do we have *righteousness?* There are two ways. One is by simply doing right. We can try to maintain that standard every day, but our sins keep us from doing so. So God has provided a second way to obtain righteousness, a way that Paul describes as "the righteousness that comes from God and is by faith" (Philippians 3:9). Thus by God's grace, we can be *filled* with the righteousness of Christ.

E. The Merciful (v. 7)

⁷ *"Blessed are the merciful,*
for they will be shown mercy.

Merciful people are grieved by the misery and pain of others, and they do what they can to relieve or end it. Often, when those who have been merciful find themselves in difficult circumstances, *they will be shown mercy* by others who benefited from or are aware of their kindness. Best of all, God will bless them and show mercy to them. Sometimes it's hard to tell the difference, as God often shows his mercy through other people (2 Corinthians 1:3, 4).

F. The Pure in Heart (v. 8)

⁸ *"Blessed are the pure in heart,*
for they will see God.

Pure gold is solid gold all the way through; it is not mixed with anything cheaper. The *pure in heart* have lives of solid good: their tastes, their thoughts, their desires, their motives are good. They do not value or desire anything evil. Even though the world sees personal purity as a matter for scorn and mockery, those who are characterized by this quality will one day *see God.*

G. The Peacemakers (v. 9)

⁹ *"Blessed are the peacemakers,*
for they will be called sons of God.

The Prince of peace commends those who are *peacemakers.* While the gospel will of necessity create division at times (Luke 14:26), believers should never seek conflict. Discord is a work of the flesh; peace is the fruit of the Spirit (Galatians 5:20, 22). To the extent that it is within our control, we are to "live at peace with everyone" (Romans 12:18). Of course, we must do so while maintaining a firm commitment to God's truth in Scripture. To compromise truth for the sake of getting along is not the kind of peace that God desires.

H. The Persecuted (vv. 10-12)

¹⁰ "Blessed are those who are
persecuted because of righteousness,
for theirs is the kingdom of heaven.

It is not by accident that the Beatitude on being persecuted follows the one on making peace, because making peace can be a risky business. The person who steps between warring sides may get shot at from both sides. In fact, all of the Beatitudes put the disciple of Jesus at odds with the world. Recognizing this fact, Jesus commends those whose distinctive difference will bring them persecution. Such persecution will not always be physical in nature; it may come in the form of verbal attacks or social exclusion. But it can be used by the disciple to display the characteristics of God.

¹¹ "Blessed are you when people insult you, persecute you and falsely say
all kinds of evil against you because of me.

In Jesus' eyes the Beatitude on persecution needed to be brought home more forcefully. Note how the *blessed are they* of verse 10 now becomes *blessed are you*. Persecution is the inevitable result in the clash of opposing value systems. Those who prefer the darkness will instinctively lash out against the light.

¹² "Rejoice and be glad, because great is your reward in heaven, for in the
same way they persecuted the prophets who were before you."

The persecution of God's people did not begin with Jesus and his disciples. God's prophets had been mistreated long before this. Consider such examples as Elijah (1 Kings 19:2, 13, 14), Micaiah (1 Kings 22:26, 27), and Jeremiah (Jeremiah 37:15; 38:6).

The book of Acts tells how disciples of Jesus were beaten and imprisoned (Acts 5:17, 18, 40; 8:3), killed (Acts 7:59, 60), and driven out of Jerusalem (Acts 8:1). But in spite of this, they rejoiced (Acts 5:41).

III. The Disciple's Influence (Matthew 5:13-16)
A. The Salt (v. 13)

¹³ "You are the salt of the earth. But if the salt loses its saltiness, how
can it be made salty again? It is no longer good for anything, except to be
thrown out and trampled by men.

Salt was a vital substance in the ancient world. It served as flavoring to make food palatable; more important, it was a preservative to keep meat from spoiling. Just as a little salt can go a long way, even a few Christians can have tremendous influence for good. Christians are the moral disinfectant that keeps a society from going bad.

But what *if the salt loses its saltiness*? If the place where salt is stored gets wet, the sodium chloride can leach out, leaving only dust-flavored remains. Such "saltless salt" *is no longer good for anything*, so it is *thrown out*.

Similarly, what if we Christians become indistinguishable from the people around us? What if we no longer mourn over sin or hunger and thirst for righteousness? What if we are not pure? It is only as we live out the Beatitudes in the preceding verses that we can become the influence God intends us to be.

B. The Light (vv. 14-16)

14 "You are the light of the world. A city on a hill cannot be hidden.

On another occasion, Jesus said, "I am *the light of the world*" (John 8:12). Here he describes his followers in the same way. Could we say that Jesus is like the sun? His light is his own; it shines from his own person. His people, then, are like the moon that reflects the light of the sun; in other words, Christians shine with the light of Jesus. Just as a *city on a hill* can be seen for miles, the light of a sincere Christian—even a small light—can do a great deal to dispel the world's darkness.

15 "Neither do people light a lamp and put it under a bowl. Instead they put it on its stand, and it gives light to everyone in the house.

In New Testament times, the ordinary household *light* was provided by a small *lamp* fueled by olive oil. Yet Jesus' words are true, whether we think of a candle, an oil-burning lamp, or an electric light bulb. Light is intended to be seen. In the same way, Christians are not intended to be invisible. We have light and truth that people in the world badly need. We should not be ashamed to let our friends and neighbors see what Christ is doing in our lives.

16 "In the same way, let your light shine before men, that they may see your good deeds and praise your Father in heaven."

Jesus was sharply critical of people who did good "for men to see" (Matthew 23:5). Later in this sermon he advised people to do good secretly (Matthew 6:1-4). Here we see him telling his people to *let* their *light shine before men, that they may see your good deeds*.

The key to understanding Jesus' teaching is in the last phrase of this verse: *and praise your Father in heaven*. God's people ought to be doing good, of course, but doing it in such a way that grateful people will praise God more than they praise his people.

IV. Jesus and the Law (Matthew 5:17-20)
A. Fulfilling the Law (vv. 17, 18)

17 "Do not think that I have come to abolish the Law or the Prophets; I have not come to abolish them but to fulfill them.

Jesus was about to say some things in this sermon that would be in sharp contrast with the Old Testament law. (They are found in the remainder of this chapter.) Hearing these statements, some people might conclude that Jesus wanted to *abolish the Law* that had been given through Moses. Jesus assured his listeners that he had no such intention.

Jesus did not elaborate on how he was going to *fulfill* the law and *the Prophets*, but the following ways should be considered. First, he fulfilled the prophecies of the Old Testament by doing what those prophecies said the Messiah would do.

Second, Jesus "filled up" the law by pouring into it the meaning that had been forgotten by the teachers of Israel. The rest of Matthew 5 shows how he did this. He applied the law to thoughts and motives as well as to actions.

Third, Jesus fulfilled the law by accomplishing what the law had failed to do. The law let people know that they were sinners, not good enough to earn eternal life (Romans 3:19, 20), but it could provide no solution to that problem. The law pointed out our need for a Savior, thus it served as a means "to lead us to Christ that we might be justified by faith" (Galatians 3:24). When we come to Christ, the law's purpose is fulfilled; "we are no longer under the supervision of the law" (Galatians 3:25).

18 "I tell you the truth, until heaven and earth disappear, not the smallest letter, not the least stroke of a pen, will by any means disappear from the Law until everything is accomplished.

Jesus was saying that not even the tiniest part of the law would be removed or discarded *from the Law until everything is accomplished*. This happened when Jesus declared on the cross, "It is finished" (John 19:30). Replacing the law was the gospel—the "good news" that God was now reconciling the world to himself through Jesus Christ (2 Corinthians 5:18, 19).

B. Keeping the Law (vv. 19, 20)

¹⁹ "Anyone who breaks one of the least of these commandments and teaches others to do the same will be called least in the kingdom of heaven, but whoever practices and teaches these commands will be called great in the kingdom of heaven.

As a general principle, Jesus' words highlight the grave responsibility of obeying and teaching others to obey the words of our heavenly Father precisely as he has delivered them in the Scriptures. God's people under the old covenant owed their undivided allegiance to the law given from God through Moses. Christians are under the divinely revealed gospel, which is to be committed to others in all generations for changeless preservation (2 Timothy 2:2; Galatians 1:8, 9, 12).

²⁰ "For I tell you that unless your righteousness surpasses that of the Pharisees and the teachers of the law, you will certainly not enter the kingdom of heaven."

Because we are aware of what Jesus had to say about *the Pharisees and the teachers of the law*, we may not be able to grasp what a bombshell these words were to the people who heard Jesus speak them. The Pharisees and the teachers of the law were considered to be the people who kept the law most precisely. How could anyone's *righteousness* ever surpass theirs?

A portion of the remainder of Jesus' sermon, particularly his words in Matthew 6:1-18, tells us how. These individuals did their giving, praying, and fasting purely for show. They claimed to possess a great devotion to the law, but their true devotion was to themselves, their prestige, and their traditions.

In the remainder of Matthew 5, Jesus contrasted the Old Testament law as understood and applied by the religious leaders of his day with his own teaching on a variety of subjects. In every instance, Jesus taught that sin and righteousness are found in one's thoughts and motives as well as in one's actions. To recognize this is to follow after the kind of righteousness that *surpasses* that of the Pharisees and teachers of the law. The next section of Scripture examines a portion of this teaching found in Matthew 5.

V. Jesus and Personal Relationships (Matthew 5:38-48)
A. Accepting Insults (vv. 38-42)

³⁸ "You have heard that it was said, 'Eye for eye, and tooth for tooth.'

Jesus was not simply referring to rabbinic tradition when he made this statement. This command was part of God's law (Exodus 21:23, 24;

Leviticus 24:19, 20; Deuteronomy 19:16-21). It provided for the just punishment of wrongdoing, but it also allowed for no more punishment than was just. It served to limit acts of personal vengeance and thus to prevent bitter feuds from escalating into something worse.

> [39] *"But I tell you, Do not resist an evil person. If someone strikes you on the right cheek, turn to him the other also.*

The words *But I tell you*, which appear elsewhere in Matthew 5 (vv. 22, 28, 32, 34, and 44), give evidence of Jesus' assertion of divine authority. Whatever the letter of the law said, God's true will for man was now being revealed directly by his Son.

A slap on the *cheek* in Jesus' day was done to insult someone more than injure him. Some have compared it with spitting in someone's face. It is clear that Jesus was speaking of the personal response to personal insults and injuries. He was not abolishing law and order or the protection of the weak and helpless from cruel treatment by criminals. The Scriptures approve the work of civic authorities in preventing and punishing crime (Romans 13:1-4).

> [40] *"And if someone wants to sue you and take your tunic, let him have your cloak as well.*

The *tunic* was the undergarment that people wore in Jesus' day. If someone wants to be mean enough to try to legally take your tunic, says Jesus, then *let him have your cloak as well*—your more costly and public outer garment. The principle seems to be this: do not be bitter or angry, even when you are treated unjustly. Rather, show your attitude of goodwill by giving more than your adversary demands.

At the same time, this verse does not mean that Christians are to be "doormats," allowing people to take advantage of them. It means that Jesus wants his people to be more concerned about relations with others than with their personal rights.

> [41] *"If someone forces you to go one mile, go with him two miles.*

In Jesus' day Israel was part of the Roman Empire. The Romans kept an army of occupation there to keep the peace and prevent uprisings. Each Roman soldier on duty was authorized to draft a civilian at will to carry his pack for a *mile*. If a civilian cursed the solider or complained, he probably would be beaten. But if he went along cheerfully and even did more than what was required, his attitude and action would disarm any hostility and promote goodwill. From this teaching of Jesus comes the familiar phrase, "going the second mile."

42 *"Give to the one who asks you, and do not turn away from the one who wants to borrow from you.*

Common sense and even love for others must qualify our response to someone *who asks* us for something. Suppose a young child wants to play with a long, sharp knife, or a man who has a drinking problem asks for money so he can buy more liquor. Obviously a Christian is not obligated to *give* what is asked for in such instances. The ideal presented here is that of helpfulness and generosity. One is not to develop a callous heart toward genuine needs, but neither is a person to grant another's requests indiscriminantly.

B. Actively Pursuing Goodwill (vv. 43-48)

43 *"You have heard that it was said, 'Love your neighbor and hate your enemy.'*

Love your neighbor was plainly written in the law (Leviticus 19:18). In contrast, *hate your enemy* is not specifically stated anywhere in the law. Even so, God's people sometimes were ordered to destroy entire nations of enemies, killing men, women, and children without mercy (Deuteronomy 7:2; 1 Samuel 15:3). It is not surprising that Jewish teachers interpreted such orders as orders to hate one's enemies.

44 *"But I tell you: Love your enemies and pray for those who persecute you,*

The Greek word for *love* that Jesus uses here refers to unselfish goodwill in action. Thus Jesus' followers must not only refuse to harbor enmity toward their *enemies*, they are told to seek what is in their best interests and to *pray* for them. This is certainly possible, but frequently it is very difficult.

45 *". . . that you may be sons of your Father in heaven. He causes his sun to rise on the evil and the good, and sends rain on the righteous and the unrighteous.*

Jesus pointed out that God gives numerous blessings to all people everywhere, even though many do not acknowledge him as the source of these blessings. In fact, many live in defiance of his will for man, following what is *evil* and *unrighteous*. The patience and kindness of our *Father in heaven* should be a constant rebuke of our pettiness and injured pride.

46, 47 *"If you love those who love you, what reward will you get? Are not even the tax collectors doing that? And if you greet only your brothers, what are you doing more than others? Do not even pagans do that?*

There is nothing unusual about responding to good treatment with a good disposition. Even people who lack any kind of spiritual depth (*pagans*) can express gratitude to those who have treated them kindly. Jesus expects his followers to do *more than others*. The Christian is to go beyond what would normally be expected.

[48] **"Be perfect, therefore, as your heavenly Father is perfect."**

The Greek word translated *perfect* means "complete" or "mature." It indicates the complete development or final form of anything. How can we ever be as complete or mature as our *heavenly Father*? We can in no way match his omnipotent power or his unlimited knowledge and wisdom. But this text is talking about such matters as loving our enemies (v. 44). We can and ought to love all those whom God loves, and we ought to do good to them as we have opportunity (Galatians 6:10). Instead of trying to excuse ourselves with the common phrase, "Nobody's perfect," let's try to improve our attitude and actions.

How to Say It

ARAMAIC. *Air*-uh-*may*-ik (strong accent on *may*).
BAAL. *Bay*-ul.
BABYLONIANS. Bab-ih-*low*-nee-unz.
CANA. *Kay*-nuh.
CAPERNAUM. Kuh-*per*-nay-um.
CEPHAS. *See*-fus.
ELIJAH. Ee-*lye*-juh.
ELISHA. Ee-*lye*-shuh.
GALILEAN. Gal-uh-*lee*-un.
GALILEE. *Gal*-uh-lee.
HEROD. *Hair*-ud.
ISAIAH. Eye-*zay*-uh.
ISRAEL. *Iz*-ray-el.
JEREMIAH. Jair-uh-*my*-uh.
JERUSALEM. Juh-*roo*-suh-lcm.
JUDAISM. *Joo*-duh-izz-um or *Joo*-day-izz-um.
JUDEAN. Joo-*dee*-un.
MESSIAH. Meh-*sigh*-uh.
MESSIANIC. mess-ee-*an*-ick.
MICAIAH. My-*kay*-uh.
NAAMAN. *Nay*-uh-mun.
NAZARETH. *Naz*-uh-reth.
PALESTINE. *Pal*-us-tine.
PHARISEES. *Fair*-ih-seez.
SABBATH. *Sa*-buth *(Sa as in sat).*
SIDON. *Sigh*-dun.
SOJOURN. *so*-jurn.
SOLOMON. *Sol*-o-mun.
SYNAGOGUE. *sin*-uh-gog.
SYRIAN. *Sear*-ee-un.
ZAREPHATH. *Zair*-uh-fath.
ZEBEDEE. *Zeb*-eh-dee.

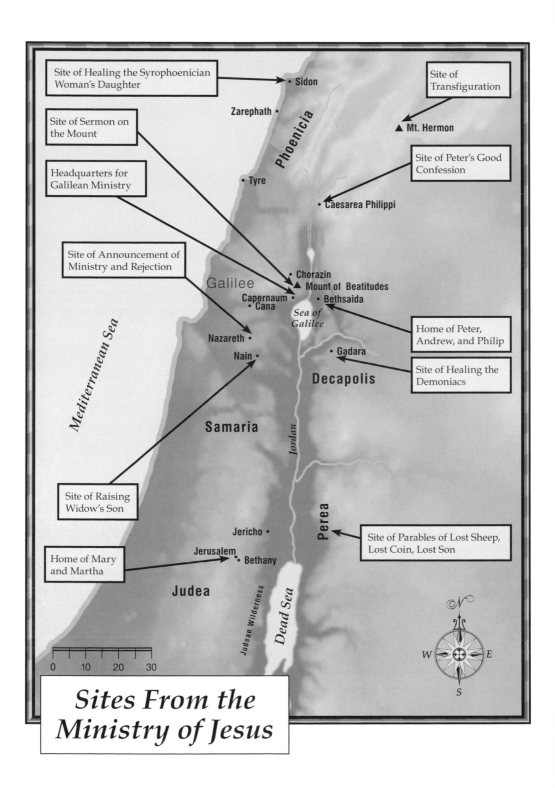

Site of Healing the Syrophoenician Woman's Daughter

Site of Transfiguration

• Sidon

Zarephath •

Phoenicia

▲ Mt. Hermon

Site of Sermon on the Mount

Site of Peter's Good Confession

Headquarters for Galilean Ministry

• Tyre

• Caesarea Philippi

Site of Announcement of Ministry and Rejection

Galilee

• Chorazin
▲ Mount of Beatitudes

Capernaum •
• Cana

• Bethsaida

Sea of Galilee

Home of Peter, Andrew, and Philip

Nazareth •

• Gadara

Site of Healing the Demoniacs

Mediterranean Sea

Nain •

Decapolis

Samaria

Jordan

Site of Raising Widow's Son

Perea

Jericho •

Site of Parables of Lost Sheep, Lost Coin, Lost Son

Jerusalem •
• Bethany

Home of Mary and Martha

Judea

Judean Wilderness

Dead Sea

0   10   20   30

N
W   E
S

Sites From the Ministry of Jesus

Chapter 7

Jesus' Galilean Ministry (Part 2)

Matthew 8:5-13; 11:2-11; Luke 7:36-50;
Matthew 12:22-32; 13:10-17

JESUS HEALS A CENTURION'S SERVANT (MATTHEW 8:5-13)

Establishing the Groundwork

It has been noted previously that Matthew has arranged his account of the life of Christ in a topical fashion, giving a series of miracles, sermons, or controversies without presenting them in the order in which they occurred. Luke's Gospel appears to be more chronological in nature, and according to his record the healing of the centurion's servant (Luke 7:1-10) took place shortly after Jesus' Sermon on the Mount (Luke 6:17-49). Matthew also places this event after the Sermon (Matthew 8:1, 5), but he groups it with other miracles of Jesus that had actually occurred earlier in his ministry, according to the order of events given by both Mark and Luke.

Examining the Text

I. The Centurion Comes to Jesus (Matthew 8:5-7)
A. Plea (vv. 5, 6)

⁵ *When Jesus had entered Capernaum, a centurion came to him, asking for help.*

Following his Sermon on the Mount, Jesus *entered Capernaum*, the headquarters of his Galilean campaign. At this point, he was some distance from the home of the *centurion*.

A centurion was the captain of a hundred troops of the Roman army. Centurions were considered the "career men" of the army. While the Jews resented the Roman presence in their land, it is interesting that every centurion mentioned in the New Testament is mentioned in a good light. The centurion at the cross declared his belief in Jesus as the Son of God (Mark 15:39). The first Gentile convert to Christianity was a centurion named Cornelius, a "devout and God-fearing" man (Acts 10:1, 2). Another centurion rescued Paul from a painful scourging (Acts 22:25, 26), and the centurion who traveled with Paul on ship to Rome treated him with courtesy and respect and followed his advice when a storm hit (Acts 27:1-3, 30-32, 42, 43).

The centurion in this account was no exception. Luke 7:3-6 tells us that the centurion had asked some elders of the Jews to bring his request for *help* to Jesus. These men gave the centurion a very high commendation, noting that "he loves our nation and has built our synagogue" (Luke 7:5).

> ⁶ *"Lord," he said, "my servant lies at home paralyzed and in terrible suffering."*

Luke's account adds the details that the centurion "valued highly" this *servant*, and that the servant "was sick and about to die" (Luke 7:2).

B. Promise (v. 7)

> ⁷ *Jesus said to him, "I will go and heal him."*

Jesus' words assured the centurion of both his compassion and his power to *heal* the servant. The fact that the centurion was a Gentile made no difference; in fact, Jesus would later use this to teach a very fundamental lesson about the kingdom of Heaven.

II. The Centurion Trusts in Jesus (Matthew 8:8-13)
A. The Centurion's Admission (vv. 8, 9)

> ⁸ *The centurion replied, "Lord, I do not deserve to have you come under my roof. But just say the word, and my servant will be healed.*

Luke tells us that after the *centurion* sent the elders of the Jews to Jesus with his request for help, he sent a second delegation of friends to Jesus. This delegation's mission was to protest the centurion's unworthiness to have Jesus come to his home and to tell Jesus to heal the servant by the power of his word (Luke 7:6-8). It may be that as Jesus drew nearer to the centurion's house, the centurion himself came and repeated this appeal. He may have been conscious of the strict regulations of the Jews forbidding them to enter the house of a Gentile (this was part of the traditions established by the Jewish teachers rather than part of the Old Testament law).

The centurion's request that Jesus merely *say the word* calls to mind the healing of an official's son from Capernaum (John 4:46-54). Jesus had healed this son from a distance by the power of his word. Perhaps the centurion, living in the same city where the official's son was healed, was aware of that miracle. The centurion's faith that *my servant will be healed* matched Jesus' promise: "I will go and heal him."

⁹ *"For I myself am a man under authority, with soldiers under me. I tell this one, 'Go,' and he goes; and that one, 'Come,' and he comes. I say to my servant, 'Do this,' and he does it."*

The centurion was aware of the power of the spoken word by one who possessed *authority*. He believed that the exercise of Jesus' divine power would produce immediate results much as the centurion's own orders in his home and in his military surroundings.

B. Jesus' Amazement (vv. 10-12)

¹⁰ *When Jesus heard this, he was astonished and said to those following him, "I tell you the truth, I have not found anyone in Israel with such great faith.*

One may wonder why Jesus, if he possessed divine insight and fore-knowledge (John 2:24, 25; 6:5, 6), would be *astonished* at this centurion's *great faith* or "amazed" at the lack of faith in Nazareth (Mark 6:6). Perhaps the best answer one can give to this is to refer to the mystery of the union of the human and the divine in the person of Jesus. When there was a need for his exercise of miraculous foresight, Jesus was always able to foresee the future or to match his conduct to its demands. But it seems that under ordinary circumstances, he accepted human limitations. His joy at the faith of this centurion was spontaneous and genuine. This man was a Gentile. His was not a background of familiarity with the law and the prophets. Therefore his great faith was all the more remarkable and served as an example to the people of *Israel*.

¹¹ *"I say to you that many will come from the east and the west, and will take their places at the feast with Abraham, Isaac and Jacob in the kingdom of heaven.*

The concept of a *feast* or banquet associated with the Messiah was rooted in some of the prophecies of the Old Testament that pictured the messianic age as a time of great abundance (Isaiah 25:6-9; Joel 3:18; Amos 9:13-15). In the New Testament, this is pictured as the "wedding supper of the Lamb" (Revelation 19:9). Those who *come from the east and the west* are Gentiles, who, like this centurion, will take their places with the patriarchs of the Jews—*Abraham, Isaac and Jacob*—in the *kingdom of heaven*.

¹² *"But the subjects of the kingdom will be thrown outside, into the darkness, where there will be weeping and gnashing of teeth."*

The phrase *the subjects of the kingdom* refers to the Jews, many of whom assumed that their descent from Abraham, Isaac, and Jacob guaranteed them a place in the kingdom of Heaven. These individuals also assumed that Gentiles would be on the *outside* since they did not share such a heritage. But Jesus taught that the roles will be reversed because entrance into the kingdom is determined by spiritual, not physical, standards. It would be hard to conceive of a more dreadful, terrifying description of the unending suffering in Hell than that conveyed by the phrase *weeping and gnashing of teeth*.

C. Jesus' Assurance (v. 13)

13 Then Jesus said to the centurion, "Go! It will be done just as you believed it would." And his servant was healed at that very hour.

Sometimes Jesus briefly delayed his miraculous healing in order to test or to cultivate faith, as in the case of the blind men mentioned in Matthew 9:27-30. But in the case of the *centurion*, nothing like that was necessary. He had made known the depth of his faith in Jesus without any prompting. *His servant was healed at that very hour*, as was the case with the official's son (John 4:51-53).

JOHN THE BAPTIST'S QUESTION FROM PRISON (MATTHEW 11:2-11)

Establishing the Groundwork

The last time we read about John the Baptist, he was introducing some of his disciples to Jesus (John 1:35-42). Eventually these men became followers of Jesus. From that point, John continued preaching, but his following decreased while Jesus' popularity grew. John accepted that change graciously, without jealousy or bitterness (John 3:25-30).

At some point, John was arrested and imprisoned for reproving Herod the tetrarch for the evils he had committed, most notably for taking the wife of his brother Philip (Luke 3:1, 19, 20). This Herod, known as Herod Antipas, was one of several sons of Herod the Great, who had ruled Judea when Jesus was born. Herod Antipas ruled the territories of Galilee and Perea, the areas where the ministries of both Jesus and John the Baptist were, for the most part, conducted.

While Jesus was in the midst of his Galilean ministry and gaining an increasing following wherever he went, messengers from John came to him with an important question.

I. John's Doubts (Matthew 11:2-6)
A. He Questioned Jesus (vv. 2, 3)

² When John heard in prison what Christ was doing, he sent his disciples

The Jewish historian Josephus tells us that *John* was imprisoned in the fortress of Machaerus, near the eastern shore of the Dead Sea. Herod had a winter palace there. Even though John was *in prison*, he was not completely isolated from the outside world. Apparently he was allowed visitors, among whom were *his disciples* who informed him of *what Christ was doing*. Most likely this included reports of both his teaching and his miracles. John was also permitted to send messages through his disciples, as this verse indicates.

³ . . . to ask him, "Are you the one who was to come, or should we expect someone else?"

John had been certain of who Jesus was after baptizing Jesus (John 1:29-34). He had confidently declared of Jesus to two of his disciples, "Look, the Lamb of God!" (John 1:35, 36). What had happened to that confidence? Why did John seem to be expressing doubts concerning Jesus at this point?

Several suggestions may be offered. First, John was a rugged person who had spent his entire adult life in the outdoors. For months (some say for six months or more), he had been confined to prison. Such a change in his surroundings and the enforced inactivity may have had a debilitating effect on his spirit. Contributing to this, perhaps, was the fact that Jesus had made no move to free him.

Second, it seems that John did not understand the kind of program that would be carried out by the Messiah, whose coming he had announced. He knew that the Messiah was going to establish a kingdom of godly rule. He may have wondered, therefore, why Jesus had not proclaimed himself as the Messiah and begun to seize the government from the hands of godless rulers. From the reports John had been receiving, Jesus was conducting a simple ministry of preaching and healing. When would he begin baptizing in the Spirit and burning the wicked "with unquenchable fire" (Matthew 3:11, 12)?

B. He Received an Answer (vv. 4-6)

⁴ Jesus replied, "Go back and report to John what you hear and see:

Jesus did not rebuke John for his question and did not view the question as a sign of unfaithfulness. Instead, he answered it in such a way that John could weigh the evidence and reach his own conclusion.

5 "The blind receive sight, the lame walk, those who have leprosy are cured, the deaf hear, the dead are raised, and the good news is preached to the poor.

The prophet Isaiah spoke of a time when God would open the eyes of the *blind* and unstop the ears of the *deaf.* He predicted a time when a *lame* person would "leap like a deer, and the mute tongue shout for joy" (Isaiah 35:5, 6). In another place, Isaiah spoke of the Messiah as one who would be "anointed . . . to preach good news to the poor" (Isaiah 61:1). Through his preaching and his performing miracles, Jesus was doing exactly what Isaiah had said the Messiah would do.

6 "Blessed is the man who does not fall away on account of me."

Jesus sent John's disciples back to him with words of encouragement. "John, keep your faith no matter what the circumstances; do not stumble now. Be assured that your message about me is true, even when the details or timing of my program seem unclear." John's faith was no doubt renewed, and it provided him with the assurance he needed when he faced his untimely death (Mark 6:27-29). His ministry had not been in vain.

II. John's Character (Matthew 11:7-11)
A. He Was Strong (vv. 7, 8)

7 As John's disciples were leaving, Jesus began to speak to the crowd about John: "What did you go out into the desert to see? A reed swayed by the wind?

As John's disciples left to return to their imprisoned teacher, *Jesus began to speak to the crowd about John.* Among those present were probably some who had been disciples of John at one time. Perhaps they were inclined to think less of John because of the doubts he had raised concerning Jesus.

By means of three questions, Jesus issued a stirring tribute to John. First, when the people had gone out to hear John speak in the *desert,* did he come across like *a reed swayed by the wind?* Obviously not! John was a strong, bold proclaimer of God's truth. So they should not interpret any doubt in John's question as an indication of weakness.

8 "If not, what did you go out to see? A man dressed in fine clothes? No, those who wear fine clothes are in kings' palaces.

In addition, John did not seek luxury or comfort. He was not *dressed in fine clothes.* He lived in the outdoors, and he dressed appropriately; his "clothes were made of camel's hair, and he had a leather belt around his waist" (Matthew

3:4). John introduced the King of kings, but he did not wear royal attire to do so! In fact, the people living *in kings' palaces* were the very ones who now held John prisoner unjustly.

B. He Was a Prophet (v. 9)

⁹ *"Then what did you go out to see? A prophet? Yes, I tell you, and more than a prophet.*

John had denied that he was "the Prophet," in the sense of being the individual to fulfill Moses' promise in Deuteronomy 18:15 (John 1:21). But in the sense of being a divinely appointed spokesman for God, there was no question in Jesus' mind or in the popular opinion that John was *a prophet* (Matthew 21:26).

Jesus went on to say that John was *more than a prophet*, for John was the immediate forerunner of the Messiah. John tied the thread of hope within the messages of the prophets to the coming of Jesus.

C. He Was a Messenger (v. 10)

¹⁰ *"This is the one about whom it is written:*
"'I will send my messenger ahead of you,
who will prepare your way before you.'

Jesus quoted the Scripture from Malachi 3:1 to explain why John was "more than a prophet." He was the special *messenger* appointed by God to *prepare* the *way* for God's chosen one. He did this by calling the nation to repentance and urging all to make the Messiah's paths straight (Matthew 3:3) so he could be welcomed when he came.

D. He Was Great (v. 11)

¹¹ *"I tell you the truth: Among those born of women there has not risen anyone greater than John the Baptist; yet he who is least in the kingdom of heaven is greater than he."*

Jesus then presented before the crowd a particularly notable tribute to John. His words gave further reassurance to any who might be inclined to denigrate John for his doubt. Jesus went on to issue a statement even more challenging to consider: *he who is least in the kingdom of heaven is greater than* John. This was not a criticism of John; rather, Jesus was emphasizing as strongly as he could what wonderful blessings would be bestowed upon those in God's kingdom—the kingdom that John announced was near and that Jesus had come to establish.

JESUS IN THE HOME OF SIMON THE PHARISEE (LUKE 7:36-50)

Establishing the Groundwork

According to Luke's record, Jesus' visit in the home of Simon the Pharisee followed the visit of John's disciples to Jesus and Jesus' words of commendation concerning John. Luke is the only Gospel writer to include this account of how Jesus' forgiveness was extended to someone who was considered an outcast in her day. But this is a key emphasis in Luke's Gospel—Jesus is the Savior for all people. No one's sins are so numerous or severe that he cannot forgive them.

The exact location where this incident occurred is not given in the text. It took place in a "town" (Luke 7:37), which could well have been Capernaum, the site so central to Jesus' Galilean ministry.

Some students confuse this incident with a similar one that happened during the final week of Jesus' ministry. Luke does not mention it, but the other three Gospel writers do (Matthew 26:6-13; Mark 14:3-9; John 12:2-8). Thus some conclude that all four writers are telling of the same event.

There are similarities: Jesus attends a feast at the home of someone named Simon and a woman (unnamed by Matthew and Mark as well as Luke) comes by surprise and anoints him with expensive ointment. But the differences are stark enough to conclude the events are distinct: the host is a different Simon, the location is Bethany, and John tells us the woman's name—Mary of Bethany (John 12:3). Also different is that Jesus' head is anointed in Bethany. Only someone who had been invited to the feast could have got close enough to anoint Jesus' head. The stranger in Luke's account could get only as close as Jesus' feet. Other significant differences involve the source and the reason for the complaints. In Luke's account the host complains about Jesus' allowing the woman to anoint him because of her sinful character. But in Bethany the disciples, led by Judas (John 12:4), complain about the wastefulness of the act. Their objections have nothing to do with the woman's (Mary's) character.

Examining the Text

I. The Intruder (Luke 7:36-38)
A. The Dinner (v. 36)

36 Now one of the Pharisees invited Jesus to have dinner with him, so he went to the Pharisee's house and reclined at the table.

We know nothing about Simon the Pharisee except what we are told in this account in Luke. (We are not told Simon's name until Jesus speaks to him in verse 40.) Since Jesus was at the height of his popularity at this point in his Galilean ministry, it is likely that he received many invitations to social functions. It is noteworthy to consider that prior to this account, Luke records how Jesus' critics sought to label him as a "glutton and a drunkard, a friend of tax collectors and 'sinners'" (Luke 7:34). But Jesus never restricted his friendship to just one segment of society.

Luke does not specifically state what Simon's motives were in inviting Jesus *to have dinner with him.* Since Simon did not extend to Jesus the customary courtesies afforded a guest (as Jesus would later point out), it seems likely that his motives were less than sincere. Perhaps the invitation was given in the hope that Jesus could be caught off guard in a more informal setting and would say something that could be used to curb his popularity. We are not told whether or not any of Jesus' disciples were invited to this dinner.

That Jesus *reclined at the table* reflects the custom of that day. Each guest at a meal such as this one would recline on a couch with his feet pointed away from the table. Leaning on his left arm, he would then eat with his right hand. This explains why the woman could carry out the actions described in verse 38.

B. The Description (v. 37)

37 When a woman who had lived a sinful life in that town learned that Jesus was eating at the Pharisee's house, she brought an alabaster jar of perfume,

The *woman who had lived a sinful life in that town* is not named. Some have suggested that she was Mary Magdalene, but there is no basis for this. Most likely her sinful life was a life of prostitution or possibly adultery. The basis for suggesting this is that such a sin would be most likely to make a woman so notorious that she would be recognized instantly as a sinner, which clearly Simon did (v. 39).

It may seem strange that such an outcast could get into a wealthy *Pharisee's house.* But the rich delighted in being able to exhibit their luxurious household, clothing, food, and learned conversation to the poor. The public was permitted to come into the house on such occasions and stand around the wall in the banquet room. In such a crowd as this, the woman would have had no difficulty slipping in. She must have known that no one looked upon her with more contempt than the Pharisees, but that did not stop her.

The woman *brought* with her *an alabaster jar of perfume.* Alabaster was a translucent, milky-white stone, which was very expensive. What this jar held was most likely an expensive perfumed ointment such as rich people used on their hair and skin.

C. The Devotion (v. 38)

38 . . . and as she stood behind him at his feet weeping, she began to wet his feet with her tears. Then she wiped them with her hair, kissed them and poured perfume on them.

As noted previously, the guests were reclining on couches with their feet pointed away from the table. Thus the woman could stand *behind* Jesus and begin to *wet his feet with her tears*. It is likely that this woman had recently heard Jesus' preaching and had been persuaded to turn from her sinful lifestyle in repentance and seek forgiveness for her past. Now she was coming to Jesus to express her gratitude.

Perhaps by accident the woman's first tears fell on Jesus' feet. The spots they made revealed that his feet were still soiled with the dust of the street, so the woman remained where she was, bathing Jesus' feet as her weeping became more intense. Having no towel to wipe his feet, she then began to do so *with her hair*. If the woman unloosed her hair in public at this point, she was committing an act considered improper and disgraceful. Such an impulsive gesture revealed the depths of the feelings of love and gratitude that filled her heart.

The woman then *kissed* Jesus' feet. The verb form used in the Greek text for kissed means to kiss repeatedly. Finally, she poured the *perfume* she had brought on Jesus' feet. Normally the head was the part of the body that was anointed, but in her deep humility the woman anointed only the feet of Jesus.

II. The Host and the Guest (Luke 7:39-47)
A. Simon's Perspective (v. 39)

39 When the Pharisee who had invited him saw this, he said to himself, "If this man were a prophet, he would know who is touching him and what kind of woman she is—that she is a sinner."

The host of this dinner still remains unnamed, but to see him identified as *the Pharisee* at this point is sufficient—for he demonstrated a typical Pharisaic attitude. His reaction to Jesus stood in direct contrast to the woman's action. While she commended Jesus by her works, he criticized Jesus by his words. While she did what she did for all to see, he said his words only *to himself.*

Simon's reasoning is most revealing. It seems he had been pondering the question of just who Jesus was. He had entertained the notion that he might be a *prophet*. Now he seriously doubted this to be so, because, in his thinking, a holy man such as a prophet would know this woman's character and order her to go away. The Pharisees prided themselves on their separation from anything unclean and sinful. That Jesus allowed such close contact with such a sinful woman was inexcusable to Simon. His statement *she is a sinner* carried with it the self-righteous implication: "and I am not."

B. Jesus' Parable (vv. 40-43)

40 Jesus answered him, "Simon, I have something to tell you."
"Tell me, teacher," he said.

Simon probably did not expect Jesus to answer his unspoken thoughts, but Jesus knew that Simon's thinking had to be confronted. He did so with a "mini-parable."

41, 42 "Two men owed money to a certain moneylender. One owed him five hundred denarii, and the other fifty. Neither of them had the money to pay him back, so he canceled the debts of both. Now which of them will love him more?"

The denarius (the singular form of *denarii*) represented a day's wages for a working man (Matthew 20:1, 2). One debt in Jesus' parable was nearly twenty months' pay, and the other about two months' pay. Yet in spite of the huge difference between the two debts, they were both canceled. Jesus concluded the parable with a question, as he sometimes did (Matthew 21:31, 40; Luke 10:36).

43 Simon replied, "I suppose the one who had the bigger debt canceled."
"You have judged correctly," Jesus said.

The principle taught by the parable is this: more gratitude flows from the person who has received more forgiveness. Simon had *judged correctly* in regard to a parable involving people without faces, but could he see how the principle applied to the situation unfolding in his own house?

C. Jesus' Point (vv. 44-47)

44-46 Then he turned toward the woman and said to Simon, "Do you see this woman? I came into your house. You did not give me any water for my feet, but she wet my feet with her tears and wiped them with her hair. You did not give me a kiss, but this woman, from the time I entered, has not stopped kissing my feet. You did not put oil on my head, but she has poured perfume on my feet.

Jesus contrasted the woman's actions with the shabby treatment he had received from his host. All of the actions that Jesus described in verses 44-46 involved common courtesies extended to houseguests in those days. Jesus had been given none of them. The woman, however, performed them, though it was not her place to do so. She even went beyond them. It is clear that Simon loathed Jesus, while the sinful woman loved him.

47 *"Therefore, I tell you, her many sins have been forgiven—for she loved much. But he who has been forgiven little loves little."*

Jesus knew full well that this woman was a sinner, contrary to Simon's earlier thinking (v. 39). In fact, it is probable that forgiveness had been granted to her at some point before the dinner. The love for Jesus that she had so fervently demonstrated here came because he had *forgiven* her. The love did not produce the forgiveness; the parable Jesus had just given indicates that forgiveness is an act of grace and cannot be purchased or earned in any way.

On the other hand, Simon had not demonstrated any love toward Jesus because he had been *forgiven little*. He did not see himself as a sinner and therefore needed no forgiveness. This issue was at the very heart of Jesus' ongoing controversy with the self-righteous Pharisees.

III. The Guest and the Intruder (Luke 7:48-50)
A. Declaration of Forgiveness (v. 48)

48 *Then Jesus said to her, "Your sins are forgiven."*

Jesus' previous statement, "her many sins have been forgiven," might have been taken as a declaration that God had forgiven her sins. But now Jesus directly addressed the woman and said, *Your sins are forgiven*. These words would have been spoken, not only to reassure the woman, but to challenge Simon and others present to consider that he was far more than a "prophet" (v. 39).

B. Doubts Expressed (v. 49)

49 *The other guests began to say among themselves, "Who is this who even forgives sins?"*

In the home of Simon, Jesus had performed no miracle to prove that he had the power to forgive *sins*, as he had done with the paralytic in Mark 2:1-12. But the manner in which he had demonstrated insight into the thoughts and actions of others had produced too much discomfort for any of the Pharisees present to care to dispute his claim publicly. As Simon had done earlier (v. 39), they kept their thoughts to *themselves*.

C. Declaration of Peace (v. 50)

50 *Jesus said to the woman, "Your faith has saved you; go in peace."*

Jesus had earlier spoken of the woman's love; now he commended her *faith*. That faith had brought her to Jesus, where she found the grace that could wash the stains from her sordid past. *Peace* comes when sins go.

We have no record of what happened to the woman after this, but one cannot doubt that her life was dramatically changed. The Pharisees were changed as well, but only in the sense that their hostility toward Jesus increased. Jesus came to save sinful women, but he had also come to save sinful Pharisees. Most of them remained too blind to acknowledge that truth.

THE BLASPHEMY AGAINST THE HOLY SPIRIT
(MATTHEW 12:22-32)

Establishing the Groundwork

Opposition against Jesus from groups such as the Pharisees continued to mount following incidents such as the one just examined from Luke's Gospel. Much of this occurred because Jesus continued to defy their traditions, which they held to be just as binding on people as the law of Moses itself. He permitted his disciples to pick grain and eat it on the Sabbath (Matthew 12:1-8). He healed a man's hand on the Sabbath (vv. 9-13). These incidents are followed by this statement: "But the Pharisees went out and plotted how they might kill Jesus" (v. 14).

The text before us recounts an occasion in which the Pharisees did not try to use physical violence against Jesus; instead, they attempted to cast doubt on his ministry by charging that he was actually an agent of Satan. The battle lines were clearly being drawn.

Matthew's arrangement seems to be topical more than chronological in chapter 12. He uses the events recounted early in the chapter (vv. 1-21) to set the stage for the confrontation described in verses 22-30. In fact, however, several weeks or even months probably separated the events.

Examining the Text

I. Kingdom of God (Matthew 12:22-30)
A. Bold Challenge (vv. 22-24)

22 Then they brought him a demon-possessed man who was blind and mute, and Jesus healed him, so that he could both talk and see.

One of the characteristics of *demon-possessed* individuals in the Bible is that demons tended to abuse their victims physically. The people Jesus confronted were often afflicted with ailments such as the lack of sight and speech (the man in this text is an example), or with torments such as causing the victim to cut himself with sharp objects (Mark 5:5) or to throw himself into a fire (Matthew 17:15).

²³ *All the people were astonished and said, "Could this be the Son of David?"*

When Jesus cast the demon out of this individual, immediately the *astonished* onlookers wondered if he might be the Messiah. *(Son of David is one of several titles for the Messiah; cf. Matthew 22:42.)*

²⁴ *But when the Pharisees heard this, they said, "It is only by Beelzebub, the prince of demons, that this fellow drives out demons."*

Beelzebub is a variant spelling of the ancient name "Baal-Zebub," which was the title of one of the local Canaanite gods in Old Testament times (2 Kings 1:2). Some believe that *Beelzebub* (meaning "lord of the flies") was a name meant to ridicule the actual name of the supposed deity, which was "Beelzebul" (meaning "lord of the house"). In fact, *Beelzebul* is the name that appears in the Greek text of this passage. The significance of the title "lord of the house" will become clear in the context of Jesus' response to the Pharisees' charge (v. 29).

The Pharisees' accusation represented the lowest form of slander against someone claiming to represent God. They were crediting Jesus' miraculous works to the power of Satan. The implication of this charge was that either Jesus was himself deceived regarding who was empowering him, or he was knowingly working in league with the devil and thus operating under false pretenses. Jesus could not allow such an accusation to go unchallenged.

B. Foolish Idea (vv. 25-27)

²⁵ *Jesus knew their thoughts and said to them, "Every kingdom divided against itself will be ruined, and every city or household divided against itself will not stand.*

Here Jesus expressed a principle that has stood the test of time: any institution or organization that allows internal conflicts to continue unchecked is bound to be *ruined*.

²⁶ *"If Satan drives out Satan, he is divided against himself. How then can his kingdom stand?*

Jesus then applied the "house divided" principle to the slanderous charge against him. Considering the aggressiveness with which Jesus had overpowered demonic spirits during his ministry thus far, did it make sense that *Satan* would support such a ministry?

²⁷ *"And if I drive out demons by Beelzebub, by whom do your people drive them out? So then, they will be your judges.*

Previously Jesus had exposed the fallacy in the Pharisees' doctrine. Now he drew attention to their practice, once more showing the foolishness (as well as the hypocrisy) of their accusation against him. They taught their own followers how to *drive out demons*. Thus for the Pharisees to argue that it required a Satanic power to cast out demons would in effect be an indictment against themselves.

Jesus' reference to the Pharisees' casting out demons raises the question of just what these men were capable of doing and by what means. We would not expect that the Pharisees were empowered by the Holy Spirit, given their opposition to the work of the Spirit in Jesus. Nor is it likely that they were empowered by Satan, using the same logic that Jesus used to defend himself. If they were successful in casting out demons, then perhaps they were doing it through the means that Jesus suggested his disciples use: prayer (Mark 9:29).

The difference between this approach and a supernatural gift such as the one Jesus and his disciples possessed is that the gift could produce an immediate release from the demon, with all the evidence of a miracle to those who observed. Prayer, on the other hand, may have taken time to accomplish its objective. It may have been this difference that accounted for the crowds' being "astonished" at the manner in which Jesus cast out demons (v. 23). His work was a powerful, instantaneous miracle of God, not simply an eventual response to fervent, persistent prayer.

C. Strong Stand (vv. 28-30)

[28] *"But if I drive out demons by the Spirit of God, then the kingdom of God has come upon you.*

Jesus could not be operating by the power of Satan, since he continually assaulted the kingdom of Satan. He was obviously doing something bigger than what was achieved through prayer, since he obtained immediate and impressive results. By the process of elimination, Jesus had proved that he was empowered *by the Spirit of God*.

Now came the challenging implication for the Pharisees: the power of the Spirit of God within Jesus confirmed the claims made by Jesus. He is indeed the Son of David, the Messiah. *The kingdom of God has come upon* them, for the King himself is standing before them. The phrase *kingdom of God* can signify the "rule" of God, and that is the meaning here. Jesus was indicating that Satan's ability to control people's lives was in jeopardy.

[29] *"Or again, how can anyone enter a strong man's house and carry off his possessions unless he first ties up the strong man? Then he can rob his house.*

Jesus provided yet another application of his "house divided" principle. Each time he freed an individual from demonic influence, he took from Satan someone whom Satan saw as his own "possession." Consider how this language was, in effect, a response to the original charge of the Pharisees. If Satan is, as the Pharisees called him, "Beelzebul" ("lord of the *house*"), then Jesus must be very powerful if he is able to enter into such *a strong man's house*, tie him up, and then *rob* him by seizing *his possessions* (people under his influence). There is only one power capable of accomplishing such a task, and Jesus must possess it: the power of God.

[30] **"He who is not with me is against me, and he who does not gather with me scatters."**

Having stated that "the kingdom of God has come upon you" (v. 28), Jesus confronted the Pharisees with their decision concerning him. They could not be neutral. The choice they faced was clear: either support Jesus in his messianic ministry or, by default, be rejected by Jesus and by God.

II. Sin Against the Spirit (Matthew 12:31, 32)
A. Unpardonable Sin (v. 31)

[31] **"And so I tell you, every sin and blasphemy will be forgiven men, but the blasphemy against the Spirit will not be forgiven.**

One of the most terrifying warnings in Scripture is this reference to what has come to be known as the "unpardonable sin." The key to understanding what this verse means (or any verse of Scripture, for that matter) is to look at the context.

Since the Pharisees were being warned about this sin, they had apparently not yet crossed the line. Even so, it was their charge—that Jesus was empowered by Satan rather than the Holy Spirit—that led to this warning. With this understanding as the starting point, some reasonable conclusions can be derived from this text.

First, *blasphemy against the Spirit* has something to do with denying the Spirit's powerful witness to Jesus Christ. Furthermore, it is a slander against the Holy Spirit; for when his divine powers are said to be Satan's powers, he is truly being "blasphemed." Blasphemy against the Spirit also seems to involve a deliberate and willful rejection of the Spirit's evidence on behalf of Jesus. Such an attitude is not an honest doubt that needs more time to reason through the data; it is a recognition of the truth and a refusal to accept it. This is the line that the Pharisees were being warned not to cross.

Perhaps this sin can best be likened to the attitude of Satan himself. He knows the truth about Jesus; he and all his cohorts "believe" in Jesus (James 2:19). And yet Satan has willfully chosen to reject the authority of God and to oppose the ministry of Jesus. This is a perversion of the will so deep that one cannot recover from it, and therefore God cannot forgive.

Let us keep in mind that this is not a sin we would expect to see often, if ever. After all, even Jesus' staunchest enemies, the Pharisees, had not yet reached this level of opposition. Thus we should continue to evangelize all those who reject the gospel of Christ, because what we will likely confront is not the willful and final rejection of a truth that these individuals know, but the resistance to a truth of which they have not yet been persuaded.

As for the Christian who is worried that he may have committed the unpardonable sin at some point in his past, the fact that he is troubled by this possibility suggests that he has never reached this level. He should repent of the sins he has committed and renew his pledge of faith to Christ.

B. Eternal Consequences (v. 32)

³² *"Anyone who speaks a word against the Son of Man will be forgiven, but anyone who speaks against the Holy Spirit will not be forgiven, either in this age or in the age to come."*

Why is speaking *against the Son of Man* more tolerable than speaking *against the Holy Spirit?* Consider that Jesus made his exceptional claims while he was in his incarnate state, and it is always reasonable to be cautious when a man claims to be God. While preaching in a human form, Jesus looked not unlike any other man who might make such an incredible claim—and there were many in his day who claimed to be great leaders (see Acts 5:34-39). There was nothing about Jesus' appearance that would have given him an advantage over these other claimants—or over those whom Jesus predicted would come after him (Matthew 24:5).

Thus to "speak against Jesus" and doubt his claims would not be unreasonable—that is, until the Holy Spirit provided an indisputable, supernatural witness to Christ through the apostles and their testimony written in Scripture (John 14:26; 16:13, 14; 17:20). A rejection at this point would not be against the Son of Man, but against the Holy Spirit, who testifies on his behalf.

The consequences of blaspheming against the Spirit and his witness to Jesus are as severe as one can imagine: it *will not be forgiven, either in this age or in the age to come.* The Holy Spirit's word concerning Jesus is God's last word. One rejects it at his own eternal peril.

JESUS' REASON FOR USING PARABLES IN HIS TEACHING (MATTHEW 13:10-17)

Establishing the Background

Matthew 13 describes an incident that took place a little past the midpoint of Jesus' three-and-a-half year ministry. In it the word *parable* appears for the first time in Matthew's Gospel. This does not mean that Jesus had never used a parable before, but it does seem that he increased his use of parables at this time. Both Matthew and Mark note that on this occasion Jesus taught only in parables (Matthew 13:34; Mark 4:34). The disciples asked Jesus why he was doing so; his explanation is the subject matter of this portion of text.

Examining the Text

I. Those Who Hear (Matthew 13:10-12)
A. Question (v. 10)

¹⁰ The disciples came to him and asked, "Why do you speak to the people in parables?"

The beginning of Matthew 13 tells us, "Such large crowds gathered around [Jesus] that he got into a boat and sat in it, while all the people stood on the shore" (v. 2). Jesus then proceeded to teach the people through a series of parables; in fact, "he did not say anything to them without using a parable" (v. 34). Mark 4:10 records, "When he was alone, the Twelve and the others around him asked him about the parables." Matthew includes one of these questions immediately after his record of the first parable, the parable of the sower (vv. 3-8), perhaps to set the stage for the further parabolic teaching that follows.

The *disciples* expressed confusion at Jesus' use of *parables*. With a huge crowd listening, Jesus was not teaching as he had done in the Sermon on the Mount. All he did was tell a series of simple stories about ordinary happenings. Even his closest followers did not understand the lessons that these stories intended to teach. It looked to them as if a great opportunity was being wasted. *Why* did Jesus teach this way?

B. Promise (vv. 11, 12)

¹¹ He replied, "The knowledge of the secrets of the kingdom of heaven has been given to you, but not to them.

The word *secrets* translates the Greek word *musterion*, which is the source of our word *mystery* and is often translated that way. (See this verse in the *King*

James Version, for example.) The *New International Version*® translates the word as "mystery" 18 times.

In the language of the New Testament, mysteries are not puzzling situations to be solved by clever detective work. They involve matters that can be known only by God's revealing them. No one can search them out; one must be told or he will never know. Jesus was revealing vital truths about the *kingdom of heaven* to his disciples, but not to the multitudes of people who cared little or nothing about those truths. *Knowledge* of the kingdom's secrets was *given* to the disciples because they wanted it. It was *not* given to most of the people in the crowds because they had not given themselves to God and to knowing his will.

> [12] *"Whoever has will be given more, and he will have an abundance.*
> *Whoever does not have, even what he has will be taken from him.*

The principle stated by Jesus in this verse is applicable to many areas of daily living. A person who learns to read can enter into the treasures of great literature. One who learns to swim can go into deeper water and use diving boards. In each case, *more* opportunities are given to the individual who has a desire to master various fields of interest and study. The disciples of Jesus had a genuine interest in Jesus' teaching; thus they had a growing knowledge, or an *abundance*, of matters pertaining to the kingdom of Heaven.

In contrast, the nonuse of abilities that a person possesses will result in the loss of those skills. The skater who stops skating for years skates very poorly when he or she tries again. The violinist who stops practicing soon loses his or her touch. So it is in the spiritual realm. The one who possesses the desire to know and obey Jesus *will be given* additional spiritual treasures. The one who is self-satisfied and who feels no need to grow in his faith will eventually lose what spiritual perception and zeal he once possessed.

II. Those Who Do Not Hear (Matthew 13:13-15)
A. Unnecessary Failure (v. 13)

> [13] *"This is why I speak to them in parables:*
> *"Though seeing, they do not see;*
> *though hearing, they do not hear or understand.*

It is possible to look at something and not *see* it in the sense of perceiving its genuine value. A jeweler, for example, can see the value of a precious gem while the novice sees only a pretty stone. When Jesus spoke *in parables*, it brought to light the fact that although many in the crowd had eyes capable of normal sight, they did not really *see* God's spiritual truths at all. And although they had ears capable of receiving normal auditory input, they did not really absorb or understand what they were *hearing*.

The parables of Jesus thus served to separate his hearers into certain spiritual categories. Some, including Jesus' disciples, were eager to accept his teachings. Others in the crowd did not have any interest in deeper spiritual truths. The teachings of Jesus only served to strengthen their obstinacy. Like the sun that melts the wax but hardens the clay, Jesus' parables either broke through to the hearts of the hearers or made them walk away in disgust. Thus the parables of Jesus can both reveal and conceal at the same time.

B. Fulfilled Prophecy (v. 14)

14 "In them is fulfilled the prophecy of Isaiah:
"'You will be ever hearing but never understanding;
you will be ever seeing but never perceiving.

Nearly eight centuries earlier God's people had been given his message through the prophet *Isaiah*, but they had rejected it. Jesus said that Isaiah's *prophecy*, found in Isaiah 6:9, 10, was also an accurate description of those to whom he spoke.

C. Stubborn Refusal (v. 15)

15 "'For this people's heart has become calloused;
they hardly hear with their ears,
and they have closed their eyes.
Otherwise they might see with their eyes,
hear with their ears,
understand with their hearts
and turn, and I would heal them.'"

Like the people in Isaiah's time, many in Jesus' day had refused to *hear with their ears*. They had willfully *closed their eyes* to spiritual matters. They did not want to *understand*. This condition of spiritual insensitivity had been self-imposed. The problem was on the part of the people, not God. God is not willing that any should perish, but that all should *turn* to him in repentance (2 Peter 3:9).

III. Those Who Are Blessed (Matthew 13:16, 17)
A. Blessing for You (v. 16)

16 "But blessed are your eyes because they see, and your ears because they hear.

The disciples resembled the good ground in Jesus' parable (v. 8). They were willing to shape their lives by what they learned from Jesus, and they became fruitful in their service to him. They did not understand all that Jesus meant in the parable of the sower; but they were willing to ask him about it (Luke 8:9), and he explained it to them (Matthew 13:18-23).

Such a blessing was not given to the twelve disciples alone; others were with them to ask and receive the explanation of the parable of the sower from Jesus (Mark 4:10). It seems, then, that anyone who cared enough to seek further instruction from Jesus could share the blessing of receiving additional insights into his message.

B. Advantage over Prophets (v. 17)

17 "For I tell you the truth, many prophets and righteous men longed to see what you see but did not see it, and to hear what you hear but did not hear it."

The people who heard Jesus speak enjoyed a special privilege. *Many prophets and righteous men longed* to experience what Jesus' hearers had the opportunity to *see* and *hear*. The prophets had foretold the coming of the Messiah, and had "searched intently and with the greatest care" to grasp "the time and circumstances" when their prophecies would be fulfilled. But God revealed to them that it was not in their own age that certain prophecies were to be fulfilled (1 Peter 1:10-12).

The spiritual truths that Jesus was teaching in parables were the answer to centuries of human longing and expectation. God's promises were being fulfilled in Jesus, and those with a desire to listen to and follow him were of all people most blessed.

How to Say It

ANTIPAS. *An*-tih-pus.

BAAL-ZEBUB. *Bay*-ul-*zee*-bub (strong accent on *zee*).

BEELZEBUB. Bih-*el*-zih-bub.

BEELZEBUL. Bih-*el*-zih-bul.

CANAANITE. *Kay*-nun-ite.

CAPERNAUM. Kuh-*per*-nay-um.

DENARII. dih-*nair*-ee or dih-*nair*-eye.

DENARIUS. dih-*nair*-ee-us.

GALILEAN. Gal-uh-*lee*-un.

GALILEE. *Gal*-uh-lee.

HEROD. *Hair*-ud.

JOSEPHUS. Jo-*see*-fus.

JUDEA. Joo-*dee*-uh

MACHAERUS. Muh-*key*-rus or Muh-*kye*-rus.

MESSIAH. Meh-*sigh*-uh.

MUSTERION. moo-*stay*-ree-on.

PEREA. Peh-*ree*-uh.

PHARISAIC. fair-ih-*say*-ick.

PHARISEE. *Fair*-ih-see.

Chapter 8

Jesus' Galilean Ministry (Part 3)

Mark 4:35-41; 5:1-17; 5:22-24, 35-43;
Matthew 14:13-21; 16:13-26

JESUS CALMS THE STORM (MARK 4:35-41)

Establishing the Groundwork

Jesus' ministry in Galilee was nearing its climax. From among his disciples, he had chosen the twelve "that they might be with him and that he might send them out to preach and to have authority to drive out demons" (Mark 3:14, 15). That called for a special teaching program in which the twelve would hear Jesus' words to the multitudes but would also have private sessions with Jesus during which he would explain truths not yet clear to them.

Both elements were present on the occasion when Jesus sat in a fisherman's boat and taught the parables found in Matthew 13 and Mark 4:1-34 to the crowds gathered on the shore, but also took time to address the concerns of the twelve and others who were interested (Mark 4:10, 34). The day's teaching left Jesus weary, seeking privacy and rest.

The time when the incident described in the following passage occurred is not easy to determine. The difficulty lies in how to interpret the word *evening*, found in Mark 4:35. According to the Jewish reckoning of time, there was a "first evening," which was the equivalent of our late afternoon and lasted from around 3:00 to 6:00 PM. A "second evening" lasted from around 6:00 to 9:00 PM. It is probably better to view the "evening" mentioned by Mark as encompassing the 6:00 to 9:00 PM time, which would create the following sequence of events. (Note that a portion of this also provides some context for the incident involving the Gerasene demoniac, the second incident covered in this chapter.)

The calming of the storm took place during the nighttime hours; thus when Jesus and the disciples arrived at the "region of the Gerasenes" and were met by the man with an evil spirit (Mark 5:1, 2) the sun was already rising on the following day. That it was daytime by then and no longer dark is based on the statement that the demoniac was able to see Jesus "from a distance" (Mark 5:6). Ordinarily it would not have taken Jesus and the disciples the entire night to cross the Sea of Galilee, but it should be noted that during a later storm the disciples were in a boat in the middle of the lake "when evening came" (Mark

6:47) and that they did not complete the crossing until after Jesus had joined them "about the fourth watch of the night" (v. 48), between 3:00 and 6:00 AM. So the disciples could have labored through the night fighting the storm, finally waking Jesus in the predawn darkness. He then could have calmed the storm and arrived with his disciples on the other side of the Sea of Galilee on the following morning, when he was met by the demoniac.

Examining the Text

I. The Storm (Mark 4:35-38)
A. Preparation (vv. 35, 36)

35 That day when evening came, he said to his disciples, "Let us go over to the other side."

That day was the day on which Jesus had given his lesson in parables, found in Mark 4:1-34. Verse 38, which notes that Jesus was "sleeping on a cushion," suggests that Jesus was tired from the day's activities and needed rest. He wanted to *go over to the other side* of the Sea of Galilee. Mark 5:1 tells us that following the stilling of the storm, Jesus and the disciples arrived at the "region of the Gerasenes," which was, it appears, on the southeastern side of the Sea of Galilee. Thus Jesus' lesson in parables may well have been delivered in or near Capernaum (on the northwestern shore of the Sea of Galilee).

36 Leaving the crowd behind, they took him along, just as he was, in the boat. There were also other boats with him.

They took him . . . just as he was implies that Jesus made no special preparation for this journey. Most likely they departed *in the boat* from which he had taught the lesson in parables without returning first to shore to pick up any additional supplies. Mark includes the detail that *there were also other boats with him.* Try as they might, Jesus and the disciples could not leave the *crowd behind* completely. No further mention is made of these other boats, leaving us to wonder what became of them. Perhaps they turned back immediately at the first sign that a storm was brewing.

B. Panic (vv. 37, 38)

37 A furious squall came up, and the waves broke over the boat, so that it was nearly swamped.

The geography of Galilee encouraged such sudden storms as that described in this verse. Lying some 600 feet below the level of the Mediterranean Sea, the

Sea of Galilee is surrounded, especially to the north and east, by hills slashed with gorges draining into the lake. Cold air from the hills is funneled down these gorges and clashes with the rising warm air over the low-lying water. A storm was a common phenomenon under these conditions, so we are a bit surprised that the fishermen-disciples were so terrified. Apparently this storm was unusually *furious*.

> [38] *Jesus was in the stern, sleeping on a cushion. The disciples woke him and said to him, "Teacher, don't you care if we drown?"*

The picture of Jesus *sleeping* in the middle of this storm should not be overlooked. References in the Old Testament present sleep as the answer of a confident believer to the dangers of this world (as in Psalms 3:5; 4:8). Jesus showed no fear because he truly had no reason to fear. His trust in his Father was complete.

The *disciples*, however, saw the situation quite differently. Since this storm was taking place most likely at night (see "Establishing the Groundwork" above), its fury may have seemed even greater than during daylight hours. For Jesus to be *sleeping* through the storm seemed incomprehensible to them. Yet they must have shown considerable constraint in not waking him earlier. Had they wakened him immediately, they would not have taken nearly so long in crossing the lake.

II. The Savior (Mark 4:39-41)
A. Speaking to the Storm (v. 39)

> [39] *He got up, rebuked the wind and said to the waves, "Quiet! Be still!" Then the wind died down and it was completely calm.*

The New Testament is very clear in its teaching that Jesus is the Creator. (See John 1:1-4; Colossians 1:15-17.) That the Creator is able to command his own creation in a miraculous way should not surprise us. The word *rebuked* echoes Jesus' earlier rebuke of the evil spirit (Mark 1:25). While it's not apparent in the *New International Version®,* Mark uses the same term to describe both events.

B. Speaking to the Disciples (vv. 40, 41)

> [40] *He said to his disciples, "Why are you so afraid? Do you still have no faith?"*

One must keep in mind that a number of Jesus' disciples were fishermen and were therefore acquainted with the whims of the Sea of Galilee. Yet they had given up all hope of surviving this storm.

The two questions that Jesus asked the disciples highlight the contrast between fear and *faith*. *No faith* may seem like a very sweeping assessment, but the presence of great fear showed the absence of great faith.

41 They were terrified and asked each other, "Who is this? Even the wind and the waves obey him!"

In the midst of the storm, the disciples had feared for their lives; now they were full of a fearsome awe of one who is more than man. Perhaps their being *terrified* included realizing that they had expressed doubt before one who is obviously able to control *the wind and the waves*.

The disciples had seen Jesus perform many miracles prior to this one, but those were in areas not wholly familiar to them: sicknesses, demon-possession, or an act such as turning water into wine. But here Jesus was in their world, where familiarity enabled them to know the elements, to measure the forces, and to realize the dangers. In this raw, elemental world, Jesus had taken command simply by speaking.

THE GERASENE DEMONIAC (MARK 5:1-17)

Establishing the Groundwork

After Jesus had quieted the storm on the Sea of Galilee, he and the disciples reached the eastern shore of that body of water. Apparently the storm slowed their progress and pushed their arrival in Gerasene country to early morning. In the light of dawn, they were observed by a troubled man in the hills, who rushed down to the shore to meet them. What resulted was another demonstration of Jesus' power—one that the locals were unable to appreciate at the time.

The disciples' reaction to this miracle is not recorded in any of the Gospels that mention it (Matthew, Mark, and Luke). But they must have reacted with a sense of awe similar to that which followed the calming of the storm.

Examining the Text

I. Jesus and the Demoniac (Mark 5:1-13)
A. The Demons and the Man (vv. 1-5)

1 They went across the lake to the region of the Gerasenes.

The exact site where Jesus and the disciples landed is a matter of some uncertainty. Mark and Luke describe it as *the region of the Gerasenes* (Luke 8:26), while Matthew's account reads "the region of the Gadarenes" (Matthew 8:28).

A town called Gerasa was located some thirty-five miles from the southeast shore of the Sea of Galilee, but this town apparently owned territory that joined the sea. In this area can be seen a fairly steep slope within forty yards of the water's edge. This could have been where the pigs rushed down into the water and were drowned (Mark 5:13). Nearby in the hills, rock-cut tombs have been discovered. These may have been where the demoniac lived (v. 3). Regardless of where the specific location may have been, Jesus and the disciples were in the general territory known as Decapolis (a Greek term meaning "ten cities" and designating ten towns in the area that had joined together in a commercial agreement).

² When Jesus got out of the boat, a man with an evil spirit came from the tombs to meet him.

Most likely this *man with an evil spirit* came running down out of the rocky hills where the *tombs* were located. Luke tells us that he wore no clothes (Luke 8:27), thus making his appearance all the more frightening.

While both Mark and Luke mention only one demoniac in their accounts, Matthew mentions two (Matthew 8:28). This does not imply a contradiction. Mark and Luke were likely focusing on only the more prominent or the more vocal of the men. Later we learn that a whole "legion" of demons actually possessed this man (v. 9), though one of them seems to have served as their leader or spokesman (v. 7).

³, ⁴ This man lived in the tombs, and no one could bind him any more, not even with a chain. For he had often been chained hand and foot, but he tore the chains apart and broke the irons on his feet. No one was strong enough to subdue him.

Mark's description of *this man* is horrifying. Because of his wild behavior, the people in the region had attempted to control him with *chains*. His strength, most likely enhanced in a supernatural way by the forces of Satan, had made him impossible to *subdue*. The Greek text, literally translated, makes this fact even more emphatic with a "triple negative": "*not* with a chain *no* longer *no* one was able to bind him."

⁵ Night and day among the tombs and in the hills he would cry out and cut himself with stones.

The demoniac remained in constant isolation from society *among the tombs and in the hills*. His condition made every day a misery. Some associate the fact that he *cut himself* with a form of demonic worship (see 1 Kings 18:28).

B. The Demons and Jesus (vv. 6-10)

⁶ When he saw Jesus from a distance, he ran and fell on his knees in front of him.

In the early morning light, the demoniac *saw Jesus* and the disciples approaching. Immediately he left the tombs and *ran* down to the shore. Then, as Jesus got out of the boat, the man approached him (v. 2).

The respect shown by this man reflects the fear that the demons have for Jesus as the Son of God. Mark's Gospel has already shown how the demons were inclined to acknowledge the truth of who Jesus is. (See Mark 1:23, 24, 34; 3:11, 12.) In particular Mark 3:11 notes that evil spirits "fell down before him."

⁷ He shouted at the top of his voice, "What do you want with me, Jesus, Son of the Most High God? Swear to God that you won't torture me!"

As previously noted, apparently one of the demons served as a spokesman for the rest. (It is interesting to note that the question raised by the disciples in Mark 4:41, "Who is this?" is answered here by the demon!) Although it was not true "worship," the demon's confession that Jesus is the *Son of the Most High God* expressed truth that the demons must acknowledge, though reluctantly.

Apparently the demon understood that God's judgment was coming on all evil spirits. Luke's account includes the demons' repeated plea with Jesus "not to order them to go into the Abyss" (Luke 8:31), which is associated elsewhere in Scripture with the abode of Satan (Revelation 9:1, 2, 11; 20:1-3). The demon that for years had tortured a human being now himself feared the place of eternal *torture*.

⁸ For Jesus had said to him, "Come out of this man, you evil spirit!"

This explains why the demon became so agitated: the words he cried out in verse 7 came as a result of Jesus' command that he leave the man. The word *for* ("because") makes clear the cause-and-effect relationship between these words of Jesus and those of the demon.

⁹ Then Jesus asked him, "What is your name?"
"My name is Legion," he replied, "for we are many."

This is the first indication of the number of demons that possessed the man. The term *Legion* refers to a Roman military force of six thousand soldiers—though the word was also used of any very large, unspecific number. Other Scriptures confirm the fact that demon possession could involve *many* demons (Matthew 12:45; Mark 16:9). By requesting this information from the demon, Jesus allowed the disciples to see the seriousness of this man's condition. Thus when Jesus cast the demons out of the man, both the man and the disciples would see unmistakable evidence of the magnitude of Jesus' power over the forces of evil.

10 And he begged Jesus again and again not to send them out of the area.

The demon's repeated entreaty for Jesus *not to send them out of the area* may have been a subtle way of asking that he and his cohorts not be cast into their place of eternal punishment.

C. The Demons and the Pigs (vv. 11-13)

11, 12 A large herd of pigs was feeding on the nearby hillside. The demons begged Jesus, "Send us among the pigs; allow us to go into them."

Now the account takes a strange turn with the mention of *a large herd of pigs* that *was feeding on the nearby hillside.* For Jews, pigs were just as unclean as tombs and evil spirits (see Leviticus 11:7, 8; Deuteronomy 14:8; Isaiah 65:4; 66:17). The presence of pigs in this area indicates that Jesus was in Gentile territory.

Since the demons recognized that they were powerless before Jesus, they *begged* for a lesser punishment. Rather than being cast into eternal torment, could they not be cast *into* the pigs? With this request, perhaps the demons also hoped to create some antagonism toward Jesus—which we see occurring in verse 17. In any case, they had no alternative but to do whatever the Son of God ordered.

13 He gave them permission, and the evil spirits came out and went into the pigs. The herd, about two thousand in number, rushed down the steep bank into the lake and were drowned.

Some have raised a question about Jesus' giving *permission* for these demons to destroy the property of others. Perhaps the drowning of the pigs was allowed in order to make clear to the man who was possessed (and to Jesus' disciples) not only the severity of his condition but also the degree of Jesus' power over demons. We should also note that Jesus did not appear eager to deal out the ultimate punishment that even the demons knew is coming. The final punishment of all demonic powers seems to be set for a specific time (Matthew 25:41; Revelation 20:10).

II. Jesus and the Residents (Mark 5:14-17)
A. Discovering What Happened (v. 14)

[14] Those tending the pigs ran off and reported this in the town and countryside, and the people went out to see what had happened.

Those tending the pigs were close enough to witness what had happened, although they may not have been close enough to hear the conversation surrounding the events. They could see the once violent man now calm. But most likely their major concern was the loss of the pigs and what the owners might do in holding them responsible.

B. Demanding Jesus to Leave (vv. 15-17)

[15, 16] When they came to Jesus, they saw the man who had been possessed by the legion of demons, sitting there, dressed and in his right mind; and they were afraid. Those who had seen it told the people what had happened to the demon-possessed man—and told about the pigs as well.

Once the residents of the area learned what had happened, they *came* out to see for themselves, perhaps skeptical of what had been reported. To see *the man* who formerly *had been possessed by the legion of demons* now *sitting* quietly and also *dressed and in his right mind* should have given them reason to marvel at the power of Jesus. Instead, *they were afraid.* Apparently they found it difficult to accept the supernatural aspects of what had happened. Their reaction was similar to the disciples' being "terrified" following the stilling of the storm (Mark 4:41).

[17] Then the people began to plead with Jesus to leave their region.

Rather than investigate further what had just taken place, *the people* of the *region* allowed their fear to control their reaction to Jesus. They saw Jesus' power as something to be avoided rather than accepted (as many do today). Whereas the demons had pleaded with Jesus "not to send them out of the area" (v. 10), the residents of the area pleaded *with Jesus to leave* that place. Jesus did not attempt to force himself and his preaching on the people. Instead, he acceded to their request for him to depart.

Verses 18-20 tell us that as Jesus started to leave, the former demoniac expressed a desire to go with him and the disciples. But Jesus sent him back to his own people to witness to them of the great blessing he had received. The man did as instructed, and it is likely that the more favorable reception Jesus received when he returned to this area (Mark 7:31—8:10) stemmed in part from this man's compelling testimony of the amazing transformation Jesus had accomplished in his life.

JESUS RAISES JAIRUS'S DAUGHTER FROM THE DEAD
(MARK 5:22-24, 35-43)

Establishing the Groundwork

Following the incident involving the Gerasene demoniac and the request from the area's residents that Jesus leave, Jesus again crossed the Sea of Galilee and arrived at "the other side of the lake" (Mark 5:21), most likely in Capernaum. This crossing probably took only an hour or two. On the shore, excited and expectant crowds awaited his coming (Mark 5:21; Luke 8:40). It was at this point that Jairus, a synagogue ruler, came to Jesus with an urgent request.

Examining the Text

I. Jairus Appeals to Jesus (Mark 5:22-24)
A. Jairus's Request (vv. 22, 23)

²² Then one of the synagogue rulers, named Jairus, came there. Seeing Jesus, he fell at his feet

As the people gathered around Jesus, *Jairus* made his way through the crowd to get to him. Jairus was *one of the synagogue rulers*. Each synagogue had a group of elders who oversaw its activities and, to a certain extent, directed the civil affairs of the Jewish community as well. Jairus was one of the officials of a synagogue either in or near Capernaum. As a synagogue ruler, Jairus was accustomed to receiving homage, not giving it. However, here he *fell at* Jesus' *feet*.

²³ . . . and pleaded earnestly with him, "My little daughter is dying. Please come and put your hands on her so that she will be healed and live."

Here we see the reason for Jairus' humble approach to Jesus. His *little daughter* was *dying*. Clearly Jairus had heard about Jesus or even seen some of his miracles. He believed in Jesus' power to heal. Although his daughter was twelve years old at the time (v. 42), Jairus, in typical fatherly fashion, spoke of her as *my little daughter*. Apparently aware that Jesus often touched a person whom he *healed*, Jairus requested that Jesus *come* and *put* his *hands on her*.

B. Jesus' Response (v. 24)

²⁴ So Jesus went with him.
A large crowd followed and pressed around him.

Jesus went with him: as someone has noted, the Great Physician made house calls! Knowing that this father came to him in faith, Jesus did not hesitate to honor his request. Even though it meant that a *large* and eager *crowd* would be denied his teaching for a time, Jesus knew that he would be able to teach far more important lessons at Jairus's house. The crowd that *followed* Jesus probably anticipated seeing another miracle. If so, their hopes were realized much sooner than they expected!

II. Jesus Goes to Jairus's Home (Mark 5:35-43)

As Jesus, along with the crowd, made his way to Jairus's house, the opportunity arose to perform another miracle. As the crowd pressed around him, Jesus was touched in faith by a woman who had suffered a hemorrhaging condition for twelve years. The woman was immediately healed, and Jesus commended her for the faith that she had shown (vv. 25-34).

Jairus, believing that any delay might be fatal to his daughter, may have been quite upset and frustrated that Jesus had stopped to heal the woman. His worst fears were realized when messengers from his house arrived.

A. Sad News (v. 35)

35 While Jesus was still speaking, some men came from the house of Jairus, the synagogue ruler. "Your daughter is dead," they said. "Why bother the teacher any more?"

Jesus was still speaking to the woman who had been healed, commending her for her faith, when *some men came from* Jairus's *house* with tragic news: *your daughter is dead.* These men did not share Jairus's faith in Jesus; to them there was nothing more that could be done: *why bother the teacher any more?* Of course, Jairus's own faith may have wavered some at this point. Perhaps he too thought that all hope for his daughter was gone. Jesus had earlier raised a young man at Nain (Luke 7:11-17), some 25 miles south of Capernaum, so Jairus could have known about that. But even at the time of Lazarus's death much later, the expectation was that Jesus could have prevented the death (John 11:21, 32, 37), not that he could reverse it.

B. Jesus' Reassurance (v. 36)

36 Ignoring what they said, Jesus told the synagogue ruler, "Don't be afraid; just believe."

Someone has suggested that the art of *ignoring*, here illustrated by Jesus, is one of the fine arts of faith. A human conclusion, even one that sounds reasonable and authoritative, is never the last word. God has the last word. Once again the contrast between faith and fear is highlighted, as with the disciples during the stilling of the storm (Mark 4:40).

C. Jesus' Arrival (vv. 37, 38)

37 He did not let anyone follow him except Peter, James and John the brother of James.

As Jesus neared Jairus's house, he asked the crowd, along with nine of the twelve disciples, to remain behind. The presence of so many people in the narrow streets around the house, added to the mourners who were already there, could very well have created additional problems. Furthermore, there likely would not have been room for even the twelve in the house, which was likely quite small by modern standards.

The three disciples whom Jesus took with him, *Peter, James and John*, seem to have formed a kind of "inner circle" of followers who accompanied Jesus in other situations: the transfiguration (Mark 9:2) and his agony in the garden of Gethsemane (Mark 14:32, 33).

38 When they came to the home of the synagogue ruler, Jesus saw a commotion, with people crying and wailing loudly.

The family, along with friends and mourners, had already assembled at Jairus's *home*. Since it was the practice to conduct the burial very shortly after the death of a person, these people needed to be present almost immediately. Word of this girl's death would have spread rapidly, especially since the family of a *synagogue ruler* was involved.

Modern funerals are quite sedate compared with the practices in Jesus' day. As soon as death occurred, lamenting began, with *people crying and wailing loudly*. Besides the weeping and wailing of family members and friends, professional mourners were likely present, as was the custom, along with flute players who performed plaintive dirges on their instruments. No wonder Mark describes this as a *commotion*.

D. Jesus' Miracle (vv. 39-43

39 He went in and said to them, "Why all this commotion and wailing? The child is not dead but asleep."

Jesus spoke with the voice of authority, declaring that the well-established customs of *commotion and wailing* were inappropriate. His statement, *the child is not dead but asleep*, reflected the authority over death that he possessed and that he was about to demonstrate. Jesus used similar language of Lazarus (John

11:11-14). Paul refers to the Christians' future resurrection as an awakening from sleep (1 Thessalonians 4:13, 14; 5:9, 10).

> **40** *But they laughed at him.*
> *After he put them all out, he took the child's father and mother and the*
> *disciples who were with him, and went in where the child was.*

Here we see evidence of the mourners' strictly professional status. They were able to change from mourners to mockers when they heard what Jesus said.

Before entering the room where the girl lay, Jesus ordered everyone except *the child's father and mother and the disciples who were with him* to leave. *The child* was probably lying on the bed or pallet where she had died, for there had hardly been time to prepare her for burial.

> **41** *He took her by the hand and said to her, "Talitha koum!" (which means,*
> *"Little girl, I say to you, get up!").*

Jesus *took* the girl *by the hand*—a gesture that would normally, under the law of Moses, demand being quarantined for uncleanness (see Numbers 19:11). But the power of life in Jesus flowed from him to the corpse rather than the reverse. He addressed the girl in Aramaic, her native language: *Talitha koum*. Mark, whose writing is generally acknowledged to be for a Roman (non-Jewish) audience, translated the words for his readers. This is the first of three times Mark cites the Aramaic words Jesus used (cf. 7:34; 15:34). Jesus would normally have spoken Aramaic, so Mark's citation of the Aramaic words in these three cases piques our curiosity. No explanation is given, however, though it does suggest the influence of an eyewitness.

> **42** *Immediately the girl stood up and walked around (she was twelve years*
> *old). At this they were completely astonished.*

As the winds and the waves had obeyed the command to be still and as the legion of demons had submitted to Jesus' authority, here death joined the ranks of those forces unable to withstand the power of the Son of God.

> **43** *He gave strict orders not to let anyone know about this, and told them to*
> *give her something to eat.*

The miracle was followed by some rather bizarre instructions from Jesus *not to let anyone know about this*. Of course, the miracle could not be hidden; for as soon as the girl left the room, people would know that she had been raised from the dead and that Jesus was responsible. But Jesus constantly sought to keep the public's enthusiasm under some restraint lest it get out of hand and bring his ministry to a premature climax.

Mark concludes his account with Jesus' further concern for the welfare of the girl: he *told them to give her something to eat.* Most likely this command was given to the parents of the girl, who would have joyfully obeyed.

JESUS FEEDS THE FIVE THOUSAND (MATTHEW 14:13-21)

Establishing the Groundwork

Some time after the stilling of the storm, Jesus gave his twelve disciples miraculous power like his own and sent them out in pairs to preach as he had been preaching (Mark 6:7-13). Mark 6:30 records how the twelve "gathered around Jesus and reported to him all they had done and taught." By this time, approximately four months had passed since the stilling of the storm.

The joy of this reunion was mixed with grief, however, for just at that time came news that John the Baptist had been put to death by Herod Antipas (Matthew 14:1-12). Jesus told the disciples to "come with me by yourselves" (Mark 6:31) away from the clamoring crowds for a time of rest and perhaps a time of mourning for John. So the men boarded a boat (probably near Capernaum) and set out to go across to the eastern side of the Sea of Galilee. (This time no storm arose as they made their way across the sea.)

Examining the Text

I. The Situation (Matthew 14:13-15)
A. Jesus' Compassion (vv. 13, 14)

13 When Jesus heard what had happened, he withdrew by boat privately to a solitary place. Hearing of this, the crowds followed him on foot from the towns.

What had happened was the murder of John the Baptist. Perhaps Jesus wanted to debrief the disciples *privately* about that, and so he chose to get away from the crowds. However, the only time the men had for any rest or private conversation was during their journey in the boat. *The crowds* saw them leave and hurried around the north end of the sea *on foot.* As they did so, they were joined by people from the villages that they passed, Thus, by the time Jesus and the disciples arrived at the eastern shore an even larger gathering was waiting for them.

14 When Jesus landed and saw a large crowd, he had compassion on them and healed their sick.

Even though Jesus' plans for a quiet retreat with his disciples had been thwarted, he refused to ignore the *large crowd* or send them away. Instead, *he had compassion on them*: he *healed their sick*. Jesus' compassion included more than just the physical needs of the crowd. Mark's account says that "he had compassion on them, because they were like sheep without a shepherd." Aware of their need for spiritual leadership, Jesus "began teaching them many things" (Mark 6:34).

B. The Disciples' Concern (v. 15)

15 As evening approached, the disciples came to him and said, "This is a remote place, and it's already getting late. Send the crowds away, so they can go to the villages and buy themselves some food."

If Jesus and the *disciples* started across the Sea of Galilee early in the morning, they must have landed on the other side before noon. People who had traveled on foot arrived ahead of them. Now *evening approached*, and many in the crowd must have been getting hungry.

The feeding of the five thousand is the only one of Jesus' miracles (other than the resurrection of Jesus) that all four Gospel writers record, and each includes different details. Perhaps Jesus himself was the first to mention the issue of feeding the crowd. He may have interrupted his teaching with an aside to Philip: "Where shall we buy bread for these people to eat?" (John 6:5). Of course, Philip was stumped: "Eight months' wages would not buy enough bread for each one to have a bite!" (John 6:7).

Jesus may have then continued his teaching while Philip quietly consulted the other disciples. To them, Jesus' suggestion seemed impractical. Even if they had any money with which to buy food, the nearest place where it could be purchased was miles away. So the disciples approached Jesus with the suggestion we see in the verse before us: *Send the crowds away, so they can go to the villages and buy themselves some food.*

II. The Solution (Matthew 14:16-21)
A. Shortage of Food (vv. 16, 17)

16 Jesus replied, "They do not need to go away. You give them something to eat."

Jesus threw the problem back into the laps of the disciples. The response must have left them both frustrated and a bit irritated. How could they feed a crowd this size when they themselves had no food? Perhaps that was when Jesus sent them to see how much bread was available within the crowd (Mark 6:38).

So the disciples searched, and Andrew found one boy who had five barley loaves and two small fish (John 6:9).

17 "We have here only five loaves of bread and two fish," they answered.

The *loaves of bread* in that time were flat and round, not at all like the loaves of bread we buy today. That they were made of barley (John 6:9) indicates a cheaper kind of bread; the boy who had them may have come from a poor family.

John uses a Greek word that indicates the fish were "small fish" (John 6:9), possibly like the sardines that are available in small flat cans. Apparently the boy was willing to share the meal he had brought along, but he must have wondered, as Andrew did, "How far will they go among so many?" (John 6:9).

B. Supply of Food (vv. 18-21)

18, 19 "Bring them here to me," he said. And he directed the people to sit down on the grass. Taking the five loaves and the two fish and looking up to heaven, he gave thanks and broke the loaves. Then he gave them to the disciples, and the disciples gave them to the people.

Mark and Luke provide additional details about how Jesus *directed the people to sit down on the grass.* Jesus had the disciples organize the crowd, and the people were then told to sit down in groups of about fifty or a hundred (Mark 6:39, 40; Luke 9:14, 15). Most likely there would have been something like aisles or paths between the groups, making it easier (and less chaotic) to distribute the food that would soon become available. This grouping would have alerted the people, making them expectant. They would watch and listen intently when Jesus spoke again.

Then Jesus took the meager supply of *loaves* and *fish* and *looking up to heaven, he gave thanks and broke the loaves.* How we would like to have a fuller description of that! Perhaps Jesus broke a fragment from a loaf, and the fragment was as big as the loaf. Both fragments and loaf could be broken and then broken again into pieces increasing in size and number. The next verse speaks of twelve basketfuls of leftovers; perhaps the *disciples* used the same twelve baskets to take the food to the hungry people.

20 They all ate and were satisfied, and the disciples picked up twelve basketfuls of broken pieces that were left over.

Jesus told the *disciples* to gather any food that remained so that nothing would be wasted (John 6:12). What became of the *twelve basketfuls of broken pieces* we are not told. Perhaps they were distributed later to the poor.

21 The number of those who ate was about five thousand men, besides women and children.

This verse informs us of the magnitude of this miracle. *Five thousand men* were fed, not counting *women and children*. The total may well have been closer to ten thousand. This miracle is not to be confused with the feeding of the four thousand (recorded in Matthew 15:32-39 and Mark 8:1-10), which occurred later in another place, the Decapolis, and differed from this account at several important points.

PETER'S GOOD CONFESSION AT CAESAREA PHILIPPI (MATTHEW 16:13-26)

Establishing the Groundwork

According to John's account, following the feeding of the five thousand, those who were present desired to make Jesus a king by force (John 6:15). So Jesus withdrew to a mountain to be alone. The next day (following Jesus' walking on the water to his disciples during the night) Jesus confronted the crowd about their real motive in wanting to follow him. Were they interested only in handouts, or did they believe that he came from God to bring eternal life to mankind, as he claimed? In his discourse on the bread of life, Jesus emphasized the spiritual nature of his ministry. As a result, many of his disciples ceased to follow him. But the twelve, led by Peter, voiced their continued loyalty to Jesus (John 6:22-71).

This apparent decline in Jesus' popularity ushered in what is often referred to as the "Year of Opposition" in Jesus' ministry. (The feeding of the five thousand took place at a time when the Passover was near, according to John 6:4; this would have been one year before the Passover at which Jesus' crucifixion took place.) The decline in popular support was followed by increased criticism from some of the Pharisees and teachers of the law. They saw in the desertion of many of Jesus' followers an opportunity to attack him at a time when his movement seemed to be on the verge of collapse.

Following the feeding of the four thousand in the Decapolis, Jesus and his disciples entered a boat and came to Magadan (sometimes called Magdala) on the western shore of the Sea of Galilee (Matthew 15:39). There he had a brief confrontation with the Pharisees and Sadducees (Matthew 16:1-4), after which he and the disciples left again by boat for the eastern shore. At Bethsaida Jesus healed a blind man (Mark 8:22-26), and then, by foot, he and his disciples proceeded north toward Caesarea Philippi. It was here that Jesus' ministry took a dramatic new direction.

Examining the Text

I. The Christ Issue (Matthew 16:13-20)
A. Popular Thinking (vv. 13, 14)

13 When Jesus came to the region of Caesarea Philippi, he asked his disciples, "Who do people say the Son of Man is?"

By this point, the *disciples* had been with Jesus for about two and a half years. They had traveled the length of Palestine with him. Now Jesus led them to *Caesarea Philippi*, which was to the extreme north, about twenty-five miles north of the Sea of Galilee. He appears to have led the disciples to where the crowds would be less likely to interrupt, so that he could have some privacy with them.

The history behind Caesarea Philippi is noteworthy, given what was about to occur there. The city was very ancient and for centuries was called Panium, because it was a center of worship of the Greek god Pan. A son of Herod the Great, named Philip, rebuilt the city and renamed it in honor of the Roman emperor and himself. It then became a center of worship of Caesar Augustus (mentioned in Luke 2:1). Thus, in a place where pagan worship had become the accepted practice, Jesus challenged his disciples to consider the crucial question of his identity. (The city should not be confused with the Caesarea that is mentioned frequently in the book of Acts. That city was located on the coast of the Mediterranean Sea.)

The timing of this question was critical. The issue of who *people say the Son of Man is* would have been an uncomfortable one for the disciples to consider at this point in Jesus' ministry. It brought up the recent rejection of Jesus and the spiritual nature of his kingdom by many who had previously followed him (John 6:66). As noted earlier, the religious leadership among the Jews had stepped up their opposition toward Jesus. He wanted to face some of these issues squarely with his disciples.

14 They replied, "Some say John the Baptist; others say Elijah; and still others, Jeremiah or one of the prophets."

The answers given by the disciples all offered partial, perhaps grudging tribute to Jesus and his teachings and mighty works. Some were rooted to a degree in Scripture. The prophet Malachi had predicted that the Lord would send his people the prophet *Elijah* (Malachi 4:5), but Jesus had earlier indicated that this prophecy was fulfilled in John the Baptist (Matthew 11:11-14). Herod Antipas had claimed that Jesus was *John the Baptist* "risen from the dead" (Matthew

14:1, 2), stimulated in part by his guilty conscience for having ordered John's beheading.

All the answers given by the disciples had this in common: they did not acknowledge Jesus to be the Christ.

B. Personal Question (v. 15)

[15] *"But what about you?" he asked. "Who do you say I am?"*

This question was far more crucial than the first. The disciples were now faced with the direct challenge as to whether they had risen above the popular opinion. The pressure of the last few months had been very intense as many had turned decisively against Jesus. The disciples were being questioned as to the status of their faith.

C. Peter's Reply (v. 16)

[16] *Simon Peter answered, "You are the Christ, the Son of the living God."*

Although Jesus addressed the entire group, *Simon Peter answered*. In typical fashion, he spoke out first: *You are the Christ*. Thus Peter confessed Jesus to be the individual who was expected to fulfill the Old Testament prophecies of a coming Deliverer and King.

But Peter said more than this; he referred to Jesus as *the Son of the living God*. The Jews did not expect the Messiah to be God himself coming to deliver them, but Peter and the others had heard and seen enough of Jesus to reach this radical and controversial, but correct, conclusion. Peter certainly did not at that point understand all of the implications of his statement (as we will see shortly). Yet throughout the centuries, no one, not even theologians with their detailed creeds, has improved upon Peter's simple "Good Confession."

D. Jesus' Praise (vv. 17-19)

[17] *Jesus replied, "Blessed are you, Simon son of Jonah, for this was not revealed to you by man, but by my Father in heaven.*

The phrase *Blessed are you*, which is reminiscent of the language of the Beatitudes, expressed Jesus' approval of what Peter had just affirmed. Jesus also observed that Peter had not learned this spiritual truth through human wisdom or agency. It had been *revealed* to him by the *Father in heaven*. It is not necessary to suppose that Peter had suddenly and miraculously been given the answer to Jesus' question as soon as he asked it. More likely Jesus meant that God had revealed Jesus' identity and nature through his words and miracles. Other men and women had experienced much of what Peter and the other disciples had seen and heard, yet they did not come to the same faith.

18 "And I tell you that you are Peter, and on this rock I will build my church, and the gates of Hades will not overcome it.

As noted in chapter 5 (in the comments under John 1:42), the name *Peter* means "rock." In the Greek text this word is masculine (spelled *petros*), and describes a small piece of rock (something like a pebble). The word used in the phrase *on this rock* is feminine (spelled *petra*) and describes a large boulder or a mass of rock such as that found at the cliffs along the seacoast. Although some have proposed that Peter was to become the rock on which the church would be built, it appears that Jesus was using a play on words that, in effect, made the very opposite point. We might paraphrase Jesus' words as follows: "You're a small rock, Peter, but upon the greater rock that you have confessed, the truth of who I am, I will build my church."

In this verse (which includes the first reference in the New Testament containing the word *church*) Jesus also promised that *the gates of Hades will not overcome* his church. *Hades* is a general word for the abode of the dead, both good and evil. Jesus was saying that death and the forces of evil will not be able to prevent the ultimate triumph of the church. Indeed, Jesus now holds "the keys of death and Hades" (Revelation 1:18).

Jesus' words picture two kingdoms locked in fierce combat. His words also portray the church as on the offensive, attacking Satan's domain much as Jesus himself attacked and shattered the gates of the devil's kingdom, opening the way for sinners to return to the family and fellowship of his Father. The Lord's soldiers continue to plunder Satan's kingdom every time a person is led to acknowledge Peter's "Good Confession" and to accept Jesus as Lord and Savior.

19 "I will give you the keys of the kingdom of heaven; whatever you bind on earth will be bound in heaven, and whatever you loose on earth will be loosed in heaven."

The hypocritical Pharisees and teachers of the law in Jesus' day were shutting the kingdom of heaven "in men's faces" (Matthew 23:13). Peter was told that he would be given *the keys of the kingdom of heaven*, implying allowing people to enter it. Peter used those keys when he preached the first gospel sermon to the Jews who were gathered on the Day of Pentecost and announced the terms by which people could be added to the church (Acts 2:14-39). Several years later he used the same keys when he opened the kingdom to the Gentiles by preaching to Cornelius and his household (Acts 10:34-48).

Jesus appears to say that any judgment Peter makes *on earth* will be acknowledged as binding *in heaven*. The reference to "binding" and "loosing" does speak of a special authority, but it is an authority to declare judgment, not to determine it. One should not think that Peter and the other apostles had the authority to make up any rules they wanted, and that these would then be approved in Heaven. Rather, as spokesmen filled with and inspired by the Holy Spirit (John 14:26; 16:13), they proclaimed what the Lord had established as binding upon his followers.

E. Jesus' Prohibition (v. 20)

20 Then he warned his disciples not to tell anyone that he was the Christ.

Jesus then *warned his disciples* not to make public the content of Peter's confession. The reason seems apparent. With emotions running high and the opposition to Jesus becoming more desperate, a public announcement of his messiahship could excite the masses and cause them to try to force him into the mold of what they thought the Messiah should be—a political savior of the nation of Israel. The authorities in turn would want to take appropriate action. Jesus, however, desired to set his own time for the cross. He would lay his life down; it would not be taken from him (John 10:18).

II. The Cross Issue for Jesus (Matthew 16:21-23)
A. Jesus' Prediction (v. 21)

21 From that time on Jesus began to explain to his disciples that he must go to Jerusalem and suffer many things at the hands of the elders, chief priests and teachers of the law, and that he must be killed and on the third day be raised to life.

The disciples' hopes had likely run high as they shared with Peter the enthusiasm of his confession of *Jesus* as the Christ. Now in almost the same breath, Jesus described coming events that would threaten to shatter the faith and trust they had just expressed. This was not the first time that Jesus had mentioned his death, but earlier declarations had been mostly veiled hints that the disciples had failed to understand (as in John 7:33, 34). The phrase *from that time on* indicates that Jesus was going to be much more open and detailed about what awaited him in *Jerusalem*. Ironically, the "holy city" was to be the scene of a heinous crime. But that was not the end of what awaited Jesus: he would also *be raised to life*. Peter's reaction, described in the next verse, indicates that his shock at Jesus' words about his death was so great that he completely missed the good news in the climax of Jesus' announcement.

B. Peter's Protest (v. 22)

²² Peter took him aside and began to rebuke him. "Never, Lord!" he said. "This shall never happen to you!"

Peter took Jesus *aside*, though Mark's account indicates that all the disciples echoed Peter's sentiments at this point (Mark 8:33). Perhaps Peter was emboldened by Jesus' earlier praise of him, but now he was leaving his place as a disciple and presuming to instruct his Master. It is clear that he did not grasp the full meaning of his earlier confession. Jesus' use of *must* in verse 21 stands in sharp contrast to Peter's insistence of *never* in this verse.

C. Jesus' Rebuke (v. 23)

²³ Jesus turned and said to Peter, "Get behind me, Satan! You are a stumbling block to me; you do not have in mind the things of God, but the things of men."

Peter's rebuke of Jesus was met with an even more stinging rebuke: *Get behind me, Satan!* Peter was not literally Satan, or possessed by Satan, but his words certainly reflected the interests of Satan. Indeed, Peter was offering the same temptation that the devil had presented in the desert, that of becoming a king by a means other than the cross. Jesus did not command Peter to leave (as he had commanded Satan), but he did order him to *get behind* Jesus in his proper place as a follower and not try to dictate the course to be followed. Peter was nothing but a *stumbling block* to Jesus when he tried to take the lead.

III. The Cross Issue for Us (Matthew 16:24-26)
A. Denying One's Self (v. 24)

²⁴ Then Jesus said to his disciples, "If anyone would come after me, he must deny himself and take up his cross and follow me.

Mark's account indicates that these words of Jesus addressed *to his disciples* were spoken to the crowd as well as to his closest disciples (Mark 8:34). While Jesus had originally sought a private setting where he could instruct his disciples, it appears by this point that word had reached some in the area of Jesus' whereabouts.

Moments earlier Peter had urged that Jesus cease all talk about suffering and dying. Here Jesus called *anyone* who *would come after* him to *deny himself, take up his cross, and follow* Jesus. Thus Jesus was being even more specific about how he would "be killed" (v. 21)—by the exceedingly cruel means of crucifixion. However, Jesus was also saying something about what would be required of any who would follow him.

To deny self does not mean that we hate self. But it does mean that we learn to say "no" to selfishness. It means that we realize we are no longer our own boss. We recognize Jesus as Lord, and we follow where he leads.

To take up the cross signals that the follower of Jesus must be prepared to face opposition and that in some cases that opposition may involve giving one's life to suffer and even die for Christ's sake. Jesus had already indicated in the Beatitudes that such suffering was to be accepted with a joyful spirit (Matthew 5:11, 12).

To follow Jesus means that we obey his teachings and follow his example in our daily lives, particularly concerning the cross. Of course, our crosses are not redemptive in the same way his was. But they must be willingly carried if the gospel is to be carried into all the world and people are to be saved.

B. Losing One's Life (vv. 25, 26)

25 For whoever wants to save his life will lose it, but whoever loses his life for me will find it.

Here Jesus gave a universal principle that is always operative in the moral and spiritual world, just as the principle of gravity always functions on earth. The one who *wants to save his life*—who hoards his life, who becomes ingrown, selfish, and unwilling to share or give of himself, will eventually *lose* his life. His gifts will depreciate, his horizons will narrow, his capacities will shrink, and he will slowly perish. However, the one who, for Jesus' sake, *loses* all claim to *his life* by giving, reaching out, and opening up his life to Jesus' leading *will find* strength, development of abilities, and enlargement of opportunities to grow and serve. He will find, as Jesus put it, life "to the full" (John 10:10).

26 What good will it be for a man if he gains the whole world, yet forfeits his soul? Or what can a man give in exchange for his soul?

To gain *the whole world* was what Satan had offered Jesus in the desert (Matthew 4:8, 9). But Jesus knew that the passing grandeur of this world is of little real value; eternal matters—matters of the *soul*—are what must be given priority. Foolish indeed is the person who *forfeits his soul* for the pleasures of this world, which eventually will be utterly destroyed.

The question *what can a man give in exchange for his soul?* is a follow-up to the previous one; in essence it asks, "If a man has forfeited his soul, by what means can he buy it back?" Even if he had the whole world of material wealth, that would not be enough. One's only hope is to turn to Jesus, whose blood has paid the price of redemption to buy us back so that we may return to our creator (1 Corinthians 6:20; Colossians 1:13, 14).

How to Say It

ANTIPAS. *An*-tih-pus.

ARAMAIC. *Air*-uh-*may*-ik (strong accent on *may*).

BETHSAIDA. Beth-*say*-uh-duh.

CAESAR AUGUSTUS. *See*-zer Aw-*gus*-tus.

CAESAREA. Sess-uh-*ree*-uh.

CAPERNAUM. Kuh-*per*-nay-um.

DECAPOLIS. Dee-*cap*-uh-lis.

DEMONIAC. duh-*moe*-nee-ak.

GADARENES. *Gad*-uh-reens.

GALILEAN. Gal-uh-*lee*-un.

GALILEE. *Gal*-uh-lee.

GERASA. *Gur*-uh-suh.

GERASENE. *Gur*-uh-seen.

HADES. *Hay*-deez.

HEROD. *Hair*-ud.

JAIRUS. *Jye*-rus or *Jay*-ih-rus.

LEGION. *lee*-jun.

MAGADAN. *Mag*-uh-dun.

MAGDALA. *Mag*-duh-luh.

MESSIAH. Meh-*sigh*-uh.

NAIN. Nane.

PALESTINE. *Pal*-us-tine.

PANIUM. *Pan*-ee-um.

PETRA. *pet*-rah.

PETROS. *peh*-tross.

PHARISEES. *Fair*-ih-seez.

PHILIP. *Fil*-ip.

PHILIPPI. Fih-*lip*-pie or *Fil*-ih-pie.

SADDUCEES. *Sad*-you-seez.

SYNAGOGUE. *sin*-uh-gog.

TALITHA KOUM. (*Aramaic.*) *tal*-i-thuh-*koom* (strong accent on *koom*).

Chapter 9

From Galilee to Jesus' Later Judean Ministry

Matthew 17:1-9; John 8:21-36; 9:1-7, 35-41;
Luke 10:25-37, 38-42

THE TRANSFIGURATION (MATTHEW 17:1-9)

Establishing the Groundwork

At the time of the transfiguration, little more than six months remained of Jesus' earthly life before the cross. About one week earlier the disciples had confessed their faith in Jesus as the Christ. Immediately after that came Jesus' devastating announcement of his upcoming death. While only Peter voiced an objection to this, none of the disciples could fathom such a turn of events. They seem to have accepted the common understanding that when the Messiah came, he would never die (John 12:34).

It seems that God wanted to counter the feeling of uncertainty and despair produced by Jesus' announcement of his death with the awe-inspiring experience of the transfiguration. By this event, God reaffirmed for the apostles who witnessed it that Jesus was indeed God's Son.

Examining the Text

I. Jesus Is Transformed (Matthew 17:1-4)
A. Three Men Taken (vv. 1, 2)

¹ After six days Jesus took with him Peter, James and John the brother of James, and led them up a high mountain by themselves.

Both Matthew and Mark (Mark 9:2) record this incident occurring *six days* following the events surrounding Peter's Good Confession, while Luke says "about eight days" (Luke 9:28). It would appear that Luke counted the days of the start and the finish of this time period, while Matthew and Mark counted only the intervening days. The disciples must have found this week very difficult, coming on the heels of Jesus' words about his suffering and death. Perhaps they slept little and spent much time pondering what Jesus' words meant, both for him and for them.

Understanding the disciples' anxiety, Jesus took the three leaders of the group apart for a time of private instruction and encouragement. While Jesus no doubt desired that the spiritual uplift the three would receive would be conveyed to the other nine disciples, it seems that certain ill feelings followed: a quarrel as to who was the greatest arose among the twelve as they journeyed south after this occasion (Mark 9:33-37). The failure of the nine to cast out a demon from a boy while the others were on the mountain with Jesus probably added to the friction within the group (Mark 9:14-29).

Peter had made the Good Confession in the vicinity of Caesarea Philippi, and it seems that Jesus and the disciples were still in this general area. The *high mountain* where Jesus took the three men is not named in the Scriptures, but it may well have been Mount Hermon, the highest in the region. It was about ten miles north of Caesarea Philippi.

> *² There he was transfigured before them. His face shone like the sun, and his clothes became as white as the light.*

The Greek word rendered *transfigured* sounds like the word for "metamorphosis" in English. From Luke's account we learn that Jesus' appearance changed while he was praying (Luke 9:29). Both *his face* and *his clothes* began to shine brilliantly. The veil of Jesus' humanity was pulled back, and the three disciples were given a glimpse of the glory Jesus had before he came to earth as a man (John 1:14; 17:5). Years later Peter wrote of this scene: "We were eyewitnesses of his [Jesus'] majesty. For he received honor and glory from God the Father when the voice came to him from the Majestic Glory . . . when we were with him on the sacred mountain" (2 Peter 1:16-18).

B. Two Men Talking (v. 3)

> *³ Just then there appeared before them Moses and Elijah, talking with Jesus.*

Moses and Elijah may be considered the key representatives of the law and the prophets, respectively. While Matthew's account simply says that Moses and Elijah were *talking with Jesus*, Luke's includes more specific information about the subject matter: "They spoke about his departure, which he was about to bring to fulfillment at Jerusalem" (Luke 9:31). The Greek word translated "departure" is the word from which we get our word "exodus," thereby pointing to Jesus' death as the means by which he would deliver his people from the bondage of sin and bring to fulfillment the work of both Moses and Elijah. Thus these two men were discussing the very topic that had caused the disciples such alarm when Jesus raised it at Caesarea Philippi (Matthew 16:21, 22). That the issue was being calmly discussed by these men indicated that Jesus' death was not to be considered a tragedy; on the contrary, it was in complete harmony with the law and the prophets.

We are not told how the three disciples recognized Moses and Elijah. Did a tradition exist concerning their appearance? Did the conversation at some point make clear their identity? Whatever the answer may be, the fact that these two men were still alive could encourage the disciples to trust what Jesus had said at Caesarea Philippi about being raised to life (Matthew 16:21).

C. One Man Thinking (v. 4)

⁴ Peter said to Jesus, "Lord, it is good for us to be here. If you wish, I will put up three shelters—one for you, one for Moses and one for Elijah."

Luke indicates that *Peter* spoke these words as *Moses* and *Elijah* started to leave (Luke 9:33). (Once again Peter speaks up and voices his opinion, even though he has not been addressed.) Mark adds, "He did not know what to say, they were so frightened" (Mark 9:6; see also Luke 9:33). Peter suggested that he be allowed to *put up three shelters—one for* Jesus, *one for Moses, and one for Elijah.* Perhaps he thought that by providing such structures, the three men would stay a while longer and prolong this thrilling experience.

In the Christian life there are occasions that we call "mountaintop experiences." Often these are times when we gather with other Christians to share our hope and joy in the Lord and thus encourage one another. We can understand Peter's desire for this experience to continue. But we also know that for God's will to be accomplished, one must come down from the mountaintop and, with Jesus, walk in the paths of service, even in the way of the cross.

II. The Father Testifies (Matthew 17:5-9)
A. Tribute to the Son (v. 5)

⁵ While he was still speaking, a bright cloud enveloped them, and a voice from the cloud said, "This is my Son, whom I love; with him I am well pleased. Listen to him!"

A *cloud* often signifies the presence of God in Scripture (Exodus 13:21; 34:5; 40:34-38; Isaiah 4:5). In addition to the sight of the cloud, *a voice* came *from the cloud.* The message was similar to the one that was spoken at the baptism of Jesus (Matthew 3:17), with the important addition of *Listen to him!*

Once again, it appears that Peter was being rebuked for his hasty comments. God wanted to make clear to him and the other disciples that Jesus, Moses, and Elijah were not to be considered equals (with one shelter erected for each of them). The law (represented by Moses) and the prophets (represented by Elijah) pointed to God's Son, and he is the one to whom they must now listen. He is superior!

As noted previously, the timing of the transfiguration was critical. Only a week before, Jesus had rejected Satan's attempt to get him to avoid the cross (Matthew 16:23). Now, while on the mountaintop, he had calmly spoken with Moses and Elijah about his coming death in Jerusalem. Then came the voice from heaven reaffirming the truth of Jesus as the Son of God. Luke 9, which records the transfiguration, also notes Jesus' unyielding determination to carry out his Father's plan: "As the time approached for him to be taken up to heaven, Jesus resolutely set out for Jerusalem" (Luke 9:51).

B. Terror of the Disciples (vv. 6-8)

⁶ When the disciples heard this, they fell facedown to the ground, terrified.

The *disciples* made the only appropriate response that weak and sinful human beings can make in the presence of Almighty God.

⁷ But Jesus came and touched them. "Get up," he said. "Don't be afraid."

Jesus' words on this occasion were not a rebuke for a lack of faith (as in Mark 4:40); rather, they expressed his compassion for them and his desire to banish whatever fears they had. His touch would have reassured them as well.

⁸ When they looked up, they saw no one except Jesus.

The sight of *no one except Jesus* reaffirmed his superiority. Moses the lawgiver and Elijah the prophet were gone; only Jesus remained. God's purpose now centered on Jesus and on him alone, and he was soon to complete the great work that he had come to earth to do.

C. Teaching from Jesus (v. 9)

⁹ As they were coming down the mountain, Jesus instructed them, "Don't tell anyone what you have seen, until the Son of Man has been raised from the dead."

As recently as a week before the transfiguration, Jesus had *instructed* the disciples not to tell the general populace that he was the Christ (Matthew 16:20). It was clear from Peter's reaction to Jesus' announcement of his coming death (v. 22) that the disciples themselves did not understand what was involved in his messiahship, namely that he must die for the sins of the people and be *raised from the dead*. If the disciples did not understand that, the public certainly would not. The people were bent on having an earthly Messiah, one who would be their political savior. To announce publicly Jesus' deity and messiahship at this time would only stir up national excitement and lead to reckless actions by the zealous militarists among the Jews.

It was for this same reason that Jesus now told the disciples not to *tell anyone* what they had *seen* on the mountaintop—not until after his resurrection. (We assume that this prohibition did not apply to the other nine disciples.) After Jesus' resurrection the disciples themselves would better understand the nature of Jesus' kingdom, and the people would be better prepared to receive their teaching concerning it.

The months that lay ahead in Jesus' ministry were going to be difficult ones for the disciples. The sight of the transfigured, glorified Christ was meant to sustain them during that time. In the same way, knowing that death could not hold Jesus should sustain every disciple today through the hard times of life.

JESUS' TEACHING DURING THE FEAST OF TABERNACLES (JOHN 8:21-36)

Establishing the Groundwork

The occasion for this teaching recorded only by John was the Feast of Tabernacles, celebrated in the fall about six months before Jesus' death. Jesus had lingered in Galilee, despite his brothers' attempts to urge him to attend the feast (John 7:1-9). However, after Jesus' brothers had left for the feast, he did go, though privately (John 7:10). Even before his arrival, he was the subject of much discussion and disagreement among the Jewish people and their leaders.

Once in Jerusalem, Jesus began to teach publicly in the temple, rebuking the leaders for their rejection of him. When soldiers were dispatched to arrest Jesus, they returned empty handed, admitting, "No one ever spoke the way this man does" (John 7:46). It was at this time that Jesus declared himself to be the source of "living water" (John 7:38) and the "light of the world" (John 8:12).

Opinions about Jesus during this time ranged from open, even murderous, hatred (John 7:1, 25) to various levels of faith and acceptance. Even though some were challenging and questioning his teaching during the Feast of Tabernacles, John 8:30 tells us, "Even as he spoke, many put their faith in him."

Examining the Text

I. Engaging the Critics (John 8:21-30)
A. Words of Warning (vv. 21-24)

21 Once more Jesus said to them, "I am going away, and you will look for me, and you will die in your sin. Where I go, you cannot come."

Verses 12-20 of John 8 tell how offensive Jesus' teaching was to some of the Pharisees. Certain of them wanted to arrest him, and some later even wanted to stone him (John 8:59); yet "no one seized him, because his time had not yet come" (John 8:20; note also 7:6, 30). Here Jesus spoke of his impending death with the phrase *going away*, but his words made it clear that he himself would choose the time and would arrange the circumstances for his death. His death would not come until he allowed it. Earlier he had spoken of going to a place where the Jews could not find him, and they had speculated that he might be going to foreign lands to teach among the scattered Jews and their Gentile neighbors (John 7:34-36). In bold contrast to Jesus' statement *Where I go, you cannot come* is his later promise to his followers: "You know the way to the place where I am going" (John 14:4).

> ²² **This made the Jews ask, "Will he kill himself? Is that why he says, 'Where I go, you cannot come'?"**

Just how would Jesus arrange his own departure so that he could not be found or followed? There was in his comment a note of finality that suggested death to his hearers. They were right to think of death, but it would not be at Jesus' own hand as they supposed.

The question *Will he kill himself?* may well have been asked in scorn or jest rather than out of a sincere desire for knowledge. The question itself was slanderous, for the Jews abhorred the idea of suicide and believed that anyone who committed suicide went into the depths of Hades lower than any ordinary Jew could go.

> ²³ **But he continued, "You are from below; I am from above. You are of this world; I am not of this world.**

Jesus pointed out the source of his critics' misunderstanding: they did not have the proper frame of reference by which to know (as we sometimes put it) "where he was coming from." The selfish interests, ambitions, and pride of the Pharisees marked them as drawing on sources *from below*, or of this world, or as Jesus would later claim, from the devil (v. 44). In contrast, Jesus was *from above*, fully committed to the will and purpose of his Father.

> ²⁴ **"I told you that you would die in your sins; if you do not believe that I am the one I claim to be, you will indeed die in your sins."**

These scoffers *would die in* their *sins* because they did not *believe* in the only one who could save them from their sins. They were in the position of being "condemned already" (John 3:18) because of their unbelief.

The Greek text of this verse literally reads, "if you do not believe that I am." The statement may have been preparatory to Jesus' later and more controversial claim: "Before Abraham was born, I am!" (John 8:58). Jesus' perplexing words were bound to produce the next question asked by the Pharisees.

B. Words of Self-Revelation (vv. 25-27)

25 "Who are you?" they asked.

"Just what I have been claiming all along," Jesus replied.

Baffled by Jesus' refusal to identify himself more clearly, the questioners demanded (literally), "You, *who are you?*" As in verse 22, the Pharisees tried to dismiss Jesus' charge of their sinfulness by turning on him with contempt. It was not yet time for Jesus to provide his enemies with a quotable declaration of his deity. That would come later when he was ready to die for what they would call "blasphemy" (Mark 14:61-64). For now, Jesus directed his questioners to what he had been *claiming all along*. From the beginning of his ministry, Jesus had been providing evidence that he was indeed the Christ. Let these questioners draw their own conclusions from the evidence available to everyone else.

26 "I have much to say in judgment of you. But he who sent me is reliable, and what I have heard from him I tell the world."

Jesus was fully aware that *much* of what he said was spoken *in judgment* of people such as the Pharisees because they had refused to believe in him or in anything he said. However, he also knew that he was not acting alone; God had *sent* him to accomplish a particular task on behalf of *the world*.

27 They did not understand that he was telling them about his Father.

This explanatory remark by John helps explain why it was necessary for Jesus to continue his remarks in the following verses. The problem of Jesus' enemies was not that they lacked the information necessary to lead to faith. Their problem was that they had so hardened their hearts that they would not accept the truth when they heard it.

C. Words of Promise (vv. 28-30)

28 So Jesus said, "When you have lifted up the Son of Man, then you will know that I am the one I claim to be and that I do nothing on my own but speak just what the Father has taught me.

The discussion continued, with Jesus speaking in veiled terms about himself, and his hearers still not understanding what he meant. Jesus had spoken about *the Son of man* being *lifted up* during his conversation with Nicodemus (John 3:14, 15). He would raise the issue again some six months later during his final week in Jerusalem (John 12:32). At that point, John adds this comment: "He said this to show the kind of death he was going to die" (v. 33). Jesus' enemies would cause him to be "lifted up" on the cross to die, but that was part of the eternal plan of God (Acts 2:23).

The statement *then you will know that I am the one I claim to be* indicates that Jesus' death and resurrection would demonstrate that the controlling hand of God was in all Jesus had said and done. His critics would have all the evidence needed to conclude that Jesus was who he claimed to be. As in verse 24, the literal reading of this verse is "then you will know that I am."

²⁹ "The one who sent me is with me; he has not left me alone, for I always do what pleases him."

God was *the one who sent* Jesus and who constantly attended and empowered Jesus in his ministry. Jesus would state that truth later in even bolder terms: "I and the Father are one" (John 10:30).

³⁰ Even as he spoke, many put their faith in him.

Then, as now, Jesus' claims made it impossible for anyone to be neutral or indifferent regarding him. At this point, *many put their faith in him.* We are not told how many believed, or how the fact that they did so was expressed. At any rate, there were enough to pose a threat to the Jewish leaders in their determination to seize and do away with Jesus. They did not dare move against him when too many who supported him were around.

II. Encouraging the Believers (John 8:31-36)
A. Knowing the Truth (vv. 31-33)

³¹ To the Jews who had believed him, Jesus said, "If you hold to my teaching, you are really my disciples.

The previous discussion had been heavily influenced by the Pharisees' opposition to Jesus. Now Jesus addressed *the Jews who had believed him.* It was one thing to follow Jesus with an initial burst of enthusiasm; it was quite another to *hold to* his *teaching* with a determined commitment to follow no matter what the cost.

³² "Then you will know the truth, and the truth will set you free."

Here is an important step in the pathway of discipleship. The way to be *free*, Jesus declared, is an intimate acquaintance with him who is the *truth* (John 14:6). Truth is much more than mere facts or data; it is a Person.

Jesus' linking of truth with freedom is significant, especially in today's world in which freedom is often equated with not adhering to any kind of absolute truth. The knowledge of Christ frees one from ignorance, superstition, and bad habits; it frees from the slaveries of pride, self, and sin. Without Christ, the pursuit of philosophical "truth"—even within the mysteries of Scripture—can become an enslavement to self-centered pride. Paul writes of those who are "always learning but never able to acknowledge the truth" (2 Timothy 3:7).

³³ They answered him, "We are Abraham's descendants and have never been slaves of anyone. How can you say that we shall be set free?"

These words are surprising if they came from some of the Jews who had earlier expressed faith in Jesus (vv. 30, 31). Apparently certain of the Jewish leaders were still present and were listening as Jesus was addressing the new believers. We know Jesus was speaking to these leaders when he later said that they were intending to kill him (vv. 37, 40) and when he described them as children of the devil (vv. 38, 41, 44).

On the surface, the claim that *Abraham's descendants* (the Jews) had *never been slaves of anyone* seems absurd. The nation had been in bondage to Egypt, Babylon, Persia, and Syria (during the intertestamental period) and was now subject to Rome. But the Pharisees' claim reflected a fierce insistence that while the children of Abraham might be enslaved politically, they would never become voluntary slaves to anyone. From a religious standpoint, they had maintained a sense of superiority to their oppressors because of their unique position as God's chosen people and his "holy nation" (Exodus 19:5, 6). To them, this was all the freedom they needed. What more could Jesus offer?

B. Turning from Sin (v. 34)

³⁴ Jesus replied, "I tell you the truth, everyone who sins is a slave to sin.

Jesus' hearers claimed that they had never been enslaved to anyone, but Jesus responded by affirming that these descendants of Abraham were trapped in a bondage that is far worse than any political oppression—the bondage of sin. *Everyone who sins*, that is, who continues in sin as a pattern of life, *is a slave to sin.* Jesus was making it clear that his definition of freedom and slavery involved far more than political constraint.

C. Accepting the Son (vv. 35, 36)

³⁵ "Now a slave has no permanent place in the family, but a son belongs to it forever.

The one who has yielded himself in obedience to sin is not only in bondage, but until a more lasting relationship is established, he is without a *family*. A servant has *no permanent place in the family* whom he serves. He may be turned out at any time. But Jesus, as God's one and only *son*, possesses an eternal claim on the rights and riches of Heaven; and he shares those freely with all who come to the Father in his name and thus become members of the family by adoption.

> [36] *"So if the Son sets you free, you will be free indeed."*

The real freedom that God's *Son* came to give was ultimately freedom from sin and all of sin's consequences. To be *free* from that kind of bondage is to be *free indeed*. And that kind of freedom can come from no other source but Jesus.

JESUS HEALS THE MAN BORN BLIND (JOHN 9:1-7, 35-41)

Establishing the Groundwork

Whether this incident happened immediately after Jesus left the temple grounds to escape those who wanted to stone him (John 8:58, 59) or on a day soon afterward, we are not told. What is most important to note is that Jesus used this man's affliction to demonstrate the truth of his claim made earlier: "I am the light of the world" (John 8:12). By bringing this man out of his physical darkness into the light of this world, he was also offering a "visual aid" to highlight the truth that he had the power to bring the souls of men from the darkness of sin into the light of God's forgiveness and acceptance. He still has that power.

Examining the Text

I. Light for the Eyes (John 9:1-7)
A. Condition Described (v. 1)

> [1] *As he went along, he saw a man blind from birth.*

This *man blind from birth* may well have been seated at an entrance to the temple where he could appeal for alms as worshipers came and went (as did the lame man described in Acts 3:1, 2). Apparently he was positioned in some public spot to be noticed, and thus helped, by those who *went along* the way.

B. Cause Sought (v. 2)

> [2] *His disciples asked him, "Rabbi, who sinned, this man or his parents, that he was born blind?"*

We do not know how the *disciples* were aware that this man had been *born blind*. Perhaps he mentioned it as he called to the passersby for help.

The disciples' question of *who sinned* reflects the popular belief of that time that any affliction such as blindness was the result of personal sin. (Recall that this was the argument made by Job's "friends" as they tried to urge him to confess his wrongdoing so that his wealth and reputation could be restored.) One could make the case that all the evil and suffering in the world is caused either directly or indirectly by sin, but much evil or suffering is caused so indirectly that it is difficult or impossible to trace it to its cause. The man born blind posed an interesting problem. Since he was blind from birth, surely he had not sinned before he was born. Was blindness imposed at his birth to punish sins he would commit later, or was his blindness a punishment for the sins of his *parents*? If the latter was true, why should this man have to suffer for sins he did not commit?

C. Clarification Provided (vv. 3-5)

³ *"Neither this man nor his parents sinned," said Jesus, "but this happened so that the work of God might be displayed in his life.*

Jesus' statement should not be taken to mean that *this man* and *his parents* had lived absolutely sinless lives. He was saying that the man's blindness should not be attributed to a particular sin that either he or his parents had committed. It would also be erroneous to say that God caused this man to be born blind and required him to suffer the effects of that handicap just so that *the work of God might be displayed* by Jesus' healing him. In fact, Jesus said nothing about the cause of this affliction and did not use this occasion to enter into a philosophical discussion of the cause of suffering. Instead, he declared that the man's affliction would result in a demonstration of God's power *in his life*. Thus even unmerited suffering can serve a divine purpose. (See Romans 8:28.)

⁴ *"As long as it is day, we must do the work of him who sent me. Night is coming, when no one can work.*

Jesus used the word *day* to describe the time allotted to man in this world to accomplish God's will and purpose. The phrases *as long as it is day* and *night is coming* reflect Jesus' understanding that his time on earth was growing short. In less than six months he would be crucified. The *night* of his death would end the *day* in which he would work as he then was working. Another *day* would come, and in it Jesus would work through "the church, which is his body, the fullness of him who fills everything in every way" (Ephesians 1:22, 23).

⁵ *"While I am in the world, I am the light of the world."*

Not long before this, Jesus had declared, *I am the light of the world* (John 8:12). He now repeated this statement, most likely in preparation for the miracle of sight that he was about to give the blind man. Although Jesus himself is no longer *in the world*, his followers have been called to continue his mission of being the light of the world (Matthew 5:14).

D. Compassion Demonstrated (vv. 6, 7)

⁶ *Having said this, he spit on the ground, made some mud with the saliva, and put it on the man's eyes.*

Jesus' words were followed with deeds. The patient could not see the procedure; others could. Why Jesus chose to heal the man by placing *mud* on his *eyes*, then sending him to wash it off (v. 7), we are not told. Some have suggested that the method was designed to arouse the blind man's faith and to challenge him to demonstrate it by obedience.

To the Jewish leaders, however, this act carried a much different message. Their tradition forbade working with clay or treating eyes for healing on the Sabbath, and this action took place on a Sabbath (v. 14).

⁷ *"Go," he told him, "wash in the Pool of Siloam" (this word means Sent). So the man went and washed, and came home seeing.*

The *Pool of Siloam* was located on the southeastern end of Jerusalem. While we are not told exactly how far the man had to go until he came to the pool, it should be noted that the pool was not far from the temple area, where the incidents recorded in John 8 took place. Most likely he did not travel much more than half a mile. We are also not told whether the man made the journey alone or whether he was guided along by others. Of greatest importance is that the man's obedience to Jesus was immediate and without question—and so was the blessing of sight: he *washed, and came home seeing.*

John includes the additional comment that the name *Siloam* means *sent.* Thus the one who was "sent" from God (v. 4) "sent" a blind man to a place called "Sent," where he would receive his sight.

After the once-blind man *came home seeing,* he was immediately the source of controversy. His neighbors were unsure whether or not he really was the man they had known as blind from birth (vv. 8-12). Then came intense interrogation from the Pharisees (vv. 13-34). The questioning involved the man first (vv. 13-17), then his parents (vv. 18-23), and then him again (vv. 24-34). Rather than yielding to pressure and softening his testimony about Jesus, he remained true to the facts and strengthened his witness. He concluded that this man called Jesus was a prophet (v. 17) and that he was sent from God (v. 33).

The man's growing conviction concerning Jesus resulted in growing hostility from the Pharisees. He accepted this, aware of the religious authorities' earlier warning that anyone who confessed Jesus as the Messiah would be put out of the synagogue (v. 22). And that is exactly what happened (v. 34), leaving the man without religious fellowship, community support, or social acceptance. This man paid a price for staying true to his convictions about Jesus.

II. Light for the Soul (John 9:35-41)
A. Spiritual Sight (vv. 35-38)

35 Jesus heard that they had thrown him out, and when he found him, he said, "Do you believe in the Son of Man?"

The outcast was probably not alone for very long. *Jesus . . . found him.* It is difficult to know what the question *"Do you believe in the Son of Man?"* meant to the man at this point. How much the man was aware of the debate concerning Jesus during the Feast of Tabernacles we do not know. Probably he had heard at least some bits of information as he sat begging, and he may have heard more extended discussions from his neighbors and his parents following Jesus' miracle.

36 "Who is he, sir?" the man asked. "Tell me so that I may believe in him."

The man indicated a desire to receive more information about the Son of Man. Apparently he had not seen Jesus since he had been given sight (Jesus had sent him to the Pool of Siloam to receive his sight), and the earlier brief encounter with Jesus was not enough to allow him to recognize Jesus' voice. But just as the man was ready to obey what he was told to do earlier (v. 7), now he was ready, with proper guidance, to *believe in* the Son of Man.

37 Jesus said, "You have now seen him; in fact, he is the one speaking with you."

In the plainest terms, Jesus said that he himself is the Son of Man. *You have now seen him* was a reminder that this man had seen nothing at all until the Son of Man had given him sight.

38 Then the man said, "Lord, I believe," and he worshiped him.

This man's confession, though simple and direct, is all the more remarkable because his faith developed in such a short time. In addition, his faith had deepened in the face of criticism and even persecution.

The Greek word translated *worshiped* can mean homage that is given either to God or to man. In the New Testament, however, it usually refers to the worship of God; and that was what this former blind man was giving to Jesus. He knew that this was not just another man; Jesus was and is the Light of the world.

B. Spiritual Blindness (vv. 39-41)

39 Jesus said, "For judgment I have come into this world, so that the blind will see and those who see will become blind."

Jesus came to save the world rather than to judge it (John 12:47), but his coming inevitably brought a *judgment*, or separation, between those who accepted the truth about him and those who did not (note also John 3:17-19). In this case, the contrasting responses of the Pharisees and the former blind man provided Jesus an opportunity to emphasize this point.

The man born *blind* and the Pharisees were witnesses to the same facts. The man accepted and believed; he received sight, both physical and spiritual. The Pharisees refused to acknowledge any need, assuming they already could *see*—that they possessed all light and truth. So they became increasingly blind, closing their eyes to the light Jesus came to bring.

40 Some Pharisees who were with him heard him say this and asked, "What? Are we blind too?"

At this point in Jesus' ministry, *some* of the *Pharisees* or their messengers were usually within hearing distance of Jesus, hoping to catch him saying or doing something questionable. They were stung by Jesus' suggestion that they might be *blind*. They were the accepted teachers and "experts" among God's people; how dare Jesus make such an accusation!

41 Jesus said, "If you were blind, you would not be guilty of sin; but now that you claim you can see, your guilt remains."

If the Pharisees had realized just how *blind* and ignorant they really were, they would have accepted Jesus' claims about himself as did the man born blind. If they had admitted their *sin*, they could have been forgiven as Jesus had forgiven others. But they were so sure of their sight and so confident in their understanding that they declared Jesus to be a sinner (v. 24), and thus they themselves sank deeper into sin. They chose darkness when they closed their eyes to the Light of the world.

JESUS' PARABLE OF THE GOOD SAMARITAN (LUKE 10:25-37)

Establishing the Groundwork

After the Feast of Tabernacles, Jesus continued to teach in Judea. He stayed in that vicinity for more than two months, observing the winter Feast of Dedication (John 10:22, 23). There he continued to avoid attempts to stone him (John 10:31) and, failing that, to arrest him (John 10:39).

During this time, Jesus sent 72 of his followers to teach and heal (Luke 10:1-12) as the 12 disciples had done in Galilee a few months earlier. These followers returned, rejoicing in the success of their mission, especially in the submission of demons (Luke 10:17). Excitement about Jesus was building among the people, but so was the hostility of those who stood opposed to his ministry. One person's attempt to "test" Jesus became the occasion for one of Jesus' best known and loved parables.

Examining the Text

I. What Must I Do? (Luke 10:25-28)
A. Knowing What to Do (vv. 25-27)

25 On one occasion an expert in the law stood up to test Jesus. "Teacher," he asked, "what must I do to inherit eternal life?"

The *expert in the law* was one of a group of scholars who were professional teachers and interpreters of the law of Moses and the traditions that had grown up around it. Because of the place of the law in Jewish life, these men exercised great influence over the people. This man may well have been a Pharisee.

On this occasion, this scholar *stood up to test Jesus.* He was not a sincere seeker after truth; his desire was to ask a question so difficult that Jesus would become confused or perhaps say something that would put him out of favor with the general public or in trouble with the religious authorities. His question was an important one: "*Teacher, what must I do to inherit eternal life?*" The belief in life after death was strong among the Pharisees but not among the Sadducees. (See Acts 23:6-8.)

26 "What is written in the Law?" he replied. "How do you read it?"

If the lawyer hoped to catch Jesus off guard, he was immediately disappointed. To offer a question in response to a question was a common practice among the rabbis. Here Jesus said in effect, "You're an expert *in the Law.* What would you say?"

27 He answered: "'Love the Lord your God with all your heart and with all your soul and with all your strength and with all your mind'; and, 'Love your neighbor as yourself.'"

The expert in the law replied by quoting from Deuteronomy 6:5 and Leviticus 19:18. At a later time, Jesus called these two commandments the greatest and the second greatest, respectively. He also stated, "All the Law and the Prophets hang on these two commandments" (Matthew 22:34-40).

B. Doing What You Know (v. 28)

28 "You have answered correctly," Jesus replied. "Do this and you will live."

Regardless of the answer the expert in the law expected or hoped for, he must have been surprised to hear a reply so brief, so approving, so conclusive. All he had to *do* to inherit eternal life was what he himself already knew and believed—what he had learned from the law that he had studied so diligently.

We Christians may be just as surprised by Jesus' reply. Don't we receive eternal life by God's grace and our faith rather than by what we do (Ephesians 2:8, 9)? Isn't it true that no one is justified by lawkeeping (Romans 3:20)? Haven't we all failed in keeping his commandments (Romans 3:23)?

Yes, all of the above is true. But Jesus and the expert in the law were speaking during a time before all of that was revealed—before Jesus died in our place. Before offering the gift of eternal life, God gave the law; and perfect obedience to that law would lead to life. But no one could keep the law well enough to earn eternal life (Romans 7:12, 13; 8:3). In this way, the law demonstrated our need for a Savior (Galatians 3:23, 24). We all deserved to die, but God sent Jesus to die in our place, offering us life as a gift.

That plan, however, was yet to be carried out. The expert in the law correctly described the means to eternal life that was in effect at that time, and Jesus agreed with him.

II. Who Is My Neighbor? (Luke 10:29-35)
A. Question Asked (v. 29)

29 But he wanted to justify himself, so he asked Jesus, "And who is my neighbor?"

As was often the case, the person who raised a question to embarrass Jesus found himself embarrassed and put on the defensive. The expert in the law shifted from trying to "test" Jesus (v. 25) to seeking *to justify himself.* He knew that he had not fully obeyed the commandments cited by Jesus, but he did not want to look bad in front of Jesus or others who may be listening to this conversation. After all, he had asked about receiving eternal life; and he did not want to look like he was *not* going to receive it! His legal mind wanted to have the word *neighbor* defined in such a way so that he could say, "I have fulfilled the law to the letter, and I am therefore entitled to eternal life."

Unlike the first question raised by the expert in the law, the question *Who is my neighbor?* could not be answered by quoting one or two verses from the law of Moses. Jesus responded with one of his most familiar parables.

B. Story Told (vv. 30-35)

30 In reply Jesus said: "A man was going down from Jerusalem to Jericho, when he fell into the hands of robbers. They stripped him of his clothes, beat him and went away, leaving him half dead.

The road *from Jerusalem to Jericho* was a place where travelers frequently *fell into the hands of robbers.* For twenty miles it wound its way through the hills, literally *going down* some thirty-six hundred feet from the capital city to the Jordan Valley. It was a narrow, rocky path with many steep turns and many places where bandits could hide, attack their prey, and then escape. In Jesus' story, the *man* who was traveling may not have had anything of value to steal; so those who robbed him took *his clothes*, then *beat him* and left him *half dead*, perhaps angry that he did not have more to take.

31 "A priest happened to be going down the same road, and when he saw the man, he passed by on the other side.

A *priest* traveling *down the same road* (from Jerusalem toward Jericho) would have left Jerusalem; perhaps he had fulfilled his duties at the temple and was returning home to Jericho, where many priests lived. Different reasons have been suggested as to why this priest, even though he *saw the man* in need, simply *passed by on the other side* and did nothing to help: he did not want to defile himself through contact with what may have been a corpse; the robbers might still be nearby; the man was probably beyond help at this point; the priest had an appointment in Jericho to keep; or he simply did not want to get involved. Yet Jesus did not mention any such excuse; he let the action (or inaction) of the priest speak for itself.

32 "So too, a Levite, when he came to the place and saw him, passed by on the other side.

A *Levite* served as an assistant to priests. He was probably more accustomed to getting his hands dirty with unpleasant or menial tasks. Perhaps he would stop to help a man who was beaten and bleeding. But sadly he too *passed by on the other side*.

> ³³ **"But a Samaritan, as he traveled, came where the man was; and when he saw him, he took pity on him.**

There must have been a stiffening among Jesus' hearers as he mentioned the word *Samaritan*, especially as he proceeded to show this man in a favorable light when compared to the priest and the Levite. (For a brief history dealing with the relations between Jews and Samaritans, see the comments under John 4:9 in chapter 5.) The contrast was immediately evident. This traveler not only *saw* the man in need (as the other two men had), but he also *took pity on him* (which the other men had not done).

> ³⁴ **"He went to him and bandaged his wounds, pouring on oil and wine. Then he put the man on his own donkey, took him to an inn and took care of him.**

The Samaritan looked beyond racial and religious differences. Seeing a man with a desperate need, he had both the resources and, more important, the desire to help. Although he had never met this man, he took the initiative and *went to him*. He freely used what he had to help the man; perhaps he tore his own clothing into strips so that he could bandage the man's *wounds*. *Wine* was sometimes used as a disinfectant, and olive *oil* served as a soothing medicine.

To this point, the Samaritan had invested his time and his resources to help a complete stranger. But he was not finished! He then *put the man on his own donkey* (thus giving up his means of transportation), *took him to an inn*, and continued to *care* for him.

> ³⁵ **"The next day he took out two silver coins and gave them to the innkeeper. 'Look after him,' he said, 'and when I return, I will reimburse you for any extra expense you may have.'"**

Here was yet another example of the depth of this Samaritan's compassion: he was willing to spend his own money on behalf of the wounded man. *Two silver coins* is "two denarii" in the Greek text, which would have been the equivalent of two days' wages. Then he offered the equivalent of a "blank check" to the *innkeeper*, promising to *reimburse* him for any *extra expense* that might be incurred in caring for the man. At no point did the Samaritan say or imply by his words or actions, "I have done enough; now someone else needs to help."

The attitudes of those who encountered the man in this parable have been summarized as follows: the thieves' attitude was, "What's yours is ours and we'll take it"; the priest and the Levite followed the thinking, "What's ours is ours and we'll keep it"; but the Samaritan lived by the principle, "What's mine is yours and I'll share it."

III. Go and Do Likewise! (Luke 10:36, 37)
A. What Do You Think? (v. 36)

36 "Which of these three do you think was a neighbor to the man who fell into the hands of robbers?"

While the expert in the law had asked, "Who is my neighbor?" Jesus concluded his story by asking, "*Which of these three* men *was a neighbor to the man in need?*" Jesus did not describe for the questioner the kind of person who must be loved according to law. Instead, he turned the questioner's thoughts inward to lead him to see that *he* was to be the neighbor to *anyone* in need, as the Samaritan had been to the beaten traveler.

B. Do What You Think! (v. 37)

37 The expert in the law replied, "The one who had mercy on him."
Jesus told him, "Go and do likewise."

The parable that had been prompted by a philosophical question resulted in a practical exhortation. What the expert in the law would *do* in addressing the needs of the people whom he confronted each day (in particular, the unscheduled, unexpected needs) would mark him as a neighbor. The lesson to him that day, as well as the lesson to us today, is that one should not define *neighbor* in terms of who the "other person" might be. The issue is this: who is willing to be a neighbor by serving and helping the "other person," regardless of who he or she is?

JESUS IN THE HOME OF MARY AND MARTHA (LUKE 10:38-42)

Establishing the Groundwork

Sometime during the two-month interval between the Feast of Tabernacles (John 7:2) and the Feast of Dedication (John 10:22), Jesus visited the home of his friends Mary and Martha in the village of Bethany, located about two miles southeast of Jerusalem. The Gospels indicate that Mary and Martha, along with their brother Lazarus, were among Jesus' closest friends. John specifically mentions Jesus' love for them (John 11:5). The sisters are mentioned in three separate incidents in the Gospels, including the one we are about to examine.

(The other incidents are the raising of Lazarus in John 11 and the anointing of Jesus by Mary in John 12:1-8.)

Examining the Text

I. Discerning Woman (Luke 10:38, 39)
A. The Setting (v. 38)

38 As Jesus and his disciples were on their way, he came to a village where a woman named Martha opened her home to him.

The phrase *on their way* indicates the journeys of *Jesus and his disciples* during their later Judean campaign. While the text says that *Martha opened her home to* Jesus, it is likely that Jesus' disciples were included as well. That this was *her home* may indicate her status as the older sister or that she was a widow at this point. That Lazarus is not mentioned in this text may indicate that he had a separate residence.

B. The Sister (v. 39)

39 She had a sister called Mary, who sat at the Lord's feet listening to what he said.

Mary, Martha's *sister*, is described as someone who *sat at the Lord's feet*—a position that calls to mind the relationship of student to teacher. (See Acts 22:3 where Paul spoke of being taught "under Gamaliel." Students familiar with the older Bible translations or with the Greek text know that this is, literally, "at the feet of Gamaliel.")

II. Distracted Woman (Luke 10:40-42)
A. Martha's Complaint (v. 40)

40 But Martha was distracted by all the preparations that had to be made. She came to him and asked, "Lord, don't you care that my sister has left me to do the work by myself? Tell her to help me!"

Assuming that *Martha* was the older sister, she felt responsible for *all the preparations* involved in hosting Jesus and his disciples. One can understand why she might have begun to feel quite irritated about Mary's failure to help her.

However (using a tactic familiar to any parent of siblings), Martha did not directly confront Mary. Instead, she came to Jesus and told him to tell Mary what to do. In fact, she appears to scold Jesus. Doesn't he *care* about Martha's being *left* to do all *the work* by herself?

B. Jesus' Counsel (vv. 41, 42)

41 *"Martha, Martha," the Lord answered, "you are worried and upset about many things,*

The repetition of the name *Martha* was probably both a rebuke and an expression of sympathy for Martha's frustration. The *many things* that she was *worried and upset about* included all the details involved in being a good hostess. Yet these were relatively inconsequential matters. Would a couple of hours until the meal was served really make that much difference? Rather than enjoying Jesus' company and taking advantage of the opportunity to learn from him, Martha was losing sight of what her priorities should be.

42 *". . . but only one thing is needed. Mary has chosen what is better, and it will not be taken away from her."*

In contrast to the "many things" that were upsetting Martha, Jesus pointed out that *only one thing is needed*. That *one thing* was what *Mary* was doing: learning from Jesus. What Martha was doing was not unimportant, but it could wait. A special opportunity was present, and Mary had *chosen* not to miss it.

Notice that Jesus did not rebuke Martha for her kindness. He was not unappreciative of her hospitality. In truth, all of us have responsibilities like Martha's that press upon us every day. However, these must not be allowed to determine our priorities and control our outlook. Specifically, we must not allow such items to crowd spiritual concerns (particularly time alone with the Lord) out of our lives.

How to Say It

ABRAHAM. *Ay*-bruh-ham.

BABYLON. *Bab*-uh-lun.

CAESAREA. Sess-uh-*ree*-uh.

DENARII. dih-*nair*-ee or dih-*nair*-eye.

EGYPT. *Ee*-jipt.

ELIJAH. Ee-*lye*-juh.

GALILEE. *Gal*-uh-lee.

GAMALIEL. Guh-*may*-lih-ul or Guh-*may*-lee-al.

HERMON. *Her*-mun.

INTERTESTAMENTAL. *in*-ter-tes-tuh-*men*-tul (strong accent on *men*).

JERICHO. *Jair*-ih-co.

JERUSALEM. Juh-*roo*-suh-lem.

JUDEAN. Joo-*dee*-un.

LAZARUS. *Laz*-uh-rus.

LEVITE. *Lee*-vite.

MESSIAH. Meh-*sigh*-uh.

METAMORPHOSIS. *met*-tuh-*mor*-fuh-suss (strong accent on *mor*).

MOSES. *Mo*-zes or *Mo*-zez.

PERSIA. *Per*-zhuh.

PHARISEES. *Fair*-ih-seez.

PHILIPPI. Fih-*lip*-pie or *Fil*-ih-pie.

SADDUCEES. *Sad*-you-seez.

SAMARITAN. Suh-*mare*-uh-tun.

SILOAM. *Sigh*-*lo*-um.

SYRIA. *Sear*-ee-uh.

TABERNACLES. *ta*-ber-*na*-kulz (strong accent on *ta*).

TRANSFIGURATION. tranz-fih-gyuh-*ray*-shun.

Chapter 10

Jesus' Ministry in Perea and His Journey Toward Jerusalem

Luke 15:11-24; John 11:20-27, 38-44;
Mark 10:17-27; 10:35-45; Luke 19:1-10

JESUS' PARABLE OF THE PRODIGAL SON (LUKE 15:11-24)

Establishing the Groundwork

Sometime after the Feast of Dedication, Jesus left Judea and "went back across the Jordan to the place where John had been baptizing in the early days" (John 10:40). This area east of the Jordan opposite Judea and Samaria was known as Perea. (The New Testament does not use this designation; it is found in Josephus and other writers.) After a brief comment on the favorable response in this area (John 10:41, 42), John says nothing more about Jesus' ministry here. He does tell of an interruption of the Perean ministry when Jesus returned to Judea for a brief period of time because of the death of Lazarus (John 11:1-44). We must look to Luke's Gospel to learn details of the first part of the Perean ministry and to all the Synoptics to learn of the concluding events.

During this time (with the cross now three to four months away), Jesus' teaching included a series of parables, three of which (the parables of the lost sheep, lost coin, and lost son) are recorded in Luke 15. These parables were given in response to criticism from some of the Pharisees and teachers of the law that Jesus "welcomes sinners and eats with them" (Luke 15:2).

While all three of these parables emphasize something or someone *lost*, they also emphasize the *joy* that results from finding what was lost. In the case of the well-loved parable of the prodigal son, the reaction of the older brother to his sibling's return exposed the haughty, self-serving attitude of Jesus' critics.

Examining the Text

I. The Departure (Luke 15:11-13)
A. Demand (vv. 11, 12)

¹¹ Jesus continued: "There was a man who had two sons.

Jesus did not give names to the characters in this parable, nor did he indicate whether or not the events included in it were taken from a real life situation.

Nevertheless, the circumstances Jesus described would have seemed quite realistic to his audience.

¹² "The younger one said to his father, 'Father, give me my share of the estate.' So he divided his property between them.

The law of Moses established some basic guidelines regarding family inheritances. The oldest son was to receive a double portion of the father's estate (Deuteronomy 21:15-17). This was to be a majority share of money and property, at least two times as much as what each of the other brothers and sisters received. In the situation described by Jesus, the process of dividing the goods was fairly simple: two-thirds would go to the older son and one-third to the younger. What is noteworthy in Jesus' parable is the demanding attitude of the *younger* son. His *give me* was not stated with any kind of respect or courtesy toward his *father*.

B. Dissipation (v. 13)

¹³ "Not long after that, the younger son got together all he had, set off for a distant country and there squandered his wealth in wild living.

As soon as he could make preparations, *the younger son* traveled to a *distant country*, separating himself as much as possible from what he considered a lifestyle too "confining." *There* he *squandered his wealth in wild living*. We can imagine what this involved—perhaps an abundance of eating, drinking, and entertaining friends and female companions. Note the older brother's later complaint to his father that "this son of yours" had "squandered your property with prostitutes" (Luke 15:30). While this accusation may have been spoken in anger rather than in truth, Jesus probably put the words in the brother's mouth to reflect accurately the prodigal's behavior. It is this young man's selfish and foolish behavior that has earned him the title "the prodigal (wasteful) son."

II. The Desperation (Luke 15:14-16)
A. Loss of Wealth (v. 14)

¹⁴ "After he had spent everything, there was a severe famine in that whole country, and he began to be in need.

No indication is given as to how much time elapsed before all the young man's resources were gone. No doubt there were many people who helped him spend his money, but whose presence suddenly became scarce when his money did. Running out of money is a hardship under any circumstance, but it is even more serious when *a severe famine* has struck.

B. Loss of Dignity (vv. 15, 16)

15 "So he went and hired himself out to a citizen of that country, who sent him to his fields to feed pigs.

It is to the young man's credit that he did not resort to stealing or begging to solve his dilemma. He *hired himself out to a citizen* of the distant *country* to which he had traveled. One finds it ironic that someone who thought he had found his independence was now more dependent than he had ever been. Such is the deceptive nature of sin.

Judging from the reference to feeding pigs, it seems the young man was no longer among his fellow Jews but was now residing in Gentile territory. Swine were among the animals that, according to the law of Moses, were to be considered "unclean" by the Jews (Leviticus 11:7; Deuteronomy 14:8). In this young man's abject desperation, with starvation looming before him, he forced himself to violate his conscience and his heritage, thus destroying whatever self-respect and dignity he may have had left. And yet even this was not the full extent of his downfall.

16 "He longed to fill his stomach with the pods that the pigs were eating, but no one gave him anything.

In his masterful telling of this story, Jesus brought his Jewish audience to a point where their hearts would have ached for this young man. For no matter how foolish he had been, no Jew deserved this fate: *he longed to fill his stomach with the pods that the pigs were eating*. These *pods* were likely what are called carob pods. This crop was specifically grown for feeding livestock, but it was sometimes eaten by the poor during times of severe hardship. Such was the plight of the prodigal. For a Jewish man to be envious of pigs indicates what little self-respect remained in him.

To emphasize further the young man's sorry plight, Jesus then added, *but no one gave him anything*. He was truly alone and helpless—quite a contrast to the cocky young man who had so rudely demanded his father's inheritance.

III. The Decision (Luke 15:17-19)
A. About Self (v. 17)

17 "When he came to his senses, he said, 'How many of my father's hired men have food to spare, and here I am starving to death!

In the fields with the pigs, the young man finally *came to his senses*. The literal reading is "he came into himself." He had been acting like a man "outside of himself," denying who he was and whose he was. Now the experience of hardship had jolted him back to reality. He was coming to a point of repentance, which is a common theme linking all three of the parables in this chapter of Luke (15:7, 10).

B. About Sin (v. 18)

18 "'I will set out and go back to my father and say to him: Father, I have sinned against heaven and against you.

The words of repentance are short and simple, yet so difficult to say: *I have sinned.* We don't like to admit that we were wrong. But genuine repentance demands that we set aside any defense of our actions and honestly confess our sin. The young man also acknowledged that his sin was both *against heaven* and *against* his *father.* All of our wrongful actions against others are ultimately sins against God. After all, our sins are a violation of the instructions God has clearly revealed to us in his Word.

C. About Status (v. 19)

19 "'I am no longer worthy to be called your son; make me like one of your hired men.'"

While the young man was still physically and legally his father's *son,* he did not feel that he deserved to be treated as a son after all he had done. Living like one of the hired men under his own father's roof would be a fitting punishment, or so he figured. Perhaps the clearest evidence of his repentant spirit is how his attitude had changed from "give me" (v. 12) to *make me.*

IV. The Delight (Luke 15:20-24)
A. The Father's Attitude (v. 20, 21)

20 "So he got up and went to his father.
"But while he was still a long way off, his father saw him and was filled with compassion for him; he ran to his son, threw his arms around him and kissed him.

Having decided on his course of action, the young man did not hesitate to carry it out. Up to this point, Jesus' parable had been primarily focused on the young man and his circumstances. Now Jesus shifted the emphasis to the father's character and conduct. (Some suggest that the parable deserves the title "The Loving Father" as much as it does "The Prodigal Son.") Though the young man's appearance had likely changed (perhaps drastically) since his departure from home, the father immediately recognized him from *a long way off*. Tossing aside all formalities, the father ran to greet his son, fell on his neck and kissed him. The reason for this dramatic reception: the father's heart was *filled with compassion* for his errant son.

> [21] **"The son said to him, 'Father, I have sinned against heaven and against you. I am no longer worthy to be called your son.'**

The *son* began the speech he had rehearsed while he was still in the "distant country." Humility had replaced the pride and arrogance he had exhibited earlier. But before he could complete his speech, the father interrupted him, disregarding any thought of humiliating his son. He had more noble plans in mind.

B. The Father's Actions (vv. 22-24)

> [22] **"But the father said to his servants, 'Quick! Bring the best robe and put it on him. Put a ring on his finger and sandals on his feet.**

The *father* did not offer any response to his son's words. Instead, he addressed his *servants*. He called for *the best robe* (often reserved for an honored guest) to replace what were likely smelly, tattered clothes. The *ring* may have been a signet ring, a sign of standing and authority in the family. *Sandals* often distinguished the freeman from the barefoot slaves.

> [23] **"'Bring the fattened calf and kill it. Let's have a feast and celebrate.**

Just as it had been not merely a robe but the "best robe," so it was *the fattened calf* and not just any animal prepared for the *feast*. The atmosphere of celebration at the son's return was similar to that portrayed in the other two parables in this chapter—when a shepherd found his lost sheep (Luke 15:5, 6) and a woman found her lost coin (v. 9).

> [24] **"'For this son of mine was dead and is alive again; he was lost and is found.' So they began to celebrate."**

The words *dead* and *lost* reflect the sad record of the son's days of rebellion, but they are overshadowed by the joyous words *alive again* and *found*. The son had been spiritually dead because of the sinful lifestyle he had pursued. The message of Jesus' parable is that an enthusiastic "welcome home" is always available for each one of us through the grace and mercy of our loving heavenly Father.

JESUS RAISES LAZARUS FROM THE DEAD (JOHN 11:20-27, 38-44)

Establishing the Groundwork

As noted in the "Establishing the Groundwork" section of the previous study, Jesus' ministry in the territory known as Perea (east of the Jordan River) was interrupted by news of the illness of his friend Lazarus (John 11:3). Jesus, however, did not immediately travel to Bethany, where Lazarus and his sisters Martha and Mary lived. He waited two days before announcing to his disciples that they were returning to Judea (John 11:7). The disciples were quite concerned about such a move and reminded Jesus of how the Jews had wanted to stone him the last time he was there (for the Feast of Tabernacles).

Jesus then told the disciples that Lazarus had "fallen asleep" and that he was going to "wake him up" (John 11:11). When the disciples expressed relief that Lazarus' condition seemed to be improving, Jesus plainly told them that Lazarus was dead. Thomas responded with a kind of despairing faith, "Let us also go, that we may die with him" (John 11:16). But this journey to Judea would mark the triumph of life, not death. As Jesus had told his disciples earlier, "This sickness will not end in death. No, it is for God's glory so that God's Son may be glorified through it" (John 11:4).

Examining the Text

I. Jesus and Martha (John 11:20-27)
A. Martha's Confrontation (vv. 20-22)

20 When Martha heard that Jesus was coming, she went out to meet him, but Mary stayed at home.

When Martha heard that Jesus had arrived, *she went out to meet him.* This is in keeping with what we know of Martha from the Gospels, for she is depicted elsewhere as an energetic, practical person. Her zeal for being a good hostess when Jesus came to visit resulted in his gentle rebuke found in Luke 10:38-42. John 12:2 recounts a dinner given in Jesus' honor at which "Martha served." By contrast, *Mary* seems to have been more reserved and contemplative. Recall her choice to sit at Jesus' feet during the aforementioned visit (Luke 10:39). Here she *stayed at home,* possibly unaware that Jesus had arrived.

21 "Lord," Martha said to Jesus, "if you had been here, my brother would not have died.

Martha appears to be scolding Jesus, reminiscent of how she had approached him when he came to visit earlier (Luke 10:40). *If* only Jesus had come sooner, Lazarus's life would have been spared! Yet we must not be too hard on Martha. Words spoken in grief may seem harsh or indignant, but they only reflect the frustration or anguish of the grieving person. Martha's words are similar to many who question, "Where was God?" in response to a tragedy. Her words, however, are spoken not just in response to a death but to a death that must have seemed totally preventable.

²² "But I know that even now God will give you whatever you ask."

At the same time, it is important to acknowledge the element of trust in Martha's words. There was in what she said a combination of criticism and tribute, of indignation and faith. Martha simply did not understand why Jesus delayed coming to Bethany. She was hurt and disappointed. And yet, she probably knew that Jesus had previously raised individuals from the dead, including the widow's son at Nain and the daughter of Jairus (Luke 7:11-17; 8:49-56). Martha did not presume to ask Jesus to raise Lazarus from the dead, but perhaps her words hinted at the possibility of that very thing occurring.

B. Jesus' Comfort (v. 23)

²³ Jesus said to her, "Your brother will rise again."

Jesus promised that Lazarus would *rise again*, but at this point he did not say when. Perhaps he kept this initial statement obscure in order to test Martha's faith.

C. Martha's Limited Faith (v. 24)

²⁴ Martha answered, "I know he will rise again in the resurrection at the last day."

Martha held to the common Jewish belief in a *resurrection at the last day*. This was based on certain Old Testament passages (Job 19:25-27; Psalm 49:15; Isaiah 26:19; Daniel 12:2), although the Old Testament is not as explicit as is the New Testament in its teachings about life after death. (This shows the impact of Jesus' resurrection.) It is also possible that Martha was testing Jesus' initial reply, hoping that it conveyed more than just a reference to the final resurrection.

D. Jesus' Declaration (vv. 25, 26)

²⁵ Jesus said to her, "I am the resurrection and the life. He who believes in me will live, even though he dies;

Jesus' response came in the form of one of his most dramatic "I am" statements: *I am the resurrection and the life.* Resurrection is not to be thought of in terms of a concept or a belief; rather, it is, like truth (John 14:6), to be found in the person of Jesus alone. He is the ultimate source of life, *even though* someone *dies*. To the one who *believes in* him, death is of no consequence. This "I am" declaration is one of seven recorded by John in his Gospel (6:35; 8:12; 10:7, 9; 10:11, 14; 11:25; 14:6; 15:1, 5). It is in keeping with John's declaration at the beginning of his Gospel concerning Jesus: "In him was life, and that life was the light of men" (John 1:4).

[26] **". . . and whoever lives and believes in me will never die. Do you believe this?"**

This statement served as an even greater challenge to Martha's faith. Whereas Jesus' declaration in the previous verse promised a resurrection of the body, the promise that *whoever lives and believes in* Jesus *will never die* seems to point to the "second death"—the eternal judgment of Hell—from which one is delivered through faith in Jesus (Revelation 20:11-15).

Jesus had clearly declared himself to be the Lord over death. But then came the question to Martha that each person must face concerning Jesus and his claims: *Do you believe this?*

E. Martha's Confession of Faith (v. 27)

[27] **"Yes, Lord," she told him, "I believe that you are the Christ, the Son of God, who was to come into the world."**

Martha's answer came in the form of her own "Good Confession" of faith in Jesus as *the Christ, the Son of God*. We sometimes think of Mary as being the more spiritual of the two sisters. She was the one who sat at Jesus' feet to learn from him while Martha busied herself with preparations. Later she was the one who poured perfume on Jesus' feet (John 12:1-3). Yet for all of her concern about the material needs of life, Martha had developed an exemplary faith in Jesus. She was not sure she understood the statements Jesus had just uttered, nor did she ask for an explanation or try to unravel their meaning. She simply expressed her own trust that whatever he meant was true and that whatever he did concerning her brother would be right.

Jesus then requested to see Mary. When she came to Jesus, she fell at his feet and expressed the same sentiments Martha had regarding Jesus' failure to come in time (v. 32). The Jews who had come with Mary were overcome with grief as she wept. Moved to tears himself (John 11:35), Jesus went to the place where Lazarus had been buried (v. 38).

II. Jesus and Lazarus (John 11:38-44)
A. Jesus' Command (v. 38-40)

38 Jesus, once more deeply moved, came to the tomb. It was a cave with a stone laid across the entrance.

Jesus seems to have experienced an additional sense of grief as he *came to the tomb* of Lazarus. The *cave* used for the burial was probably in the side of a hill. A large, flat slab of *stone* was usually cut into a circular shape, resembling a wheel. This was rolled *across the entrance* to close the tomb (or rolled aside to open it). A groove wide enough to match the thickness of the stone was cut in the ground to provide a "track" for the stone when it closed the entrance.

39 "Take away the stone," he said.
"But, Lord," said Martha, the sister of the dead man, "by this time there is a bad odor, for he has been there four days."

Martha, practical person that she was, objected to Jesus' command to *take away the stone*. Since effective embalming was not practiced in Palestine, the body would have started to decompose almost immediately. The result of *four days* of that decomposition would be a very unpleasant *odor*. To open the tomb now would be an embarrassment and would probably result in a fresh outburst of grief.

40 Then Jesus said, "Did I not tell you that if you believed, you would see the glory of God?"

This specific language about seeing *the glory of God* is not recorded in the account of Jesus' earlier conversation with Martha, but he may have said more than is recorded. Perhaps he was simply summarizing what he had told her. It appears that Martha was still experiencing an inner struggle between the reality of her brother's death and the promise of life that Jesus had spoken.

B. Jesus' Prayer (vv. 41, 42)

41 So they took away the stone. Then Jesus looked up and said, "Father, I thank you that you have heard me.

The *stone* was taken away as Jesus had asked. Then Jesus *looked up* to his *Father* in heaven and gave thanks that his prayer had been *heard*, which here implies both *heard* and *answered*. Jesus was certain of the miracle that was about to take place.

42 "I knew that you always hear me, but I said this for the benefit of the people standing here, that they may believe that you sent me."

Jesus' audible prayer was *for the benefit* of those who were hearing him. If it was clear to them that the miracle was performed through the power of God, they would be more likely to *believe* that God had *sent* Jesus.

C. Jesus' Miracle (vv. 43, 44)

⁴³ When he had said this, Jesus called in a loud voice, "Lazarus, come out!"

Like the giving of thanks for answered prayer (v. 41), the *loud voice* was for the benefit of the people present. They heard Jesus speak, and they would see Lazarus obey.

⁴⁴ The dead man came out, his hands and feet wrapped with strips of linen, and a cloth around his face.
Jesus said to them, "Take off the grave clothes and let him go."

The dead man came out. Death, the "last enemy" (1 Corinthians 15:26), is powerless before him who is "the resurrection and the life." The suggestion that Lazarus's being wrapped with strips of linen would prevent movement is overstated. Obviously, the wrapping would not be that much of an obstacle. In any case, no *grave clothes* can hold the person of one in the grave when Jesus cries, "Come out!"

Some who witnessed this miracle were led to put their faith in Jesus (John 11:45). But when the Pharisees learned of it, they became even more determined in their hostility toward Jesus (vv. 46-53). How tragic that a miracle that gave someone new life produced in some people more intense hatred, and a desire for the death, of the miracle worker!

JESUS AND THE RICH YOUNG RULER (MARK 10:17-27)

Establishing the Groundwork

Because of the increasing antagonism toward him following the raising of Lazarus, Jesus "withdrew to a region near the desert, to a village called Ephraim, where he stayed with his disciples" (John 11:54). This village is mentioned nowhere else in the New Testament; it has been identified by archaeologists with a village located on the road from Samaria to Jericho, about fifteen miles from Jericho. It is uncertain how long Jesus remained in this territory before resuming his ministry in Perea.

The tenth chapter of Mark records an interesting variety of situations that Jesus encountered during his later ministry in Perea. As usual, crowds of people were gathering to hear him teach (v. 1) when some Pharisees approached him with a question concerning the sensitive issue of divorce (v. 2). Like the expert in the law whose question about eternal life eventually led to Jesus' parable of the good Samaritan, these Pharisees "tested" Jesus in an effort to place him in an embarrassing or controversial position and thereby stifle his popularity.

At a later time, people were bringing little children to Jesus so he could touch them and bless them. When the disciples rebuked those who did this, Jesus became "indignant" (v. 14). He emphasized the importance of receiving God's kingdom like a little child (v. 15).

There were also occasions when an individual could approach Jesus with a question. This was the desire of the young man whose encounter with Jesus is described in the following passage.

Examining the Text

I. Jesus Instructs a Seeker (Mark 10:17-22)
A. The Sincere Request (v. 17)

17 As Jesus started on his way, a man ran up to him and fell on his knees before him. "Good teacher," he asked, "what must I do to inherit eternal life?"

It appears that this incident followed Jesus' blessing of the children (Mark 10:16). *Jesus started on his way*, a way that at this point included the eventual arrival at Jerusalem where Jesus had said he would be killed. Later in this chapter we are told how alarmed the disciples and other followers of Jesus were at what lay ahead (vv. 32-34).

Nothing about the man who approached Jesus on this occasion is mentioned in this verse. Later Mark describes him as having "great wealth" (v. 22). Matthew's account says that he was a young man as well as one with great wealth (Matthew 19:22). Luke records that he was "a certain ruler" (Luke 18:18) and also uses the words "great wealth" to describe him (v. 23). Thus, since this man's name is not given in any account, he is generally known simply as the "rich young ruler."

One is immediately impressed with this man's enthusiasm. He *ran up to* Jesus, then *fell on his knees before him*. He was eager yet respectful, even reverent. His question is similar to the one raised by the expert in the law in Luke 10:25: *Good teacher, . . . what must I do to inherit eternal life?*

B. Jesus' Reply (vv. 18, 19)

18 "Why do you call me good?" Jesus answered. "No one is good—except God alone.

Jesus began his response to the young man by challenging him to think about the language he had just used to describe Jesus. What did he mean by calling Jesus *good?* Was he merely trying to flatter Jesus? Did he mean that Jesus was good in spite of some faults, as many people are? Or did he mean that Jesus was divine, good as *God alone* is good. It can be very easy to use "religious" language without any depth of understanding.

19 "You know the commandments: 'Do not murder, do not commit adultery, do not steal, do not give false testimony, do not defraud, honor your father and mother.'"

Jesus cited the last six of the *commandments* within the Ten Commandments. These summarize God's instructions concerning human relationships. (The first four Commandments, not cited by Jesus, include God's instructions for man's relationship with him.) The command *do not defraud* may be a summation of the Tenth Commandment concerning coveting. It may also refer to the teaching in such portions of the law as Deuteronomy 24:14, 15, which warns that wealth should not come at the expense of the poor. (This would be especially relevant to a rich person.) According to Matthew's account, Jesus also cited the command to "love your neighbor as yourself" (Matthew 19:19).

Jesus' response to the young man was similar to what he told the expert in the law who had inquired about eternal life (Luke 10:25-28). Until the church was established, the Old Testament law was still in effect.

C. The Sincere Claim (v. 20)

20 "Teacher," he declared, "all these I have kept since I was a boy."

The young man's answer is reminiscent of Paul's description of himself prior to his conversion as being "faultless" regarding "legalistic righteousness" (Philippians 3:6). Outwardly he may well have been a "good moral man." But it is not likely that he had any idea of the deeper meaning that Jesus gave to the law in the Sermon on the Mount (Matthew 5:21-48). In any case, such an answer in the presence of the "good teacher" sounds rather arrogant! But he was apparently sincere and perhaps not as arrogant as he sounds here. Matthew tells us he recognized he was still missing something. "What do I still lack?" he asked (Matthew 19:20).

D. Jesus' Challenge (v. 21)

²¹ Jesus looked at him and loved him. "One thing you lack," he said. "Go, sell everything you have and give to the poor, and you will have treasure in heaven. Then come, follow me."

Obviously Jesus loves everyone, so Mark's notation that *Jesus looked at him and loved him* must indicate a special compassion for this man. He saw this young man's heart and knew that a barrier existed between him and God and therefore the eternal life he sought. He had another god—his wealth. The solution was a radical step: *sell everything* he had and *give* his wealth *to the poor*. This man's *treasure in heaven* could be laid up only as his treasure on earth was laid down. This does not mean that every follower of Jesus must do this, but this young man had to in order to find what he desired. Jesus was giving a personal prescription here, not a general command to all. At the same time, he challenges all of us to consider where our hearts truly are (Mathew 6:19-21; 1 Timothy 6:17-19). Anything we put before God in our hearts is an idol and must be dealt with in the same decisive manner in which Jesus was telling the rich young ruler to deal with his wealth.

E. The Sad Response (v. 22)

²² At this the man's face fell. He went away sad, because he had great wealth.

The young man was afraid he would be unhappy if he gave up all he had, but he was unhappy because he did not. His real problem was not that *he had great wealth*, but that his great wealth had him. He had the right desire, but was unwilling to make the right investment.

We have no further information in Scripture about the rich young ruler. We do not know whether he ever changed his outlook and decided that he would do what Jesus commanded. But it is worth noting that Jesus did not pursue him or change his terms. The man *went away sad*, yet we can be sure there was a greater sadness in the heart of Jesus.

II. Jesus Instructs the Disciples (Mark 10:23-27)
A. The Problem of Riches (vv. 23-25)

²³ Jesus looked around and said to his disciples, "How hard it is for the rich to enter the kingdom of God!"

We can only imagine the reaction of Jesus' *disciples* at this turn of events. They were probably shocked and speechless. How could Jesus ask so much?

How could he let this man just walk away? Will he ask the same of them at some point? Aware of their lack of understanding, Jesus proceeded to instruct them on *how hard it is for the rich to enter the kingdom of God.*

24, 25 *The disciples were amazed at his words. But Jesus said again, "Children, how hard it is to enter the kingdom of God! It is easier for a camel to go through the eye of a needle than for a rich man to enter the kingdom of God."*

The disciples held to the common view of that time that riches constituted evidence of God's approval of one's life. Jesus then noted *how hard it is* for anyone *to enter the kingdom of God,* a statement similar to his teaching in the Sermon on the Mount (Matthew 7:13, 14). But it is especially so for those who are rich. There is nothing wrong with wealth in and of itself. The problem with wealth is that it often keeps people from following God's instruction to trust in him. *A rich man* has so large a stake in this world that it can be very hard for him to think beyond it and to consider preparations for the world to come.

To further highlight this truth, Jesus used a hyperbole—an exaggerated statement. Some have suggested that an ancient city wall may have had a small gate called the needle's eye, through which a camel might pass with some difficulty, but only without any baggage or cargo. Even if such a gate existed, however (and it is questionable that it did), this would not fit with Jesus' lesson here. He was talking about something completely impossible with men (v. 27), and he emphasized that impossibility with this illustration of a huge *camel* going *through* the tiny *eye of a needle.*

B. The Disciples' Amazement (v. 26)

26 *The disciples were even more amazed, and said to each other, "Who then can be saved?"*

The *disciples* immediately understood the implications of Jesus' illustration and *were even more amazed.* Some of the most honored religious leaders were wealthy men. If it was impossible for a rich man to be *saved,* what hope was there for the less favored?

C. Jesus' Answer (v. 27)

27 *Jesus looked at them and said, "With man this is impossible, but not with God; all things are possible with God."*

It is not impossible for a rich man to enter the kingdom of God. *With man this is impossible,* but salvation is always a gift of God's grace, whether it is received by the rich or the poor. Poverty is not a key to Heaven, and riches are not a door to Hell. One may have great wealth and love God more than all, or he may have very little and love it more than God. It is the condition of the heart and not the state of the bank account that makes the difference.

The rich young ruler sounds a warning to people who want a Christian faith that will not upset their values or change their worldly lifestyles. Jesus does not command every seeking sinner to sell everything he has and give away the money, but he does put his finger of conviction on anything with which we are being dishonest and that comes between ourselves and him.

JESUS' TEACHING ABOUT GREATNESS (MARK 10:35-45)

Establishing the Groundwork

By this point, Jesus' Perean ministry was nearing its end. Mark 10:32 notes that Jesus and the disciples "were on their way up to Jerusalem." The verse also describes the disciples as "astonished" and others who followed as "afraid." They probably recalled the danger that had confronted Jesus the last time he was in Jerusalem for the Feast of Tabernacles. Again (for the third time according to Mark's account) Jesus explained that, yes, danger, in fact death, awaited him in Jerusalem. But death would not be a conclusion for Jesus; it would merely set the stage for his greatest miracle—his own resurrection (Mark 10:32-34).

Following the record of Jesus' first two explicit predictions of his death, Mark notes how the disciples misunderstood what Jesus was saying (Mark 8:31-33; 9:30-32). The second prediction was followed by an argument among the disciples as to who among them would be the greatest (Mark 9:34). After the third prediction came yet another controversy involving greatness, but it was sparked by the request of two of the disciples.

Examining the Text

I. Request (Mark 10:35-37)
A. The Presumption (v. 35)

35 Then James and John, the sons of Zebedee, came to him. "Teacher," they said, "we want you to do for us whatever we ask."

In an earlier study, we saw how *James and John, the sons of Zebedee*, were called to leave their fishing business to follow Jesus, and how (along with Peter) they became part of Jesus' "inner circle," accompanying him during the raising of Jairus's daughter and the transfiguration. Apparently they felt close enough to Jesus to make this rather bold request: *to do for us whatever we ask.*

B. The Petition (vv. 36, 37)

36 "What do you want me to do for you?" he asked.

Since Jesus "knew what was in a man" (John 2:25), he knew what James and John were about to ask and might have reprimanded them from the outset. But it was better for their instruction (and ours) to have them state their request. When we see what they wanted, their reluctance to put it into words is understandable.

37 They replied, "Let one of us sit at your right and the other at your left in your glory."

The seats at the *right* and the *left* of a king's throne were the places of highest honor, the places for the king's most trusted and respected aides. Despite all that Jesus had said to this point about the spiritual nature of his kingdom, the disciples were still thinking in terms of a physical and political realm. Recall that Peter had already been promised an important role in Jesus' kingdom (Matthew 16:17-19); perhaps James and John felt that, as part of the "inner circle," it was "their turn."

It is important to note that the parallel account in Matthew adds that James and John's mother came to Jesus (even kneeling before him) with this request (Matthew 20:20, 21). This woman, whose name was Salome, appears to be the sister of Jesus' mother Mary (comparing John 19:25; Matthew 27:56; and Mark 15:40), making James and John cousins to Jesus. Perhaps the two disciples devised this plan by which their mother (Jesus' aunt) would serve as their spokesperson, thinking he would be more apt to grant their request if it came from her.

II. Response (Mark 10:38-41)
A. Jesus' Challenge (vv. 38-40)

38 "You don't know what you are asking," Jesus said. "Can you drink the cup I drink or be baptized with the baptism I am baptized with?"

The cup and *the baptism* were figurative expressions for the suffering and death that Jesus faced in the near future. In Gethsemane, Jesus prayed, "Take this cup from me" (Mark 14:36), referring to the suffering that lay ahead (see also John 18:11). On another occasion, he used baptism to describe his suffering (Luke 12:50). Jesus was asking these aspiring leaders if they were willing to bear the consequences that would be faced by those who identified themselves with him and his cause.

> *39 "We can," they answered.*
> *Jesus said to them, "You will drink the cup I drink and be baptized with the baptism I am baptized with,*

Jesus' promise that James and John would *drink the cup* he drank and *be baptized with* his *baptism* did not mean that their experiences would be identical to Christ's, either in extent or significance. But they did suffer for Christ's sake. James later died at the hands of King Herod (Agrippa I) as the first of the apostles to be martyred (Acts 12:1, 2). John suffered imprisonment and beatings (Acts 5:17, 18, 40), and near the end of his life he was banished to the island of Patmos (Revelation 1:9).

> *40 ". . . but to sit at my right or left is not for me to grant. These places belong to those for whom they have been prepared."*

The places of honor to which James and John aspired were not the kind that could be given simply to fulfill a request. Probably they had no concept of the multiplied millions across the centuries who would experience some aspect of the "cup" and the "baptism" that Jesus described. When we think of some of the heroic souls who have been "faithful, even to the point of death" (Revelation 2:10), we must pause as we consider who might be thought "most worthy" of the homage that James and John sought. When we remember Jesus' teaching that "many who are first will be last, and the last first" (Mark 10:31), we must acknowledge that the choice of who should receive such an honor is best left with the Father (Matthew 20:23).

B. The Disciples' Confrontation (v. 41)

> *41 When the ten heard about this, they became indignant with James and John.*

By its very nature, the conversation that James, John, and Salome had with Jesus must have been in private. Yet the other *ten* disciples somehow learned about it or perhaps overheard portions of the conversation. Their indignation *with James and John* reveals the content of their own hearts. Earlier all of the twelve had argued over which of them was the greatest (Mark 9:33, 34). Most likely the ten were indignant because James and John had "beaten them to the draw" in getting to Jesus first.

III. Reproof (Mark 10:42-45)
A. The World's Way (v. 42)

42 Jesus called them together and said, "You know that those who are regarded as rulers of the Gentiles lord it over them, and their high officials exercise authority over them.

At this point, the disciples were acting like products of the world around them. Greatness in the secular Gentile culture (among the Romans in particular) meant having a position of authority and exercising it by giving orders to subordinates. The mindset that defines greatness according to power, perks, and possessions is still very much a part of the way the secular world thinks.

B. The Kingdom Way (vv. 43-45)

43 "Not so with you. Instead, whoever wants to become great among you must be your servant,

Not so with you. With these words, Jesus set before his followers (then and now) a totally different concept of greatness in the kingdom he came to establish. His kingdom is "not of this world" (John 18:36), and neither is his understanding of greatness. Greatness in Jesus' kingdom comes only from cultivating the heart of a *servant.* It is not determined by how much honor one can receive, but by how much help one can render.

44 ". . . and whoever wants to be first must be slave of all.

Again the importance of greatness through service is emphasized, but here Jesus used the word *slave* rather than *servant* to indicate the degree to which his followers must give serving others the highest priority. Any reward that comes will be the unsought result of that service.

45 "For even the Son of Man did not come to be served, but to serve, and to give his life as a ransom for many."

With the words *even the Son of Man*, Jesus showed that he was willing to do more than just define true greatness. He himself remains the prime example of his teaching. Jesus had left his position at the right hand of the Father, not *to be served* by others, but *to serve* the entire human race. His was no token service of merely going through the motions just to impress people. Jesus came *to give his life as a ransom for many*—the perfect sacrifice given at the cross to die for imperfect humanity. There is no greater model of servanthood than this.

Once more, however, the disciples failed to grasp what Jesus meant. Again they seemed to miss completely the ominous reference to his approaching death. Even at the Last Supper, on the night before Jesus would give his life as a ransom, they were still quarreling about who would be the greatest in his kingdom (Luke 22:24-27).

JESUS AND ZACCHAEUS (LUKE 19:1-10)

Establishing the Groundwork

As Jesus continued to make his way toward Jerusalem and his crucifixion, he crossed the Jordan River, re-entering the territory of Judea. A few miles west of the Jordan, he came to the city of Jericho. As in other locations, great crowds accompanied him and his disciples. In Jericho Jesus gave sight to two blind men (Matthew 20:29-34), though Mark (10:46-52) and Luke (18:35-43) mention only one man, whom Mark identifies as Bartimaeus. Word of this miracle quickly spread throughout the city, increasing the size of the crowd that followed Jesus and probably hoped to see another miracle.

Another miracle did occur that day in Jericho; and while it was not the kind that gained a public following, it was the kind that reflected why Jesus came to our world and why he was determined to go to Jerusalem.

Examining the Text

I. The Setting (Luke 19:1, 2)
A. The Place (v. 1)

¹ Jesus entered Jericho and was passing through.

The city of *Jericho* was located approximately twelve miles northeast of Jerusalem. More than eight hundred feet below sea level and at one of the lowest points in the Jordan Valley, Jericho enjoyed a warm and pleasant climate. It was known as "the City of Palms" (Deuteronomy 34:3). Jericho was also an important point on the trade route that ran to and from Jerusalem.

B. The Person (v. 2)

² A man was there by the name of Zacchaeus; he was a chief tax collector and was wealthy.

The term *chief tax collector* is used only here in the New Testament. It probably designates someone in charge of a district, with other tax collectors under him. The intense contempt in which tax collectors were held by the general populace was noted previously (see the comments on Luke 3:12 in chapter 4).

Given Jericho's location on a major trade route, *Zacchaeus* and his subordinates were probably able to levy some measure of tax on the various goods that passed through the city. That he was *wealthy* becomes even more apparent when one reads of the significant amount of his riches with which he was willing to part (v. 8).

II. Zacchaeus Meets Jesus (Luke 19:3-7)
A. Being Seen (vv. 3, 4)

3 He wanted to see who Jesus was, but being a short man he could not, because of the crowd.

Perhaps Zacchaeus had heard of Jesus' reputation for befriending "tax collectors and sinners." Possibly Zacchaeus had reached a point in his life where his riches had left him feeling spiritually empty. Or perhaps he had heard Jesus was coming and was following the *crowd* out of curiosity. But the crowd posed a problem for Zacchaeus, who was *a short man*. And the general dislike for him made it improbable that anyone would step aside and give him a place closer to the front.

4 So he ran ahead and climbed a sycamore-fig tree to see him, since Jesus was coming that way.

One has to give credit to Zacchaeus for being creative and resourceful. Knowing he would never make it to the front of the crowd, he *ran ahead* of everyone and *climbed a sycamore-fig tree* so he could *see* Jesus when he passed by. This tree was a wide, sturdy tree with low limbs that allowed even a short man like Zacchaeus to climb into it. It was also well-known for the shade it provided from the heat.

Also worth noting is Zacchaeus's willingness to cast aside the dignity that his office and his wealth afforded him in order to see Jesus. Surely many would be quick to ridicule a chief tax collector perched in a tree like some curious little boy.

B. Being Known (vv. 5, 6)

5 When Jesus reached the spot, he looked up and said to him, "Zacchaeus, come down immediately. I must stay at your house today."

Zacchaeus probably intended to get a look at Jesus without Jesus noticing him.

He did not consider the fact that Jesus knew full well what Zacchaeus had done and where he was. How surprised Zacchaeus must have been when Jesus *looked up* and addressed him by name! Even more stunning was Jesus' sense of urgency in wanting to spend time with Zacchaeus. Notice the words: *immediately, must, today*. Jesus knew that Zacchaeus would welcome him into his *house*, but would hesitate to offer an invitation.

⁶ So he came down at once and welcomed him gladly.

Zacchaeus responded to Jesus' urgency with his own: *he came down at once*. He *welcomed him gladly*—yet another illustration of how Jesus was the "friend of tax collectors and 'sinners'" (Luke 7:34).

C. Being Judged (v. 7)

⁷ All the people saw this and began to mutter, "He has gone to be the guest of a 'sinner.'"

The people in the crowd responded to Jesus' actions toward Zacchaeus just as the Pharisees had done on previous occasions when Jesus welcomed social outcasts. Wasn't he aware of Zacchaeus's position and reputation? How could he socialize with such a man? But Jesus never permitted his agenda to be determined by the reactions of others. He had associated with tax collectors before; in fact, one of his twelve disciples had been a tax collector when Jesus called him (Matthew 9:9). Yes, the people were right about Zacchaeus; he was indeed a *sinner*—but so was each of them.

III. Zacchaeus Follows Jesus (Luke 19:8-10)
A. A Changed Man (vv. 8, 9)

⁸ But Zacchaeus stood up and said to the Lord, "Look, Lord! Here and now I give half of my possessions to the poor, and if I have cheated anybody out of anything, I will pay back four times the amount."

We are not told the contents of what was said in the home of Zacchaeus; we know only its impact on him. At some point, he was apparently challenged to follow a new Master. He responded by making a radical promise to the Lord. Once more a sense of urgency was present: *here and now* he would give half of his possessions to the poor and offer a quadruple repayment to anyone he had cheated. Such a fourfold return went far beyond the requirements of the law of Moses, which stipulated that one restore twenty percent more (one-fifth) than he had wrongfully taken (Leviticus 6:1-5; Numbers 5:5-7).

It is easy to express repentance in words. To follow up with actions is more difficult. True sorrow for sin manifests itself in a change of direction that is reflected in a desire to make amends for one's wrong actions wherever possible.

Zacchaeus went from being a taker to being a giver. Needless to say, the contrast in response to Jesus between him and the rich young ruler is striking.

> *⁹ Jesus said to him, "Today salvation has come to this house, because this man, too, is a son of Abraham.*

Jesus' reference to Zacchaeus's *house* perhaps highlighted the impact of his decision upon all his relationships. His wife and children (if he had any), his relatives, his employees, his friends—all could not help but notice the difference in Zacchaeus's life from this day forward. Jesus had provided physical sight to the blind men in Jericho; spiritual sight was the result of Zacchaeus's encounter with Jesus.

Jesus described Zacchaeus as a *son of Abraham*. Certainly he was that by birth and was the beneficiary of Jesus' ministry to "the lost sheep of Israel" (Matthew 15:24). But now, by committing his life in faith to Jesus, Zacchaeus had become a spiritual son of Abraham (Galatians 3:7, 29). Observe that at this point, Jesus could declare *salvation* for someone whenever he deemed it appropriate. This was not a "conversion" such as what we see described in the book of Acts, because the New Covenant did not become effective until after the death of Jesus on which it is based (Hebrews 9:15-17).

B. A Compassionate Savior (v. 10)

> *¹⁰ "For the Son of Man came to seek and to save what was lost."*

This was Jesus' explanation of the urgency he had earlier expressed: "I must stay at your house today" (v. 5). It is also a summation of his purpose for coming into the world. The picture is that of a good and faithful shepherd who leaves his comfortable surroundings and goes out into dangerous and rugged places to seek his lost sheep. It is a theme that Jesus used at other times to describe his mission (Luke 15:3-7; John 10:11-18). It is the same mission he has given to his church.

How to Say It

ABRAHAM. *Ay*-bruh-ham.

AGRIPPA. Uh-*grip*-puh.

ARCHAEOLOGIST. ar-key-*ah*-luh-jist.

BARTIMAEUS. *Bar*-tih-*me*-us (strong accent on *me*).

BETHANY. *Beth*-uh-nee.

CAROB. *care*-ub.

EPHRAIM. *Ee*-fray-im.

GENTILE. *Jen*-tile.

GETHSEMANE. Geth-*sem*-uh-nee (*g* as in *get*).

HEROD. *Hair*-ud.

HYPERBOLE. high-*per*-buh-lee.

JAIRUS. *Jye*-rus or *Jay*-ih-rus.

JERICHO. *Jair*-ih-co.

JERUSALEM. Juh-*roo*-suh-lem.

JOSEPHUS. Jo-*see*-fus.

JUDEA. Joo-*dee*-uh.

LAZARUS. *Laz*-uh-rus.

MOSES. *Mo*-zes or *Mo*-zez.

NAIN. Nane.

PATMOS. *Pat*-muss.

PEREA. Peh-*ree*-uh.

PHARISEES. *Fair*-ih-seez.

PRODIGAL. *prah*-dih-gul.

SALOME. Suh-*lo*-me.

SAMARIA. Suh-*mare*-ee-uh.

SAMARITAN. Suh-*mare*-uh-tun.

SYCAMORE. *sih*-cuh-more.

SYNOPTICS. Sin-*op*-ticks.

TABERNACLES. *ta*-ber-*na*-kulz (strong accent on *ta*).

TRANSFIGURATION. tranz-fih-gyuh-*ray*-shun.

ZACCHAEUS. Zack-*key*-us.

ZEBEDEE. *Zeb*-eh-dee.

The last week of Jesus' life

Bethany
- Jesus is anointed

SAT

Mount of Olives and Jerusalem
- The Triumphal Entry

On the road between Bethany and Jerusalem
- Jesus curses the fig tree

Jerusalem
- Jesus cleanses the Temple

SUN

MON

On the road between Bethany and Jerusalem
- Jesus and the disciples discuss the withered fig tree

Jerusalem
- Jesus' authority is questioned by the chief priests and the elders
- Jesus teaches in the temple using parables and answers questions

Jerusalem
- Chief priests, scribes, and elders plot against Jesus
- Judas agrees to betray Jesus

TUES

WED

Jerusalem, the Upper Room
- Preparation for the Passover meal
- The last supper with the disciples
- Jesus washes His disciples' feet
- Judas identified as the traitor
- The Lord's Supper instituted
- Jesus comforts and prays for the disciples and later believers

Jerusalem
- Trials before Annas, Caiaphas, and the Sanhedrin
- Trials before Pilate and Herod; torture by Roman soldiers

THURS

Golgotha, outside Jerusalem
- Jesus' crucifixion and death

FRI

Joseph's Tomb
- Jesus' burial

Gethsemane, on the Mount of Olives
- Jesus prays in the garden
- Jesus' betrayal and arrest

Chapter 11

The Early Days of Passion Week

John 12:1-8; Matthew 21:1-13;
Mark 11:27-33; 12:28-34; Matthew 25:31-46

JESUS IS ANOINTED BY MARY (JOHN 12:1-8)

Establishing the Groundwork

This chapter's studies bring us to the final week of Jesus' earthly life—often referred to as "Passion Week." The first event to be considered actually occurred "six days before the Passover" (John 12:1), on a Sabbath, since the "next day" (v. 12) was the day on which the triumphal entry took place (the first day of Passion Week). The setting was a dinner that had been prepared for Jesus and the disciples. Needless to say, this was an extremely tense time. Speculation ran high as to whether Jesus would attend the upcoming Passover (John 11:56). The chief priests and Pharisees, whose hostility toward Jesus had been steadily rising, "had given orders that if anyone found out where Jesus was, he should report it so that they might arrest him" (v. 57).

In the midst of this tension, Mary of Bethany, whose devotion to Jesus has already been noted (Luke 10:39), expressed her love for Jesus and perhaps her anxiety for his safety in a very dramatic way.

Examining the Text

I. An Act of Devotion (John 12:1-3)
A. Gathering with Friends (vv. 1, 2)

¹ Six days before the Passover, Jesus arrived at Bethany, where Lazarus lived, whom Jesus had raised from the dead.

John specifically mentions three different Passovers in his Gospel (2:13, 23; 6:4; and this one). This third *Passover* is the most significant, because it was during this feast that Jesus would be crucified. Indeed, his primary purpose for coming to Jerusalem at this precise time was so that he might die in fulfillment of prophecy and accomplish a spiritual deliverance from the bondage of sin.

Six days before the Passover, Jesus came to *Bethany*, where his close friends Martha, Mary, and Lazarus lived. This village was located about two miles southeast of Jerusalem on the eastern slope of the Mount of

Olives. The previous chapter of John's Gospel (11) records how Jesus *raised* Lazarus *from the dead.*

> *² Here a dinner was given in Jesus' honor. Martha served, while Lazarus was among those reclining at the table with him.*

In both Matthew's and Mark's accounts of this occasion, we find that it took place in the house of a man called Simon the Leper (Matthew 26:6; Mark 14:3), who had most likely been healed by Jesus. Even though this *dinner* was not at her house, *Martha served.* This is certainly in keeping with her tendency to be involved with such matters (Luke 10:38, 40), but the fact that she would do this at another person's house may indicate that she was respected both in Bethany and among Jesus' followers. This dinner would have been quite a testimonial to Jesus' miracle-working power, with both a former leper and *Lazarus,* a former dead man, present!

B. Gesture of Honor (v. 3)

> *³ Then Mary took about a pint of pure nard, an expensive perfume; she poured it on Jesus' feet and wiped his feet with her hair. And the house was filled with the fragrance of the perfume.*

Matthew and Mark relate this anointing in the midst of their narratives concerning the observation of the Passover (Matthew 26:6-13; Mark 14:3-9). Apparently John provides the chronological arrangement of events, while Matthew and Mark seem to place the anointing in such a way as to achieve a certain dramatic effect. When we compare how the Jewish leaders assembled to plot against Jesus (Matthew 26:3-5; Mark 14:1, 2) with the reason for the assembly at Simon's house (a dinner "given in Jesus' honor," according to John 12:2), the contrast is quite startling.

It was customary to take some oil and anoint the heads of guests when they arrived in someone's home (Luke 7:46), but this gesture of *Mary* is extraordinary in more than one respect. Since this was not her home, Mary must have come prepared with the *perfume.* It is described as *about a pint of pure nard* and as *expensive* (since it was pure). Nard (or spikenard) was the name of both a plant that grew in India and the fragrant oil it yielded.

Whereas John states that Mary poured the perfume on Jesus' feet, Matthew (Matthew 26:7) and Mark (Mark 14:3) record that Jesus' head was anointed. Evidently Mary did both. Perhaps she came to anoint Jesus' head as was customary, then saw that his feet were dirty from his travels and poured perfume on them as well. Like the woman who anointed Jesus in the home of Simon the Pharisee (Luke 7:38), perhaps the extent of Mary's action was spontaneous.

Having no towel to wipe Jesus' *feet*, she used her *hair*. For a woman to loosen her hair (which Mary likely would have done) in mixed company was considered immodest, as was noted in the study of Luke 7:36-50 (see chapter 7). But just as Mary defied expectations earlier when Jesus visited the home of Martha (Luke 10:39, 40), here she did the same; and both actions were the product of a heart devoted to Jesus.

II. An Attitude of Selfishness (John 12:4-8)
A. Judas Criticizes Mary (vv. 4-6)

⁴ But one of his disciples, Judas Iscariot, who was later to betray him, objected,

In contrast to Mary's selfless, noble gift to Jesus stood the attitude of *Judas Iscariot*. Judas was the one *who was later to betray* Jesus, although neither John nor any of the other disciples knew this at the time this event occurred. Writing years later and guided by the Holy Spirit, John could provide this information.

⁵ "Why wasn't this perfume sold and the money given to the poor? It was worth a year's wages."

Far from being moved by Mary's act of devotion to Jesus, Judas was indignant at what he considered a blatant waste of such a valuable commodity. He did not criticize her or the act directly, but he suggested an alternative use of the *perfume* that seemed "spiritual." It even sounds similar to the command that Jesus gave to the rich young ruler: sell the perfume and let the *money* be *given to the poor*. Judas also cited the *worth* of the perfume at *a year's wages*—a great deal of money indeed!

Matthew describes the criticism of Mary's action as coming from all the disciples (Matthew 26:8, 9), while Mark attributes it to "some of those present" (Mark 14:4, 5). Most likely Judas voiced his objection first, then all the disciples followed suit.

⁶ He did not say this because he cared about the poor but because he was a thief; as keeper of the money bag, he used to help himself to what was put into it.

Again, John was not aware of this information about Judas at the time this incident occurred. Only later was he able to shine the light of truth upon Judas's professed concern for *the poor*. In reality, Judas *was a thief* who cared nothing for those in need. Since he was *keeper of the money bag* and served as the disciples' "treasurer," his protest over Mary's act sprang only from the thought of how much money had slipped through his fingers because she used her perfume for something as "foolish" as anointing Jesus.

It is interesting to consider the fact that Jesus undoubtedly knew what Judas was doing with the group's finances, yet apparently did not confront him about his actions or entrust the money bag to someone else in the group. (Perhaps the other disciples rather than Jesus had chosen Judas for this task, or Judas may have volunteered for it.) Jesus had earlier alluded to the malicious character of one of his disciples without naming Judas (John 6:70, 71). Judas must have been aware at that point that Jesus was aware of his actions and could have come to him in repentance and confessed his wrongdoing. But he continued to live a life of greed and deception.

B. Jesus Commends Mary (vv. 7, 8)

7 "Leave her alone," Jesus replied. "It was intended that she should save this perfume for the day of my burial.

With his words *leave her alone*, Jesus rebuked Judas and anyone else who judged Mary's actions as absurd and wasteful. By saying that *it was intended that she should save* the *perfume for the day of* his *burial*, Jesus showed that he knew that his death and burial were only a few days away. With this in mind, he considered Mary's anointing a preparation for this event, since various perfumes and spices were used in preparing a body for burial (Luke 23:56). It is possible that Mary herself grasped to some degree the significance of her act.

8 "You will always have the poor among you, but you will not always have me."

On the surface it may appear that Jesus was minimizing the concern we are to have for *the poor*. Actually he was reaffirming a teaching from the law of Moses, found in Deuteronomy 15:11. Jesus' recognition that the poor will *always* be *among* us indirectly acknowledges our need to minister to them. That will not change until he returns.

We should also recognize that some service opportunities are timeless, while others are more time bound. When the window of opportunity to serve in the time-bound cases is shut, it is permanently lost. When Jesus said that those who surrounded him at this dinner would not always have him with them, he knew that the opportunity for his followers to honor him in the final tragic hours of his earthly ministry was severely limited. On the stage of history, Mary had seized the opportunity of a lifetime.

THE TRIUMPHAL ENTRY (MATTHEW 21:1-13)

Establishing the Groundwork

The day after the dinner at Simon the leper's house, Jesus made his "triumphal entry" into Jerusalem. The day we now call "Palm Sunday" commemorates that electrifying day when Jesus was given a royal welcome as he entered the city toward which he had "resolutely set out" (Luke 9:51) and where he would fulfill his Father's plan in fulfillment of prophecy.

Examining the Text

I. Obeying the Master (Matthew 21:1-6)
A. Finding an Animal (vv. 1-3)

¹ As they approached Jerusalem and came to Bethphage on the Mount of Olives, Jesus sent two disciples,

The day after the dinner in Bethany, *they* (meaning Jesus and his disciples) began to walk the approximately two miles to *Jerusalem*. This road would have taken them over the *Mount of Olives*, down a steep descent, and into Jerusalem from the east side.

The Mount of Olives is a ridge running north and south just across the Kidron Valley from Jerusalem. It is the highest peak on the east side, providing a strategic view of Jerusalem. Historical sources of Jesus' day indicate that a person could stand upon the top of the mount and see clearly into the temple courts. In ancient times the terrain was thick with olive groves, thus providing the origin of the mount's name. Somewhere on the lower slopes of the Mount of Olives was a place known as Gethsemane, which means "olive press."

While the village of *Bethphage* (which means "house of figs") has never been located, scholars believe that it was situated somewhere on the eastern slope of the Mount of Olives. As they neared the village, Jesus *sent two* unnamed *disciples* on a special mission.

² . . . saying to them, "Go to the village ahead of you, and at once you will find a donkey tied there, with her colt by her. Untie them and bring them to me.

Jesus knew exactly what the two disciples would *find* when they entered the *village* of Bethphage: *a donkey tied there, with her colt by her.* Mark and Luke mention only the colt (Mark 11:2; Luke 19:30), since that was the animal upon which Jesus rode. Mark also notes that the colt had not yet been ridden by any person (Mark 11:2). Perhaps the reason his mother was also brought along was to steady the young animal during his first experience at being ridden.

³ *If anyone says anything to you, tell him that the Lord needs them, and he will send them right away."*

In a small village such as Bethphage, one might expect that two strangers taking off with someone else's property would be challenged. Mark and Luke tell us that the two disciples were, in fact, questioned about taking the animals; and Luke notes that they were questioned by the animals' owners (Mark 11:5; Luke 19:33). However, when informed that *the Lord needs them*, the owners were pleased to oblige (Mark 11:6).

B. Fulfilling God's Will (vv. 4-6)

⁴ *This took place to fulfill what was spoken through the prophet:*

Matthew notes that Jesus' triumphal entry on this colt was a fulfillment of the prophecy found in Zechariah 9:9. In a chapter that speaks of God's judgment coming on Israel's enemies, Zechariah (a little over five hundred years before the time of Christ) foretold the coming of the Messiah-King to Jerusalem, at which time he would establish among God's people a peace that would never come to an end (Zechariah 9:8-10; 14:11).

⁵ *"Say to the Daughter of Zion,*
'See, your king comes to you,
gentle and riding on a donkey,
on a colt, the foal of a donkey.'"

The prophecy in Zechariah 9:9 was addressed to the *Daughter of Zion*. Zion was the principal hill on which Jerusalem was built. The phrase *Daughter of Zion* described the inhabitants of the city (a city or town was often considered the "mother" of its residents).

The *gentle* appearance of the Messiah-King as he came to Jerusalem *riding on a donkey* was meant to symbolize the peace that he would establish on the earth. In contrast, for royalty to parade on a white horse symbolized military might and a readiness to do battle with the enemy—a most appropriate symbol for Jesus' second coming (Revelation 19:11).

We know that through Jesus' death and resurrection, which occurred a few days later, peace has indeed been established among God's people—a peace between sinners and God, as well as a peace between Jews and Gentiles (Ephesians 2:11-22). However, many who witnessed Jesus' triumphal entry taking place were not thinking in such "spiritual" terms. They did not want a king who was *gentle*, but one who was forceful and aggressive, one who would reflect the power of Israel's past kings (such as David) and reaffirm Israel's place of distinction among the nations.

⁶ The disciples went and did as Jesus had instructed them.

The two *disciples*, although they *did as Jesus had instructed them*, likely did so with a certain amount of apprehension about what lay ahead. Only a few months earlier in Jerusalem, during the Feast of Dedication, the religious authorities had attempted to kill Jesus (John 10:31, 39). When Jesus wanted to return to Judea after the death of Lazarus, the disciples were concerned about possible threats against him (John 11:14-16). Yet here they obeyed the Master's directives without hesitation.

II. Honoring the King (Matthew 21:7-11)
A. Preparing His Way (vv. 7, 8)

⁷ They brought the donkey and the colt, placed their cloaks on them, and Jesus sat on them.

Lacking a saddle, the disciples *placed* some of *their cloaks* (their outer garments) on the backs of *the donkey and the colt*. Since they did not know which animal Jesus planned to ride, they spread cloaks on both animals. Amazingly the *colt* quietly accepted Jesus as a rider rather than becoming frightened and unmanageable. Perhaps the same quality of gentleness that endeared Jesus to children also calmed the fears of animals.

⁸ A very large crowd spread their cloaks on the road, while others cut branches from the trees and spread them on the road.

The reaction of the *crowd* to Jesus' arrival was spontaneous. Jerusalem was rapidly filling with visitors who had come to the city to celebrate the Passover. (The number of people in the city grew, according to some estimates, by as many as five times during this occasion.) No doubt some of these visitors, especially those from Galilee, already knew of Jesus and his reputation. Not long before this, Jesus had raised Lazarus from the dead. Word of this miracle would have spread among the visitors as well, increasing their excitement and their desire to see Jesus.

As the crowd saw Jesus approaching, the people quickly caught the spirit of a royal procession. In a special gesture of homage (and perhaps in imitation of the disciples' removal of their cloaks), they *spread their cloaks on the road* for Jesus to ride upon (see 2 Kings 9:13). (This would be the equivalent of our "red carpet treatment.") Since the road passing over the Mount of Olives went through a heavily wooded area, many in the crowd *cut branches from the trees* and *spread them* in Jesus' path. The Gospel of John specifically refers to the use of palm branches (John 12:13), thus our designation of this day as "Palm Sunday."

B. Praising His Name (vv. 9-11)

⁹ The crowds that went ahead of him and those that followed shouted,
"Hosanna to the Son of David!"
"Blessed is he who comes in the name of the Lord!"
"Hosanna in the highest!"

All four Gospel writers record the triumphal entry, although there are differences in the accounts, especially in what the *crowds . . . shouted*. This should not surprise us because this was a spontaneous outpouring of joyous praise, not a carefully planned and orchestrated gathering. Some of the people *went ahead of* Jesus, while others *followed*. This indicates that there were likely two crowds. One was made up of those who had come with Jesus from Jericho and others who had gathered in Bethany when they learned that he was there. They followed Jesus as he proceeded to Jerusalem. The other crowd, already in Jerusalem, heard the shouts of those already with Jesus and came out of the city and up the slopes of the Mount of Olives to meet him. Once they reached the procession, they turned around and led the way back into the city.

The accolades directed toward Jesus by the crowds included various messianic tributes of praise. *Son of David* was one of the most widely used messianic titles, expressing the hopes that the Messiah-King would establish a kingdom no less glorious than that of his father David. This king would come *in the name of the Lord*—that is, with the authority and power of God.

On this day the crowds wished for Jesus nothing but God's finest blessings. They shouted *Hosanna*, from a Hebrew word meaning, "Save, we pray." They expressed a desire that God save and preserve the life of his king and grant him success with his messianic plans. How ironic that only five days later many in this same crowd would be crying, "Crucify him!" (Matthew 27:22).

¹⁰ When Jesus entered Jerusalem, the whole city was stirred and asked,
"Who is this?"

As Jesus and the crowd *entered Jerusalem*, it quickly became apparent to those inside the city that something unusual was happening. Such a large crowd and commotion suggested that an important person was arriving, but apparently they could not tell *who* it was. Some were probably visitors in the city who did not know anything about Jesus.

¹¹ The crowds answered, "This is Jesus, the prophet from Nazareth in Galilee."

Despite the messianic overtones of the crowd's earlier tributes, they gave a more moderate answer when asked about Jesus' identity. To describe him as a *prophet* was far less controversial than to label him the Messiah. Perhaps this indicates already the highly fickle nature of the *crowds*. It may also reflect their hesitancy to say anything about Jesus that would get them in trouble with the religious authorities. John notes how the Pharisees observed the celebration surrounding Jesus and commented, "Look how the whole world has gone after him!" (John 12:19).

Mark's account notes that it was near evening when Jesus arrived at Jerusalem. Thus he did not stay in the city for very long that day, but went back to Bethany with his disciples (Mark 11:11). The events recorded in the next two verses took place on the following day (Monday).

III. Respecting the Lord (Matthew 21:12, 13)
A. Expelling the Money Changers (v. 12)

¹² Jesus entered the temple area and drove out all who were buying and selling there. He overturned the tables of the money changers and the benches of those selling doves.

As noted above, the "cleansing of the temple" took place on the day following Jesus' triumphal entry. No doubt Jesus deliberately planned to separate the two events to allow the crowd to settle down. Had he immediately *entered the temple area* and proceeded to rid it of the abuses taking place there, the frenzied crowd might well have broken out into a riot. By waiting until the next day, Jesus was able to cleanse the temple in a manner that demonstrated his authority as Messiah-King. This was no mob action, but wholly the act of Jesus.

By the time of Jesus, the chief priests and Pharisees had turned the temple into a religious marketplace. Initially, their intentions may have been quite commendable. Those traveling to the temple from great distances for the Passover or other occasions would find it more convenient to buy their sacrificial lambs and birds at the temple rather than having to transport them to Jerusalem. Likewise, money brought to pay tithes and offerings had to be converted to acceptable Jewish coins by the *money changers*.

At some point, however, this convenience had turned into nothing more than a racket. Some sources indicate that perfectly good animals were often rejected as inadequate in order to coerce travelers into purchasing from the temple market. The exchange fees charged by the money changers became exorbitant. The system had become corrupt and was badly in need of reform.

In his role as Messiah, Jesus *drove out all who were buying and selling* in the temple area and *overturned the tables of the money changers and the benches of those* who sold *doves* for sacrifices. Furthermore, he would not allow pedestrians to take shortcuts across the temple grounds while they conducted their business (Mark 11:16). There is no indication that Jesus harmed anyone, but there was a clear expression of his anger against the defilement of God's holy temple.

B. Explaining His Actions (v. 13)

¹³ "It is written," he said to them, "'My house will be called a house of prayer,' but you are making it a 'den of robbers.'"

The phrase *den of robbers* was taken from the prophet Jeremiah, who lamented the fact that the people who gathered for worship in his day were so malicious to each other throughout the week that the temple became, whenever they were present, a "den of robbers" (Jeremiah 7:11). The situation was even worse in Jesus' day, for the thievery that once had been practiced outside the temple was now actually being conducted, under priestly sanction, on temple grounds.

However, there was more to Jesus' actions. Using the language of the prophet Isaiah (Isaiah 56:7), Jesus also declared that the temple was meant to be a *house of prayer*. What God intended to be a holy place had been turned into a site where profits were more important than prayer.

Mark's comment following this incident is quite noteworthy and marks a change of direction in how Jesus' enemies sought to deal with his escalating popularity. "The chief priests and the teachers of the law heard this and began looking for a way to kill him, for they feared him, because the whole crowd was amazed at his teaching" (Mark 11:18). Jesus' earlier critics had attempted to discredit him and to undermine his influence with the people. Realizing that these efforts had only served to increase Jesus' popularity with the people, his enemies now resorted to more drastic measures. His cleansing of the temple must have been the proverbial "last straw" for any who might have had reservations about killing him.

THE AUTHORITY OF JESUS IS QUESTIONED (MARK 11:27-33)

Establishing the Groundwork

At the end of the day on which he cleansed the temple, Jesus left Jerusalem and returned to Bethany for the night (Matthew 21:17; Mark 11:19). It seems likely that Jesus spent each night through Wednesday of Passion Week in Bethany with Martha, Mary, and Lazarus. While returning to the temple the next morning (Tuesday), the disciples viewed with astonishment the fig tree that Jesus had cursed the previous day (Mark 11:12-14). Jesus proceeded to draw lessons on faith, prayer, and forgiveness of others from the withered fig tree (vv. 20-26).

Tuesday of Passion Week was an especially busy one for Jesus. In Matthew's Gospel, four entire chapters and portions of two others are devoted to it (Matthew 21:20–26:5). The day was characterized by a series of attempts by Jesus' enemies to embarrass him with what they considered difficult questions. Perhaps members of groups such as the Pharisees and the Sadducees met on Monday night to plan their strategy and proceeded to carry out their assaults on Jesus the following day.

Examining the Text

I. The Jews' Question (Mark 11:27-30)
A. The Issue of Jesus' Authority (vv. 27, 28)

27 They arrived again in Jerusalem, and while Jesus was walking in the temple courts, the chief priests, the teachers of the law and the elders came to him.

Luke's Gospel notes that on this occasion, Jesus "was teaching the people in the temple and preaching the gospel" (Luke 20:1). As he did so, *the chief priests, the teachers of the law and the elders came to him.* The Jewish high court, or the Sanhedrin, was composed of members of these three groups. These are the very men whom Jesus had predicted would reject him, condemn him, and deliver him to death at the hands of the Gentiles (Mark 8:31; 10:33).

28 "By what authority are you doing these things?" they asked. "And who gave you authority to do this?"

The Jewish leaders raised the question of Jesus' *authority.* By *these things*, they were referring to what Jesus had been saying and doing since his entry into Jerusalem. The manner of his entry into the city, his acceptance of messianic honor, and his preaching and teaching in the temple were all bad enough, but the climax of his unacceptable actions lay in halting and forbidding the established temple business involving sacrificial animals and the exchange of money.

By raising the issue of Jesus' authority and its source, the Jewish leaders undertook to make Jesus give such a clear and public declaration of his messiahship and divine nature that they would have grounds for legal charges against him. In his own time, Jesus would provide such a declaration. But his response to this inquiry was not to answer the question but to expose the questioners.

B. The Issue of John's Baptism (vv. 29, 30)

29 Jesus replied, "I will ask you one question. Answer me, and I will tell you by what authority I am doing these things.

The questioners were well aware that Jesus claimed the *authority* of God. A few months earlier the Jewish leaders (perhaps some of whom were standing before Jesus now) had been prepared to stone Jesus for that claim (John 10:29-33). At this point, Jesus did not give a direct answer to the question asked of him, most likely because he did not want to precipitate a repetition of that attack. Instead, he countered with a *question* of his own.

30 "John's baptism—was it from heaven, or from men? Tell me!"

The specific issue of *John's baptism* was a central part of his preaching; indeed, it provided the title ("the Baptizer") by which he had become known. Because his baptism was an innovation and because nothing like it had been commanded in the law of Moses, the source of his authority could be questioned as well.

As experts in matters religious, the members of the Sanhedrin were expected to examine all who claimed to be prophets and to determine the validity of their claims. The people expected it as protection against false prophets, and Rome expected it as a measure of control in the religious community. The members of the Sanhedrin had witnessed John's claim to be God's messenger. Let them now present their conclusions. Did John have the right to set up an institution for the forgiveness of sins when the law plainly declared that animal sacrifices were to be offered for that purpose? Of course, in addition to this John had declared that Jesus was the Christ (Luke 3:15-17).

II. The Jews' Quandary (Mark 11:31-33)
A. Conference Among Themselves (vv. 31, 32)

31 They discussed it among themselves and said, "If we say, 'From heaven,' he will ask, 'Then why didn't you believe him?'

Jesus' question confounded the members of the Sanhedrin. So before they responded to Jesus, the men *discussed* his question *among themselves*, perhaps gathering into a huddle to discuss their options while the *people* looked on with great interest in what they would say. Their choices were only two: first, if they acknowledged that John's authority was *from heaven*, then Jesus would confront them with their refusal to accept John and his preaching. (The Jewish leaders had spurned John's call to baptism, according to Luke 7:30.) But worse, from their viewpoint, Jesus would strengthen his own claim to authority because John testified that he was the Christ. The questioners dared not say that John's authority came from God, for they would condemn themselves as despising and defying God.

> [32] *"But if we say, 'From men'* . . . ." *(They feared the people, for everyone held that John really was a prophet.)*

The questioners' refusal to say "from heaven" was followed by their quotation of what Jesus would say in response. But their refusal to say *from men* is broken off. Mark states their reason in his own words: *they feared the people, for everyone held that John really was a prophet.* One glance at the throngs of people gathered in the temple awaiting their answer to Jesus was enough to convince them that they dare not say out loud that John was nothing more than a hoax, who claimed to be sent from God but who really concocted the whole idea of baptism. Obviously these men were concerned with preserving their reputation and status rather than with examination of the facts.

B. Confession to Jesus (v. 33)

> [33] *So they answered Jesus, "We don't know."*
> *Jesus said, "Neither will I tell you by what authority I am doing these things."*

The questioners' weak answer of *we don't know* was a complete evasion of responsibility. If they *could* not give an answer, they were incompetent in an area where they were supposed to be the experts. If they *would* not, they were self-serving cowards interested in pleasing people more than pleasing God. They refused to put their reply into words, so Jesus refused to answer their original question. But he did not have to. By linking his authority to John's, he showed its divine nature; but the members of the Sanhedrin could not accuse him of the claim because they refused to acknowledge John's credentials.

Jesus followed this question with a parable that unmistakably portrayed him as God's Son and the Jewish leaders as men bent on his destruction (Mark 12:1-11). This meaning may have been missed by the crowds, but not by the leaders: "they knew he had spoken the parable against them. But they were afraid of the crowd; so they left him and went away" (Mark 12:12). For the moment, the confrontation had resulted in a stand-off; in reality, it had only fueled the fires of hatred that would burn beneath the surface until they flared forth at Calvary.

JESUS IS QUESTIONED CONCERNING
THE GREATEST COMMANDMENT (MARK 12:28-34)

Establishing the Groundwork

The parable told by Jesus in Mark 12:1-11 reignited the animosity against Jesus (v.12). Afterward, two other attempts were made to trap Jesus by means of questioning him about highly sensitive issues. First, the Pharisees and the Herodians asked him whether it was lawful to pay taxes to Caesar (vv. 13-17). Then the Sadducees, who denied the resurrection, posed a question to Jesus that they thought would stump him and make him look inept before the crowds (vv. 18-27). In both cases, the tables were turned on the interrogators, as Jesus responded confidently and with authority. Then one of the teachers of the law came with yet another question. This man's response to Jesus' answer distinguished him from the majority of the religious leaders who confronted Jesus during Tuesday of Passion Week.

Examining the Text

I. A Crucial Question (Mark 12:28)
A. The Issue of Jesus' Authority (v. 28)

28 One of the teachers of the law came and heard them debating. Noticing that Jesus had given them a good answer, he asked him, "Of all the commandments, which is the most important?"

One of the teachers of the law noticed that Jesus *had given them a good answer.* The word *them* refers to the Sadducees, whose effort to trap Jesus is recorded in verses 18-27. According to Matthew's account, this teacher was a Pharisee (Matthew 22:34, 35), and was thus pleased with the defense of the resurrection that Jesus had given the Sadducees, since the Pharisees believed in the resurrection of the body. In the passage just cited, Matthew also notes that this man "tested" Jesus and implies that his question came as the result of a discussion among some of the Pharisees regarding how to trap Jesus.

The question about *the most important* commandment in the Law reflected a long-standing debate among Jewish scholars of that day. First-century Judaism had systematized the instructions written by Moses and created a list of some 613 commands, with 248 of them positive ("do this") and 365 negative ("do not do this"). For these who desired to undermine Jesus' authority, the question probably looked quite promising. No matter which command Jesus proposed as the greatest, his questioners could argue for other possibilities, thereby suggesting that Jesus was not as wise as he claimed or even implying that he did not really care about the commandments he passed over in his answer.

II. A Clear Answer (Mark 12:29-31)
A. Love God (vv. 29, 30)

29 "The most important one," answered Jesus, "is this: 'Hear, O Israel, the Lord our God, the Lord is one.

Jesus quoted from Deuteronomy 6:4, a verse of Scripture well known among the Jews. It was called the *Shema*, which is the Hebrew word for *hear* and is the first word in this verse. The *Shema* was held in such high esteem that it was quoted as the invocation for every synagogue service (and is still used as such in Jewish services today). The reason this passage was so highly valued among the Jews was that it succinctly expressed the monotheism (belief in one God) that formed the foundation of the Jewish faith.

30 "'Love the Lord your God with all your heart and with all your soul and with all your mind and with all your strength.'

By quoting the verse that followed the *Shema* (Deuteronomy 6:5), Jesus proposed that the entire passage be treated with great esteem, not just the first part. The Scripture text that defined one's most important belief also supplied, to use the teacher's words, the "most important" commandment.

It is possible to take the different terms Jesus used (*heart, soul, mind,* and *strength*) and treat them as distinct aspects of man's nature. However, knowing the Jewish penchant for speaking in "parallelism" (that is, repeating an idea several times with phrases that are roughly synonymous), we cannot say for certain whether Jesus intended for us to make such fine distinctions. What we can reasonably conclude from his statement is that every aspect of the human personality should be devoted to obeying the command to *love the Lord your God*.

B. Love Your Neighbor (v. 31)

31 "The second is this: 'Love your neighbor as yourself.' There is no commandment greater than these."

Jesus had not been asked to give the *second* greatest commandment, but he took this opportunity to do so and thus to teach a more complete view of one's primary duty to God. This second quotation is taken from Leviticus 19:18. In first-century Jewish thought, this was recognized as a legitimate command; however, its full force was often blunted by attempts to limit the scope of the word *neighbor*. Recall how an "expert in the law" had earlier tried to "justify himself" by asking Jesus, "And who is my neighbor?" (Luke 10:29).

Loving God and loving one's neighbor are God's highest expectations for mankind; in fact, Jesus treated them as one commandment in his statement, *There is no commandment greater than these*. Why are they so closely linked? Because the latter logically follows from the former. One who truly loves God cannot help but love those who carry within them the image of God. (See 1 John 4:20.)

III. A Courteous Response (Mark 12:32-34)
A. Agreement Expressed (vv. 32, 33)

32 "Well said, teacher," the man replied. "You are right in saying that God is one and there is no other but him.

This is not the kind of admission we might expect from one working within the ranks of those attempting to discredit Jesus. But then, sometimes truth is so powerful that an honest man cannot deny it, no matter how much he may dislike the source of that truth. Coming when it did, this man's willingness to rise above the hatred and prejudice of his fellow Pharisees was a "breath of fresh air" amidst an otherwise tense series of exchanges.

33 "To love him with all your heart, with all your understanding and with all your strength, and to love your neighbor as yourself is more important than all burnt offerings and sacrifices."

The teacher's reference to burnt offerings and sacrifices may indicate that until now he had been inclined to consider the commandments regarding those actions to be "most important" (v. 28). No doubt many in his day so believed. But now the man understood that the observance of any religious ceremony, devoid of a sincere, loving spirit toward God and others, was not really what God desired.

B. Assurance Given (v. 34)

34 When Jesus saw that he had answered wisely, he said to him, "You are not far from the kingdom of God." And from then on no one dared ask him any more questions.

Here was a man who was not yet in full stride with God's messianic plan, but he was *not far* from being so. We do not know any more about him, but we can hope that he was one of those who later accepted Jesus as the promised Messiah, perhaps on the Day of Pentecost.

For now, the challenges from the various religious groups ceased. Each challenge had been met authoritatively and without the religious leaders' intended effect, so none of them now *dared ask* Jesus *any more questions*. Jesus continued teaching the people, part of which included a scathing denunciation of the teachers of the law and the Pharisees (Matthew 23:1-39). No doubt those groups continued to meet, even more determined than ever that Jesus must die.

JESUS' DESCRIPTION OF THE FINAL JUDGMENT (MATTHEW 25:31-46)

Establishing the Groundwork

As Jesus left the temple following the busy day of teaching the people and facing challenges from the Jewish leaders, his disciples called his attention to the impressive buildings that made up the temple complex. Jesus responded by telling them that one day all of those structures would be destroyed (Matthew 24:1, 2). Later, when the disciples were alone with Jesus on the Mount of Olives, he told them what to expect in the future, concerning both the fall of Jerusalem (which took place in AD 70) and his second coming. (See Matthew 24, which records what is often referred to as Jesus' "Olivet discourse.")

Then Jesus told two parables to show his disciples (both then and now) that they needed to be ready for his return. Both of these are found in Matthew 25. The first was the parable of the ten virgins (vv. 1-13); the second was the parable of the talents (vv. 14-30). The chapter closes with a dramatic picture of the day of final judgment, which will take place when Jesus returns. It is not a true parable, because Jesus does not say that the kingdom of heaven is "like" something, as he does with the parables of the ten virgins and the talents (vv. 1, 14). What he says is more accurately a prophetic statement describing the coming judgment and using the kind of symbolic language that one often encounters in prophetic material. The account furnishes a powerful climax to all that Jesus had been saying about his return. It underscores his royal authority and the absolute finality of his judgments.

Examining the Text

I. The Judge (Matthew 25:31-33)
A. The Judge's Glory (v. 31)

³¹ When the Son of Man comes in his glory, and all the angels with him, he will sit on his throne in heavenly glory.

No one knows the day *when the Son of Man* will come, but the fact of his return is certain. Unlike his lowly entrance into this world as a baby in Bethlehem, at his second coming he will appear *in his glory*. In addition, Jesus will be accompanied by *all the angels* of Heaven at his return. The "great company of the heavenly host" that praised him at his birth (Luke 2:13, 14) will rejoice to see his final and total triumph over all evil.

B. The Judge's Gathering (vv. 32, 33)

³² All the nations will be gathered before him, and he will separate the people one from another as a shepherd separates the sheep from the goats.

In the dramatic scene described by Jesus, *all the nations* will be summoned to stand trial before him. People will not be able to go to the god of their choice; all will answer to Jesus. Then, just *as a shepherd separates the sheep from the goats*, Jesus will separate the righteous from the wicked. In the same way that a shepherd has no difficulty telling which is which, Jesus will be able to make a clear and flawless judgment.

³³ He will put the sheep on his right and the goats on his left.

To be at a ruler's *right* was to be in the place of approval and acceptance (for example, see Psalm 110:1 and Acts 7:55, 56), and it is here that the *sheep* are placed. Observe that Jesus describes only two groups: sheep and *goats*. When he examines the hearts of people on the Day of Judgment, there will be no middle ground. We are either for him or against him (Matthew 12:30). While we may see human behavior in shades of gray, Jesus will be able to pronounce judgment clearly and decisively.

II. The Blessed (Matthew 25:34-40)
A. Approval for the Blessed (v. 34)

³⁴ Then the King will say to those on his right, "Come, you who are blessed by my Father; take your inheritance, the kingdom prepared for you since the creation of the world.

Once the peoples of all nations have been separated and assigned to their rightful places on one side or the other, *the King*, Jesus, will announce his reward for those *on his right*. The *kingdom* to which he refers is that realm beyond this world where God's rule is complete, where nothing will mar the peace and joy of those permitted to enter it. Even as God was creating "the heavens and the earth" (Genesis 1:1), he was preparing a place for his faithful children to spend eternity. Heaven has been described as a *prepared* place for a prepared people.

B. Acts of the Blessed (vv. 35, 36)

35 "For I was hungry and you gave me something to eat, I was thirsty and you gave me something to drink, I was a stranger and you invited me in,

King Jesus then lists the various acts of mercy done to him by those on his right. They are the ones who gave him food when he was *hungry* and something to *drink* when he was *thirsty*. They gave him shelter when he needed it. The King will not overlook or forget any kindness they have shown. For people who really know God, meeting human needs is a part of what constitutes "pure and faultless" religion (James 1:27).

36 ". . . I needed clothes and you clothed me, I was sick and you looked after me, I was in prison and you came to visit me.'

The King continues to list the ways in which he was served by the sheep. Such a heavy emphasis on doing good to others may well make us think that Judgment Day will be merely a time for counting up good deeds and merit points. How does Jesus' commendation of good works square with the biblical teaching on salvation by grace? In truth, there is both divine initiative and human response in salvation. Salvation by God's grace must be followed by appropriate good works (Ephesians 2:8-10). Salvation based on faith in Jesus must allow that faith to express itself through love (Galatians 5:6). It is not true that we are saved *by* works, but it is true that we are saved *for* works.

C. Amazement of the Blessed (vv. 37-40)

37-39 Then the righteous will answer him, "Lord, when did we see you hungry and feed you, or thirsty and give you something to drink? When did we see you a stranger and invite you in, or needing clothes and clothe you? When did we see you sick or in prison and go to visit you?"

There is a wonderful innocence in the questions asked by the *righteous*. They are completely unaware of ever having done any acts of mercy for their *Lord*. It is generally true that those who are most devoted to others are least self-conscious of that devotion. Their attention is directed outwardly to needs, rather than inwardly to their own virtue. Their good deeds are a natural outgrowth of hearts that know the love of God and of eyes that see people the way he sees them.

40 The King will reply, "I tell you the truth, whatever you did for one of the least of these brothers of mine, you did for me."

Because *the King* loves his people and identifies with them, anyone who helps them is helping the King. Even serving *one of the least* is not overlooked.

Jesus calls these people in need *brothers of mine*. To those who believe in him, Jesus gives "the right to become children of God" (John 1:12). Therefore, he is "not ashamed to call them brothers" (Hebrews 2:11). Any help given to these *brothers* Jesus counts as help given to him personally.

This does not mean that we have the freedom to ignore the needs of any who are not followers of Jesus. Paul's words in Galatians 6:10 are instructive on this matter: "Therefore, as we have opportunity, let us do good to all people, especially to those who belong to the family of believers."

III. The Cursed (Matthew 25:41-46)
A. Condemnation for the Cursed (v. 41)

41 Then he will say to those on his left, "Depart from me, you who are cursed, into the eternal fire prepared for the devil and his angels.

Notice how precisely the command to the group on the *left* is the opposite of that given to the group on Jesus' right. One group is invited to come; the other is ordered to *depart*. One is called blessed; the other is called *cursed*. One is called to a kingdom; the other is sent to *eternal fire*. Those in one group inherit a kingdom prepared for them. Those in the other have no place prepared for them; they can only share the place *prepared for the devil and his angels*. There is nowhere else to go. Notice that Hell is not a place *prepared* for human beings. God wants no one to go there (2 Peter 3:9).

B. Carelessness of the Cursed (vv. 42, 43)

42, 43 "For I was hungry and you gave me nothing to eat, I was thirsty and you gave me nothing to drink, I was a stranger and you did not invite me in, I needed clothes and you did not clothe me, I was sick and in prison and you did not look after me."

Observe that these people on the left, condemned to eternal fire, are not accused of doing anything horribly evil: no murder, mayhem, assault, adultery, arson, or theft. They are condemned for doing nothing. They had opportunities to do good, just as the people on Jesus' right; but they chose to do nothing.

C. Complaint of the Cursed (vv. 44-46)

44 They also will answer, "Lord, when did we see you hungry or thirsty or a stranger or needing clothes or sick or in prison, and did not help you?"

Just as the "blessed" are unaware of the good they had done, so these "cursed" are unaware of the evil with which they are being charged. They attempt to defend themselves by implying that if they had known that a needy person was actually the *Lord*, they would certainly have helped him.

> ⁴⁵ *He will reply, "I tell you the truth, whatever you did not do for one of the least of these, you did not do for me."*

Those on the left have learned too late that by ignoring the King's people, they have ignored the King himself. If even *the least of these* is slighted, he takes it personally.

> ⁴⁶ *Then they will go away to eternal punishment, but the righteous to eternal life.*

Jesus describes eternity in terms of only two destinies: *eternal punishment* and *eternal life*. There is no "in-between" place. The endless punishment of the wicked will be the place of "eternal fire" (v. 41), a place where "the fire is not quenched" (Mark 9:48). If this is not literal fire, then it stands for a punishment equivalent to or worse than such fire. (In figurative descriptions found in the New Testament, the reality conveys more than the figure.) Hell is a place of unspeakable torment.

In contrast, the *righteous* will enter *eternal life*. Nothing is said here about this life, but other passages of Scripture give us some hints concerning it. Passages particularly in Revelation reveal a heavenly city, eternally bright, inhabited only by the redeemed, where there will be freedom from all sin, absence of sorrow and death, and a constant awareness of the very presence of God.

How to Say It

BETHANY. *Beth*-uh-nee.

BETHLEHEM. *Beth*-lih-hem.

BETHPHAGE. *Beth*-fuh-gee.

GETHSEMANE. Geth-*sem*-uh-nee (*g* as in *get*).

HERODIANS. Heh-*roe*-dee-unz.

ISCARIOT. Iss-*care*-e-ut.

JERUSALEM. Juh-*roo*-suh-lem.

JUDEA. Joo-*dee*-uh.

KIDRON. *Kid*-ron.

LAZARUS. *Laz*-uh-rus.

MESSIANIC. mess-ee-an-ick.

MONOTHEISM. *mon*-uh-thee-izm (th as in thin)

PENTECOST. *Pent*-ih-kost.

PHARISEES. *Fair*-ih-seez.

SADDUCEES. *Sad*-you-seez.

SHEMA *(Hebrew)*. shih-*mah.*

SPIKENARD. *spike*-nahrd.

ZECHARIAH. *Zek*-uh-*rye*-uh (strong accent on *rye*).

ZION. *Zi*-un.

Chapter 12

Events Leading to the Crucifixion

Matthew 26:1-5, 14-16, 17-30;
John 15:1-11; 17:1-11, 20, 21;
Matthew 26:36-46

JUDAS PLANS HIS BETRAYAL OF JESUS (MATTHEW 26:1-5, 14-16)

Establishing the Groundwork

A portion of the previous chapter's studies focused on the events of Tuesday of Passion Week. The day was an especially busy one for Jesus, characterized by frequent exchanges with his enemies who were trying to curb the excitement created by his triumphal entry into Jerusalem.

When the day had concluded, Jesus told his disciples that the Passover was but two days away (Matthew 26:1, 2). For Jesus, this particular Passover would be not merely an act of faithful observance of the law but one of ultimate obedience to his Father. Jesus would be preparing himself to fulfill his mission as, in John the Baptist's words, "the Lamb of God, who takes away the sin of the world" (John 1:29; see also 1 Corinthians 5:7).

Wednesday of Passion Week appears to have been, as best as we can determine, a "silent day" in the sense that the Gospels do not record any major happenings involving Jesus. But his enemies were fine-tuning their plots against him and so, tragically, was one of his own disciples.

Examining the Text

I. Plotting a Murder (Matthew 26:1-5)
A. Jesus' Awareness (vv. 1, 2)

[1, 2] When Jesus had finished saying all these things, he said to his disciples, "As you know, the Passover is two days away—and the Son of Man will be handed over to be crucified."

The phrase *all these things* refers to the teachings of Jesus included in chapters 23–25 of Matthew's Gospel. With this, Jesus' public teaching had ended. John records a later lengthy discourse (John 14:1–17:26, including Jesus' prayer in John 17), but Jesus spoke these words in private to his disciples following the events in the upper room.

Jesus observed that *the Passover is two days away*. As previously noted, it appears that these words were spoken on Tuesday evening of Passion Week. The Passover lamb would have been sacrificed on Thursday afternoon, followed by the Passover supper that evening. While the Passover was meant to be a time of celebration for the Jews, this Passover was going to be marked by what would appear to be a devastating tragedy: *the Son of Man will be handed over to be crucified*.

B. The Jews' Assembly (vv. 3-5)

3, 4 Then the chief priests and the elders of the people assembled in the palace of the high priest, whose name was Caiaphas, and they plotted to arrest Jesus in some sly way and kill him.

That *the chief priests and the elders of the people assembled* for this meeting may indicate a gathering of the Sanhedrin, the "supreme court" of Israel. However, the fact that they met *in the palace of the high priest* rather than in the regular meeting place in the temple area may reflect a very hastily called meeting to deal with the problem that Jesus posed. Most likely this was an unofficial meeting with some members of the Sanhedrin absent. It is hard to imagine that someone like Nicodemus was present and did not raise a protest against the proceedings, much as he did on another occasion (John 7:50-52).

Following Jesus' raising of Lazarus from the dead, *Caiaphas*, the *high priest*, had expressed his position that the only way to solve the problem of Jesus was to kill him (John 11:46-53). At that time, he had apparently convinced others in the Sanhedrin that his view was the proper course of action. At the present time, during the week of Passover, the situation had become so critical that a concrete plan of action had to be devised. Of course, it had to be carried out *in some sly way* for the reason given in the next verse.

5 "But not during the Feast," they said, "or there may be a riot among the people."

Undoubtedly the chief priests and elders had kept a close watch on Jesus following the triumphal entry. Their problem was to find a way to arrest him secretly without arousing the crowds that had become enthralled by his teaching (Luke 21:37, 38). Furthermore, the Passover *Feast* was a profitable time for the temple establishment, and the Jewish leaders had no intention of doing anything that would interrupt the flow of money into the temple treasury. They also feared antagonizing the Roman authorities—a concern voiced earlier by Caiaphas (John 11:48).

II. Plotting a Betrayal (Matthew 26:14-16)
A. Securing a Price (vv. 14, 15)

14 Then one of the Twelve—the one called Judas Iscariot—went to the chief priests

It is impossible for us to know exactly what happened in the heart of *Judas Iscariot* to change him from one of the loyal twelve to a betrayer. Students have offered many suggestions, including disillusionment with Jesus when he did not set up an earthly kingdom as Judas might have expected. Others believe that Judas may have been attempting to "force the hand" of Jesus. In other words, by putting Jesus in a life-threatening situation, Judas may have hoped that Jesus would move with more urgency to establish his kingdom. It is clear, from Judas's response to Mary's anointing of Jesus, and from John's additional comment about Judas's thievery (John 12:6), that he was someone often driven by selfishness and greed. Perhaps Judas's dissatisfaction with Jesus had been building for some time prior to the anointing; Jesus' rebuke of Judas during that incident was the proverbial "last straw."

15 . . . and asked, "What are you willing to give me if I hand him over to you?" So they counted out for him thirty silver coins.

Once Judas had made up his mind to betray Jesus, he knew exactly where to go; for the hostility of the religious leaders was no secret. When one of Jesus' own followers came to them with an offer, they must have been quite surprised but pleased nonetheless. Judas's gesture would provide them with the "sly way" to arrest Jesus that they were seeking (v. 4). The price of *thirty silver coins* was no more than what the Old Testament required as compensation for the death of a slave (Exodus 21:32). Note that this action constituted another fulfillment of prophecy (Zechariah 11:12).

B. Seeking an Opportunity (v. 16)

16 From then on Judas watched for an opportunity to hand him over.

We cannot be certain exactly when Judas approached the chief priests with his scheme, whether late on the Saturday after the anointing by Mary or late on Tuesday of Passion Week after Jesus' lengthy day of confrontation and teaching had ended. Once the thirty silver coins had changed hands, Judas began the cold-blooded search for *an opportunity to hand* Jesus *over* to his enemies.

THE LAST SUPPER (MATTHEW 26:17-30)

Establishing the Groundwork

The events narrated in this text occurred on Thursday of Passion Week, as the Jews prepared to observe the Passover. The seven days following the Passover were called the Feast of Unleavened Bread, although sometimes the latter term covered the entire eight-day observance.

A tense and ominous atmosphere was present in the upper room when Jesus shared the Passover there with his disciples. While this event is often described as the "Last Supper," it was a time when Jesus would institute a new kind of "Supper" that continues to be an integral part of Christian worship.

Examining the Text

I. Preparations for the Passover (Matthew 26:17-19)
A. The Disciples' Inquiry (v. 17)

¹⁷ On the first day of the Feast of Unleavened Bread, the disciples came to Jesus and asked, "Where do you want us to make preparations for you to eat the Passover?"

The *Feast of Unleavened Bread* was originally a celebration of seven days beginning on the fifteenth day of the month of Nisan (formerly called "Abib"; see Exodus 23:15; 34:18; Leviticus 23:5, 6). This corresponds to late March or early April on our calendar. The *first day of the Feast* was the day when the Passover lamb was killed (Mark 14:12) and other preparations were made for the Passover supper.

The primary ingredient of the *Passover* meal was the lamb. This was an animal that had been specially selected ("without defect," as commanded in Exodus 12:5) and prepared for the meal. Ordinarily the meal was shared by members of a family, but sometimes small families would group together and observe the meal. While Jesus and his *disciples* did not constitute an actual family, it was not uncommon for such groups to eat the Passover together. Probably they had eaten the Passover together in previous years.

From Luke we learn that it was not the entire group of *disciples* that *asked* Jesus about making *preparations* for this meal. Jesus had summoned two of them, Peter and John, and given them this task. They then asked Jesus *where* the preparations were to be made (Luke 22:7-9).

No doubt Judas was listening intently for Jesus' answer to the disciples' question. At the time of the Passover supper, every family would be gathered for its own meal. Jesus and his disciples would be alone. This would provide just the opportunity Judas needed to direct Jesus' enemies to him.

B. Jesus' Instructions (vv. 18, 19)

18 He replied, "Go into the city to a certain man and tell him, 'The Teacher says: My appointed time is near. I am going to celebrate the Passover with my disciples at your house.'"

The disciples had no need to worry about a room for the Passover meal. Jesus had already made arrangements for it (just as he had for the donkey that he rode into Jerusalem). And just as Jesus had sent two disciples for the donkey, he now sent two disciples to make the arrangements for the Passover. Jesus told them that as they entered *the city* (Jerusalem), they would see a man carrying a jar of water; and they were to follow him to the house Jesus had chosen. Carrying water jars was ordinarily done by women, and so a man carrying one would stand out (Mark 14:13, 14; Luke 22:10, 11). Both Mark and Luke include the detail that the specific area of the house was a "large upper room" (Mark 14:15; Luke 22:12).

Thus Judas was kept in ignorance of the location and could not yet give directions to the Jewish leaders. At the same time, Jesus was fully aware that all that was happening was unfolding according to a plan: *My appointed time is near.*

19 So the disciples did as Jesus had directed them and prepared the Passover.

Peter and John, the two disciples appointed by Jesus for this task, *did as Jesus directed them and prepared the Passover.* Perhaps the owner of the house or his servants assisted with some of these arrangements, but we have no information of this.

II. Prediction of Betrayal (Matthew 26:20-25)
A. Assembly and Announcement (vv. 20, 21)

20 When evening came, Jesus was reclining at the table with the Twelve.

Probably not until *the Twelve* arrived at the appointed location did Judas know where the Passover meal would be. His problem was then to slip away and disclose this information to the Jewish leaders without attracting the attention or suspicion of the others.

None of the Gospel writers gives a complete account of all that took place in the upper room. Luke 22:24-30 reveals that the disciples revived their argument over who should be the greatest among them. Jesus repeated his teaching that greatness consists of service. John 13:1-17 adds that he illustrated this principle by washing the disciples' feet (the group would have included Judas at this point).

Many are familiar with Leonardo da Vinci's painting *The Last Supper*, which depicts Jesus sitting at a table with the twelve disciples. However, the practice in the first century was to recline on low benches, resting on the left elbow with the right hand free to take food from the *table*. This arrangement makes Jesus' washing of the disciples' feet easier to picture in one's mind than if the group were seated with their feet under a table.

²¹ *And while they were eating, he said, "I tell you the truth, one of you will betray me."*

After Peter's confession of Jesus as the Son of God, Jesus had begun to reveal in plain terms that he would be rejected by the Jewish leaders, suffer, and be killed (Matthew 16:21). This was the first time, however, that they had heard Jesus say that *one of you will betray me.*

B. Sorrow and Response (vv. 22-25)

²² *They were very sad and began to say to him one after the other, "Surely not I, Lord?"*

Jesus' comments left the disciples in extreme anguish: *they were very sad.* It is to their credit that each of them began to search his own heart instead of pointing a finger of accusation at someone else. Each asked, *"Surely not I, Lord?"* With the exception of Judas, the disciples all knew that they would never intentionally commit such an act.

²³ *Jesus replied, "The one who has dipped his hand into the bowl with me will betray me.*

During the Passover meal, it was a common practice for those participating to dip their bread into *the bowl* that contained the bitter herbs (Exodus 12:8). It is likely that all of the disciples had *dipped* their bread into this bowl at one point or another during the evening. In the ancient Near East, sharing a meal with a host constituted a sacred trust. It was considered most reprehensible for a person to violate that trust by harming the host in any way. At this point, Jesus' words reemphasized the fact that the betrayal would indeed come from within the group of those present at this meal.

John's account of this Passover indicates that Jesus went a step further in identifying the traitor. When Peter urged John to ask Jesus specifically about who the traitor was, Jesus replied, "It is the one to whom I will give this piece of bread when I have dipped it in the dish" (John 13:26). Then Jesus dipped a piece of bread and gave it to Judas. The rest of the group missed even this seemingly clear signal, however. Some of them thought that Jesus was giving instructions to Judas about money (John 13:27-29).

> [24] *"The Son of Man will go just as it is written about him. But woe to that man who betrays the Son of Man! It would be better for him if he had not been born."*

Jesus never stopped loving Judas. With these words he seems to have been reaching out to the betrayer one last time, giving him one more chance to repent. But Judas rejected this final opportunity; at this point "Satan entered into him" (John 13:27). The judgment that Judas brought upon himself for his actions was so tragic and severe that it would have been *better for him if he had not been born*. Notice that although Jesus would proceed to carry out all that was *written about him* by the Old Testament prophets, this did not excuse Judas for doing what he did.

> [25] *Then Judas, the one who would betray him, said, "Surely not I, Rabbi?" Jesus answered, "Yes, it is you."*

Judas, knowing full well that he was the betrayer, must have been reluctant to ask this question. But the others were all asking it, and to remain silent might have drawn suspicion toward him. Apparently the other disciples did not hear Jesus' response of *Yes, it is you*. Had they understood that Judas was *the one who would betray* Jesus, they surely would have tried to stop him.

It is likely that this exchange between Jesus and Judas occurred at almost the same time as the giving of the piece of bread mentioned earlier. After Judas had received the piece of bread and Satan had entered into him, Jesus told him, "What you are about to do, do quickly" (John 13:27). John 13:30 states, "As soon as Judas had taken the bread, he went out. And it was night." Apparently Judas was not present when Jesus instituted the Lord's Supper.

III. Institution of the Lord's Supper (Matthew 26:26-30)
A. The Bread (v. 26)

> [26] *While they were eating, Jesus took bread, gave thanks and broke it, and gave it to his disciples, saying, "Take and eat; this is my body."*

While they were eating the traditional Passover meal, Jesus took a dramatic departure from the usual Passover observance. He *took* some of the unleavened *bread* that was left over from the meal, *gave thanks*, *broke* it, and *gave* it to the disciples with the instructions, *"Take and eat; this is my body."* His words must have been somewhat puzzling to his followers. But they had been accustomed to Jesus' use of figurative language on many previous occasions. They would not be likely to take his words literally, any more than when he said, "I am the light of the world," or "I am the door."

B. The Cup (vv. 27, 28)

27 Then he took the cup, gave thanks and offered it to them, saying, "Drink from it, all of you.

In a traditional Passover service, there were four occasions when the participants would *drink* a *cup* of the fruit of the vine. Each cup had a distinctive theme, often accompanied by prescribed words, songs, and prayers. The first two cups were taken prior to the main meal, and the latter two cups were taken after the meal. The third cup was called the Cup of Redemption, which celebrated the fact that God had redeemed Israel from bondage in Egypt and that he continues to redeem his people in times of distress. It is likely that this was the cup that Jesus used in instituting the Lord's Supper, giving it a new and richer meaning than before—a celebration of the ultimate redemption that God would give his people through the death of his Son on the cross.

28 "This is my blood of the covenant, which is poured out for many for the forgiveness of sins.

The Jewish people were quite familiar with the idea of *covenant*. They knew of the covenant that God had made with his people through Moses at Mount Sinai. They were aware that this covenant was sealed by blood. Moses sprinkled sacrificial blood on the people, saying, "This is the blood of the covenant that the Lord has made with you in accordance with all these words" (Exodus 24:8). Now as Jesus passed the cup from which all the disciples present would drink, he pointed them toward a new covenant that would be sealed with his *blood*.

The Jewish people also understood the link between the shedding of blood and the *forgiveness of sins* (Leviticus 17:11). However, the animal blood that was offered under the Old Covenant was inadequate to provide complete forgiveness. Hebrews 10:4 says, "It is impossible for the blood of bulls and goats to take away sins." A perfect sacrifice was necessary in order for our sins to be forgiven, and Jesus came to provide that sacrifice at the cross.

C. The Future (vv. 29, 30)

29 "I tell you, I will not drink of this fruit of the vine from now on until that day when I drink it anew with you in my Father's kingdom."

Jesus' promise concerning drinking the *fruit of the vine* in his *Father's kingdom* is taken by some to mean that he will not share in this feast again until the saints join with him in the triumphant "wedding supper of the Lamb" in Heaven (Revelation 19:9). Others hold that Jesus was referring to the spiritual union that Christians enjoy with him when they celebrate the Lord's Supper. If this is the meaning, then that union was experienced only a few weeks later when the church began on the Day of Pentecost and began to observe the "breaking of bread" (Acts 2:42).

30 When they had sung a hymn, they went out to the Mount of Olives.

That Jesus and the disciples sang a *hymn* probably refers to the Psalms that were usually sung or chanted at the close of the Passover Feast. Psalms 115–118 were the ones used on this occasion. Some of the verses in these Psalms were particularly appropriate, given what was about to transpire (116:3, 4; 118:6, 7, 22-26).

Jesus then led the group from the upper room. The conversation recorded in the next few verses (31-35) took place as they walked through the dark streets of Jerusalem and across the brook Kidron to the Mount of Olives east of the city. John places Jesus' words, "Come now; let us leave" at the end of Jesus' teaching found in John 14, perhaps indicating that all the words of John 15–17 were spoken after the group left the upper room and during this walk to the Mount of Olives.

JESUS' TEACHING ON THE VINE AND THE BRANCHES (JOHN 15:1-11)

Establishing the Groundwork

John is the only Gospel writer who records the lengthy discourse given by Jesus to his disciples following the institution of the Lord's Supper (John 14:1—17:26, including the prayer in John 17). It is possible that, as Jesus and the disciples made their way to the Mount of Olives, certain sights along the way helped to introduce the figure of the vine that is found at the beginning of John 15. Perhaps they walked through the temple area where a golden vine ornamented the entrance to the sanctuary. To reach the Mount of Olives, they would have passed through the Kidron Valley, where fires of vine prunings may have been burning. As they approached the Mount, vines could have been growing along the path. In addition, they had just come from the upper room where Jesus had instituted the Lord's Supper with the "fruit of the vine." Any one of these sights or a combination of them could have led to Jesus' use of the object lesson of the vine.

Examining the Text

I. The Authentic Vineyard (John 15:1-3)
A. The Vine (v. 1)

¹ I am the true vine, and my Father is the gardener.

The Old Testament refers to God's people Israel as a vine, but often those references are negative (Isaiah 5:1-7; Jeremiah 2:21; Ezekiel 15:1-6; Hosea 10:1). Jesus described himself as the *true vine* in contrast with disobedient Israel, which was an imperfect foreshadowing. Elsewhere John records Jesus' statement that he is the "true bread" compared with the manna that God provided for Israel (John 6:31-33). At the beginning of his Gospel, John calls Jesus the "true light" compared with the light provided by John the Baptist (John 1:6-9).

Earlier during Passion Week, Jesus had spoken a parable about a vineyard and the wicked farmers who abused their responsibility to care for it (Mark 12:1-12). Those "farmers" were the Jewish leaders. Here Jesus refers to his *Father* as the *gardener* of the true vine. Whatever the "wicked farmers" among the Jews may seek to do to Jesus, his Father's higher purpose will be fulfilled.

B. The Branches (vv. 2, 3)

² He cuts off every branch in me that bears no fruit, while every branch that does bear fruit he prunes so that it will be even more fruitful.

Jesus is stating a principle by which God the gardener continues to operate: as a gardener *cuts off* the dead branches, so God will cut off those who profess to follow Christ yet are living unproductive lives. In addition, *every branch that is fruitful God prunes so that it will be even more fruitful*. This pruning serves to remove those habits, activities, and attitudes that hinder us from being productive. In some cases God may strip from us those items we think are necessities in order to make us aware of our dependency on him. Such action on his part reminds us that "the Lord disciplines those he loves" (Hebrews 12:6).

What is the *fruit* that we are to *bear*? Sometimes the term refers to converts to Christ (Romans 1:13, KJV; the Greek here uses the same word as translated "fruit" in John 15:2). Here, however, it more likely refers to one's character, as it does frequently in the New Testament. (See, for example, Matthew 3:8; 7:16-20; 12:33; Galatians 5:22, 23.)

³ You are already clean because of the word I have spoken to you.

The Greek word rendered *clean* comes from the same root as the verb meaning "to prune." (It is actually the source of our word *catharsis.*) The disciples to whom Jesus was speaking were *already* clean, or pruned. The tool for accomplishing this was Jesus' *word.* Concerning the church, Paul writes that it is Jesus' desire "to make her holy, cleansing her by the washing with water through the word" (Ephesians 5:26).

II. The Abiding Branches (John 15:4-6)
A. The Challenge of Abiding (vv. 4, 5)

⁴ Remain in me, and I will remain in you. No branch can bear fruit by itself; it must remain in the vine. Neither can you bear fruit unless you remain in me.

A *branch* cannot detach itself from the *vine.* It has no choice in the matter. And it is certain that a branch that has been detached—left *by itself*—cannot survive. But human beings do have a will, the freedom of choice. Therefore Jesus admonished the disciples (both then and now), *remain in me.* If they did this, he would remain in them just as surely as the life principle of the vine permeates all the branches. The danger that Jesus' disciples would no longer remain in him was so real that Jesus used the word *remain* or *remains* 11 times in this passage!

⁵ I am the vine; you are the branches. If a man remains in me and I in him, he will bear much fruit; apart from me you can do nothing.

Mutual remaining is needed to produce the *fruit* that God desires. Neither Jesus nor his disciples can keep the relationship right without the cooperation of the other. However, it is the disciples who determine whether the relationship is fruitful or not. Jesus never fails to do his part, but he does not compel his disciples to do their part. Each one must decide for himself to keep in touch with Jesus and then must actively do so. The result of such "remaining" will be bountiful. It is not just that we will bring forth fruit, but *much fruit.*

As every coin has two sides, so every truth has a positive and a negative side. The negative side of this illustration is that *apart from* Christ, we can *do nothing.* No real spiritual good can be accomplished without him.

B. The Cost of Not Abiding (v. 6)

⁶ If anyone does not remain in me, he is like a branch that is thrown away and withers; such branches are picked up, thrown into the fire and burned.

Jesus next stated the consequences for *anyone* who *does not remain in* him. Such a person becomes fruitless; he withers spiritually, since he has cut himself off from his source of life, and he is then described as *thrown into the fire and burned*. The destiny awaiting those who are fruitless reminds us of the Scriptures' frequent warnings about the punishment of the wicked (Matthew 13:42, 50; Mark 9:48; Luke 16:24; Jude 7; Revelation 20:14, 15). These warnings ought to cause us to take frequent inventory of our lives.

III. The Anticipated Rewards (John 15:7-11)
A. Answered Prayer (v. 7)

⁷ If you remain in me and my words remain in you, ask whatever you wish, and it will be given you.

Jesus gives an additional promise to those who *remain in* him: they may *ask whatever* they *wish, and it will be given*. Whenever we read such promises as this (similar ones are found in Matthew 21:22; Luke 11:9; and John 16:23), we may immediately think of instances in which our personal experience with prayer did not seem to confirm Jesus' promise. However, we must keep in mind the condition stated by Jesus: *if you remain in me and my words remain in you*. The petitions of those who remain in Christ will reflect a desire to achieve his will and his purpose (note the promise in 1 John 5:14). The faithful disciple of Jesus, whose perspective is being guided by the words of Jesus, will not desire nor ask for anything contrary to him and his word. Jesus was certainly not promising to satisfy each and every one of our whims. No wise and loving parent gives a child everything the child asks for—and God is our Father. His knowledge of what we need is perfect (Matthew 6:8).

B. Glorifying God (v. 8)

⁸ This is to my Father's glory, that you bear much fruit, showing yourselves to be my disciples.

God was glorified through the work of his Son (John 13:31, 32). He is also given *glory* through the work, or *fruit*, of the *disciples* of his Son.

C. Love (vv. 9, 10)

⁹ As the Father has loved me, so have I loved you. Now remain in my love.

At this point in his discourse, Jesus turned from the lesson he was giving his disciples through the figure of the vine and the branches to express his *love* for them. He assured them in this solemn hour that he *loved* them just as the

Father in Heaven loved him. Of course, Jesus would continue to love them if they turned away from him; but if they did, they would forfeit the blessings and the fruitfulness that walking in his love can bring.

> *¹⁰ If you obey my commands, you will remain in my love, just as I have obeyed my Father's commands and remain in his love.*

The relationship between *love* and obedience is mutual. If we love Jesus, we will *obey* his *commands* (John 14:15). On the other hand, if we obey his commands, it is evidence that we *remain in his love*. This ideal union between the believer and Christ is exemplified by the complete harmony and close relationship that exists between Jesus and his Father. John records other instances where Jesus declared his obedience to his *Father's commands* (John 5:30; 8:29; 14:31).

D. Joy (v. 11)

> *¹¹ I have told you this so that my joy may be in you and that your joy may be complete.*

Despite the tragic hour that lay ahead, Jesus was able to speak freely of *joy*. (Read his words in John 16:20-24.) Just as he had promised his peace to his disciples, he now promised them his joy. This is a joy that the world cannot know, even as the peace that Jesus gives is not "as the world gives" (John 14:27).

JESUS' PRAYER FOR HIS FOLLOWERS (JOHN 17:1-11, 20, 21)

Establishing the Groundwork

At one point during Jesus' words of both warning and encouragement to his disciples, and before they crossed the brook Kidron (which ran between Jerusalem and the Garden of Gethsemane), he paused to offer the prayer found in John 17. We often hear the prayer that begins, "Our Father in heaven, hallowed be your name" (Matthew 6:9) referred to as the "Lord's Prayer." However, we must realize that strictly speaking this is the disciples' prayer, since Jesus prefaced this prayer by saying, "This, then, is how you should pray" (Matthew 6:9). John 17 records the true Lord's Prayer; for it is Jesus' own personal prayer, deliberately prayed in the hearing of his closest followers. In it we learn much about Jesus and about his passion for his disciples, both those who were present with him and those who would believe in him because of their testimony.

Examining the Text

I. A Petition on Behalf of Jesus (John 17:1-5)
A. About His Present Situation (v. 1)

¹ After Jesus said this, he looked toward heaven and prayed:
"Father, the time has come. Glorify your Son, that your Son may glorify
you.

The word *this* refers to the words of Jesus' discourse with his disciples, found in John 14–16. This instruction ended on an encouraging note, in spite of the fact that the cross was just a few hours away: "In this world you will have trouble. But take heart! I have overcome the world" (John 16:33). At this point, Jesus turned from teaching his disciples and *looked toward heaven and prayed.* He knew that his ability to overcome the world was tied to his communion with his *Father.*

Jesus' first words were the acknowledgment that *the time has come.* John has noted in his Gospel thus far several occasions when either Jesus observed that his time had not come (John 2:4; 7:6, 8) or his enemies did not make a move against him because his time had not come (John 7:30; 8:20). Then, as the cross drew near, Jesus began to change his language to say that his time, or "hour," had come (12:23, 27; 13:1). This is how Jesus spoke as he began his prayer. We are reminded that the cross did not come as a surprise to Jesus. He knew that it was imminent. But he also knew that what men were plotting to do to shame him would in fact *glorify* both the *Son* and his *Father* by fulfilling the Father's plan for the world's salvation from sin.

B. About His Past Activities (vv. 2-4)

² "For you granted him authority over all people that he might give eternal
life to all those you have given him.

Life is one of the most prominent themes in John's Gospel. Jesus declares himself to be the source of "a spring of water welling up to eternal life" (4:14). He also describes himself as the "bread of life" (6:35); the "light of the world" who provides the "light of life" (8:12); "the resurrection and the life" (11:25); and "the way and the truth and the life" (14:6).

Jesus' words in this verse explain how God was about to glorify him and how he in turn would glorify God (v. 1). Jesus had been given *authority* to *give eternal life to all those* whom the Father had *given him.* The act of giving on the part of both the Father and the Son is stressed in this prayer (vv. 6-9, 11, 12, 14, 22, 24). Yet it is also clear that God's "giving" of people to Jesus does not negate their choice in the matter. Jesus' own disciples are described as those who "obeyed" (v. 6), "accepted" (v. 8), and "believed" (v. 8) his message. Future disciples are described as "those who will believe in me through [the apostles'] message" (v. 20) and through whom "the world may believe that you have sent me" (v. 21).

³ *"Now this is eternal life: that they may know you, the only true God, and Jesus Christ, whom you have sent.*

To experience *eternal life,* one must *know . . . the only true God,* which can be done only by knowing *Jesus Christ* (John 14:6). Notice that Jesus did not define eternal life in terms of endless years in Heaven. It is not a relationship with time, but with God.

⁴ *"I have brought you glory on earth by completing the work you gave me to do.*

In one sense, of course, Jesus' *work* was not yet completed. The cross was still before him, and there he would declare, "It is finished" (John 19:30). These words indicate his readiness to proceed with this ultimate step in fulfilling the will of his Father.

C. About His Future (v. 5)

⁵ *"And now, Father, glorify me in your presence with the glory I had with you before the world began.*

Jesus not only looked ahead to the cross, but he also looked beyond the cross to what lay ahead for him. In doing so, he looked back to the *glory* he *had with* the Father *before the world began.* The prologue to John's Gospel notes that "in the beginning" Jesus shared the divine glory of Heaven (John 1:1, 2). He laid that heavenly glory aside when he came to earth as a man (Philippians 2:5-8). But now his work on earth was coming to an end, and he prayed that God would restore to him the glory that had previously been his. God did exactly that after Jesus died and rose again (Philippians 2:9-11; Hebrews 1:3).

II. A Petition on Behalf of the Disciples (John 17:6-11)
A. About Their Position (v. 6)

⁶ *"I have revealed you to those whom you gave me out of the world. They were yours; you gave them to me and they have obeyed your word.*

From his prayer that he be glorified, Jesus turned the focus of his prayer to his disciples. Through his teaching, his miracles, and his very life, Jesus had *revealed* the Father to them. Earlier that evening, Jesus had told the disciples, "Anyone who has seen me has seen the Father" (John 14:9). The Twelve (now reduced to 11 because of the departure of Judas) had been especially selected to serve as Jesus' followers. They had *obeyed* the Father's *word* as revealed through his Son, even when many had turned away from Jesus (John 6:66).

B. About Their Perspective (vv. 7, 8)

7, 8 "Now they know that everything you have given me comes from you. For I gave them the words you gave me and they accepted them. They knew with certainty that I came from you, and they believed that you sent me.

The disciples had heard Jesus' teaching, seen his miracles, and obeyed his commands. Thus by hearing, observation, and personal experience they had become convinced that whatever Jesus said or did came *from* the Father and that the Father himself had *sent* Jesus. After his resurrection, Jesus would tell these men, "As the Father has sent me, I am sending you" (John 20:21).

C. About Their Unity (vv. 9-11)

9 "I pray for them. I am not praying for the world, but for those you have given me, for they are yours.

Jesus' statement *I am not praying for the world* does not mean that Jesus was unconcerned about the world. Jesus' mission included the world, as John 3:16 clearly indicates. He later expressed his concern for the world in this prayer (vv. 21, 23). But at this point in his prayer, Jesus was concentrating more on the men whom he was leaving in the world to carry on his work. Only through their efforts would the world begin to hear the message of salvation.

10 "All I have is yours, and all you have is mine. And glory has come to me through them.

The unity embracing the Father, the Son, and the disciples of the Son is reflected in Jesus' words, *all I have is yours, and all you have is mine*. It is the kind of unity that Jesus later prayed would be present among all his followers (vv. 20, 21). His statement that *glory has come to me through them* should remind us of our responsibility to "let your light shine before men, that they may see your good deeds and praise your Father in heaven" (Matthew 5:16).

11 "I will remain in the world no longer, but they are still in the world, and I am coming to you. Holy Father, protect them by the power of your name— the name you gave me—so that they may be one as we are one."

Once again Jesus looked ahead. He knew that a time was coming when he would *remain in the world no longer*. He knew the hazards his disciples would face because that world would be, for the most part, as hostile to them as it had been to him (John 15:18-21). However, he had already promised to the disciples the Holy Spirit, whom the *Holy Father* would send in Jesus' name (John 14:26). The Spirit is "another Counselor" (John 14:16), whose presence fulfills Jesus' promise, "I am with you always, to the very end of the age" (Matthew 28:20).

The phrase *protect them by the power of your name* reflects the Jewish understanding that the ideas of *power* and *name* are closely linked (as they are by us when we say, "in the name of the law"). Jesus did not intend for his followers to be secluded from the world, but to remain untarnished by the world's evil influences (v. 15).

Jesus also prayed that his disciples *be one as we are one*. Recall that in the upper room, the group had been arguing "as to which of them was considered to be greatest" (Luke 22:24). Jesus' concern for unity, however, included more than just his immediate followers, as the next portion of our printed text indicates.

Verses 12-19 record Jesus' additional prayer concerns for the eleven disciples. Having prayed for those men who were to become his apostles, Jesus then focused his prayer on future followers.

III. A Petition on Behalf of Future Disciples (John 17:20, 21)
A. About Our Position (v. 20)

²⁰ *"My prayer is not for them alone. I pray also for those who will believe in me through their message,*

Certainly we who are Christians today are included among those who *believe in* Jesus *through* the apostles' *message*. It is their testimony, written for us in the New Testament, that brings us to faith in Christ as Savior and that forms the only foundation upon which genuine Christian unity can rest. The feelings or experiences of individuals or groups can never provide such a foundation; only the objective truth of the Scriptures will suffice. We should possess the confidence that Jesus had in the power and the priority of the apostolic message.

B. About Our Unity (v. 21)

²¹ *"... that all of them may be one, Father, just as you are in me and I am in you. May they also be in us so that the world may believe that you have sent me."*

Few factors have been more damaging to the growth of the church through the centuries than divisions among followers of Jesus. We know from our own experiences that non-Christians often cite the division in the church as a reason for their lack of interest in the Christian message. Aware that this would be a problem, Jesus prayed that his followers would *be one.*

Jesus' prayer for the unity of his followers is not an organizational unity accomplished by man-made resolutions or the decisions of ecclesiastical bodies. Jesus describes unity in this manner: *as you [Father] are in me and I am in you.* This unity is spiritual in nature—a oneness in mind, will, and purpose that is expressed in our love for God and for all who have accepted Christ and are therefore God's children.

Naturally there are areas in which one person's opinion differs from another's, but the differing opinions cannot be the foundation of unity. Opinions must be confined to their proper areas; only in the explicit word of the inspired apostles do we have a solid basis for Christian unity. The Christian finds unity in the essentials of God's Word, and freedom of opinion in those areas where God has not given specific directions.

JESUS PRAYS IN GETHSEMANE (MATTHEW 26:36-46)

Establishing the Groundwork

Following Jesus' prayer recorded in John 17, he and the eleven disciples came to Gethsemane, a garden just outside of Jerusalem on the western slope of the Mount of Olives. Up to this point, Jesus had not allowed Judas to know the exact location of his whereabouts because of the need for uninterrupted time with his disciples. Concerning Gethsemane, however, Judas "knew the place, because Jesus had often met there with his disciples" (John 18:2). (Gethsemane may have been the usual place of retreat for Jesus and the disciples following the Passover each year.) It was only a matter of time until the betrayer, intent on carrying out his evil plot, arrived with an armed guard to take Jesus into custody. But before that time came, Jesus would turn once again to his heavenly Father in prayer, knowing that he could not face the agony that lay ahead of him without the Father's help.

Examining the Text

I. Jesus' Preparation (Matthew 26:36-38)
A. The Place (v. 36)

36 Then Jesus went with his disciples to a place called Gethsemane, and he said to them, "Sit here while I go over there and pray."

Previously it was noted that the name *Gethsemane* means "oil press," which tells us what this hillside area was used for. The human side of Jesus shines through his request to his *disciples*, as he desired their companionship during these moments of spiritual conflict. At the same time, there was also a need for solitude and space, allowing Jesus the freedom to wrestle in private prayer. Thus Jesus had the disciples *sit* at a certain location, perhaps at the garden's entrance, while he went some distance away to *pray*. Luke's account notes that he told all the disciples to pray as well (Luke 22:40).

B. The People (v. 37)

37 He took Peter and the two sons of Zebedee along with him, and he began to be sorrowful and troubled.

Previously Jesus had allowed *Peter and the two sons of Zebedee* (James and John) to accompany him at the raising of Jairus's daughter from the dead (Mark 5:35-42) and at the transfiguration (Matthew 17:1-8). James and John were about to get a taste of the cup they had promised to drink with Jesus (Mark 10:35-40), and Peter would have the opportunity to demonstrate the loyalty to Jesus that he had earlier claimed to possess (Matthew 26:31-35).

Already this evening Jesus had prayed to his Father in the presence of his disciples (John 17). But now as he approached this time of intense, agonizing private prayer, his distress made him *sorrowful and troubled*. A sense of deep anguish that is impossible for any human being to fathom overcame Jesus as he began to think upon what lay ahead.

C. The Plea (v. 38)

38 Then he said to them, "My soul is overwhelmed with sorrow to the point of death. Stay here and keep watch with me."

During his ministry, Jesus had seldom asked anything for himself. With endless compassion he had poured himself out for the sake of others. Now he was speaking of his own need and was pleading with his disciples to *stay* and *keep watch* with him. Was this not the "baptism"—the experience of being *overwhelmed with sorrow*—of which he had spoken to James and John (Mark 10:38)? Those close *to the point of death* often desire the nearness of friends and family. This was Jesus' desire as well, as the cross loomed ever closer.

II. Jesus' Prayer (Matthew 26:39-46)
A. The First Petition (vv. 39-41)

39 Going a little farther, he fell with his face to the ground and prayed, "My Father, if it is possible, may this cup be taken from me. Yet not as I will, but as you will."

Luke's account says that Jesus "withdrew about a stone's throw beyond" where the disciples were and then began to pray (Luke 22:41). Mark's account adds that Jesus used the term *Abba* when he addressed his *Father* (Mark 14:36). *Abba* is an Aramaic term that conveys an additional measure of intimacy and tenderness. At this point Jesus prayed that if it were *possible, this cup* (his suffering for the sins of all humanity) might be *taken from* him. Could the purpose for which Jesus came into the world still be served without the agony of the cross? The enemies of Jesus answered that question at his crucifixion: "He saved others," they said, "but he can't save himself!" (Matthew 27:42).

Jesus' statement, *Yet not as I will, but as you will*, says something of how the human and the divine elements wrestled within Jesus during this intense inner struggle. Being human he shrank from the ordeal before him, but in the end he always submitted himself to the Father's will. There could be no shortcuts; the cross was the only way.

40 Then he returned to his disciples and found them sleeping. "Could you men not keep watch with me for one hour?" he asked Peter.

Jesus addressed his question to *Peter* in particular, for he had so recently declared his unshakable loyalty to his Lord (Matthew 26:33-35). However, the *you* in this verse is plural in the Greek text (thus the translation *you men*). It is noteworthy that Peter was quite eager a short time later to become the aggressor and attack those who came to arrest Jesus, but he could not prove steadfast in prayer with Jesus.

41 "Watch and pray so that you will not fall into temptation. The spirit is willing, but the body is weak."

To *watch* means to be alert to *temptation* so as not to be caught unprepared for it. Prayer brings strength from God to help us face temptation when it comes. These admonitions were especially appropriate for the disciples. They had already shown that they were susceptible to temptation; previously that evening they had bickered over who was the greatest, and Judas had already set the wheels of betrayal into motion. The upcoming hours and days would be fraught with opportunities to fall into even more temptation. These temptations could lead the disciples into momentary setbacks (such as Peter's denial of Christ) or complete rejections of Christ (such as Judas's actions).

That evening in the upper room, Jesus had told Peter, "I have prayed for you, Simon, that your faith may not fail" (Luke 22:32). But Peter and the others must also *pray*. In the realm of spiritual conflict, good intentions are not enough. *The spirit is willing, but the body is weak.* If the Son of God recognized his need for prayer, who are we to think that we can survive without it?

B. The Second Petition (vv. 42, 43)

42 He went away a second time and prayed, "My Father, if it is not possible for this cup to be taken away unless I drink it, may your will be done."

Again, the turmoil in Jesus' soul found him contemplating some other way to save the world. And again, he avowed that if the only way to achieve the Father's purpose is for him to *drink* the *cup* of suffering and death, then *may your will be done*!

43 When he came back, he again found them sleeping, because their eyes were heavy.

Jesus had hoped that the three disciples would muster the strength to watch and pray with him, but sadly this was not the case. Mark's Gospel adds this note: "They did not know what to say to him" when he wakened them the second time (Mark 14:40). What excuse could they give for failing Jesus again?

C. The Third Petition (v. 44, 45)

44 So he left them and went away once more and prayed the third time, saying the same thing.

Luke adds two noteworthy details concerning Jesus' intense prayer in the garden. The first is that "an angel from heaven appeared to him and strengthened him" (Luke 22:43). A special measure of divine aid was given to Jesus, much as it was following his time of being tempted (Matthew 4:11). The second detail is that "being in anguish, he prayed more earnestly, and his sweat was like drops of blood falling to the ground" (Luke 22:44). Only Luke, the physician, records this testimony to how earnestly Jesus *prayed*.

45 *Then he returned to the disciples and said to them, "Are you still sleeping and resting? Look, the hour is near, and the Son of Man is betrayed into the hands of sinners.*

Jesus must have asked this question with a tinge of sadness. The *disciples* had missed an important opportunity to pray. It seems that only a brief period of time elapsed before the time for prayer became the time for action.

D. Arrival of the Betrayer (v. 46)

46 *"Rise, let us go! Here comes my betrayer!"*

Jesus most likely heard the voices and saw the lighted torches of the men who were coming with his *betrayer* to arrest him. He spoke with urgency to awaken and warn the sleeping disciples of their arrival. It is a sobering contrast: the eleven sleeping disciples and Judas, wide awake and anxious to carry out his plot of betrayal. This man, who could have been sent into the world with a message of hope, now sent his Master on a journey toward death.

Jesus, however, had prepared himself for the fast-moving series of events that were about to unfold. His words *rise, let us go!* were not words of resignation or retreat, but a courageous call to face the enemy and carry out his Father's will no matter what the cost.

How to Say It

ABBA *(Aramaic)*. *Ab*-buh.

ABIB. *A*-bib.

CAIAPHAS. *Kay*-uh-fus or *Kye*-uh-fus.

CATHARSIS. kuh-*thar*-sus.

GETHSEMANE. Geth-*sem*-uh-nee (*g* as in *get*).

ISCARIOT. Iss-*care*-c-ut.

JAIRUS. *Jye*-rus or *Jay*-ih-rus.

JERUSALEM. Juh-*roo*-suh-lem.

KIDRON. *Kid*-ron.

LAZARUS. *Laz*-uh-rus.

LEONARDO DA VINCI. Lee-uh-*nard*-oh duh *Vin*-chee.

NICODEMUS. *Nick*-uh-*dee*-mus (strong accent on *dee*).

SANHEDRIN. *San*-huh-drun or San-*heed*-run.

ZEBEDEE. *Zeb*-eh-dee.

THE CITY OF JERUSALEM

Calvary

Garden Tomb

to Bethany
2 miles

Pilate's
Praetorium

Mount of Olives

Garden of
Gethsemane

Temple Area

Palace of Herod

House of Caiaphas

Upper Room

Kidron Valley

Chapter 13

Trial, Crucifixion, and Resurrection

Mark 14:53-65; 15:1, 2, 12-15; Matthew 27:32-50;
Mark 15:42-47; Matthew 28:1-10; 28:16-20

JESUS IS TRIED BEFORE THE SANHEDRIN AND PILATE
(MARK 14:53-65; 15:1, 2, 12-15)

Establishing the Groundwork

Once Jesus had been betrayed by Judas and taken into custody in Gethsemane, the Jewish authorities had to move quickly to carry out their murderous intentions against him. The portions of Scripture examined in this first section show Jesus appearing before two different "courts." The first was the Sanhedrin, the ruling council of religious leaders (though the individuals who comprised it were hardly acting in a "religious" manner). The Sanhedrin had a strong interest in preserving its own power and influence (John 11:47, 48). In their eyes, Jesus was a threat to that power and influence because of his popularity with the general public. He had to be eliminated.

The second court was a political tribunal with a similar set of interests. Pontius Pilate, the Roman governor in Jerusalem, wanted to maintain his position. To do so, he had to keep the peace, particularly among the Jews, or face the consequences from Rome.

In confronting the issue of Jesus, each of these tribunals needed the other. The Sanhedrin could not legally execute a prisoner (John 18:31); only the Romans could do that. On the other hand, Pilate did not have the support of the Jews whom he governed. His success in maintaining control over them depended on the backing of the Sanhedrin. Each party's self-interest was the primary motivation in how each would deal with Jesus. Because of that, justice was almost non-existent throughout the entire process of what can only loosely be called a "trial."

Examining the Text

I. Jesus Before the Sanhedrin (Mark 14:53-65)
A. Condemned by Lies (vv. 53-61a)

53 They took Jesus to the high priest, and all the chief priests, elders and teachers of the law came together.

John 18:13 records that Jesus was first taken to Annas, father-in-law of the *high priest* currently in office, Caiaphas. Perhaps Annas questioned Jesus, while Caiaphas hurriedly assembled the other members of the Sanhedrin (comprised of *chief priests, elders and teachers of the law*) and tried to secure witnesses who would speak against Jesus. Annas had held the office of high priest from AD 6 to 15, but he had been deposed by the Roman authorities. By Jewish custom, however, he was entitled to hold the office for life; so the Jews continued to regard him as high priest even while Caiaphas carried out the official duties of the priesthood. Mark describes Jesus' appearance before Caiaphas and the Sanhedrin.

54 Peter followed him at a distance, right into the courtyard of the high priest. There he sat with the guards and warmed himself at the fire.

Although all the disciples had forsaken Jesus when he was seized in Gethsemane (Mark 14:50), *Peter followed him at a distance.* Perhaps he felt pangs of guilt for having deserted Jesus after declaring so boldly that he would never do so. Whatever his motives, the stage was being set for his denials of Jesus (vv. 66-72). That Peter came *right into the courtyard of the high priest* to see what was happening indicates that the Sanhedrin was meeting in the house of Caiaphas rather than in the usual temple site. This reflects the hastily called nature of the assembly along with the desire of the Sanhedrin to cloak their efforts in secrecy.

55, 56 The chief priests and the whole Sanhedrin were looking for evidence against Jesus so that they could put him to death, but they did not find any. Many testified falsely against him, but their statements did not agree.

It is obvious that those assembled had no intention of giving Jesus a fair trial. Ever since the triumphal entry at the beginning of this week, they had been looking for a way to *put him to death* (Mark 11:18). One can only imagine the frustration of the members of the Sanhedrin at their failure to find witnesses *against Jesus* whose *statements* agreed.

57-59 *Then some stood up and gave this false testimony against him: "We heard him say, 'I will destroy this man-made temple and in three days will build another, not made by man.'" Yet even then their testimony did not agree.*

John's Gospel records the incident that was the basis for the *testimony* offered by these witnesses (John 2:18-21). At the first cleansing of the temple three years earlier, Jesus had been challenged to produce a sign to establish his authority. Jesus replied, "Destroy this temple, and I will raise it again in three days" (John 2:19). He was talking about his death and resurrection (v. 21), but those who heard him (including his disciples) missed the figurative meaning of his reference to "this temple." Whether these witnesses who came before the Sanhedrin differed in their interpretation of Jesus' statement or in the wording of his statement, *their testimony did not agree.*

60 *Then the high priest stood up before them and asked Jesus, "Are you not going to answer? What is this testimony that these men are bringing against you?"*

Caiaphas seems desperate at this point. His plot to do away with Jesus had hardly begun and was already in danger of unraveling because of the lack of integrity in his witnesses. He decided to try to get Jesus to incriminate himself.

61a *But Jesus remained silent and gave no answer.*

Recognizing that the testimony of the self-contradictory witnesses had no merit whatsoever, Jesus *remained silent and gave no answer* to the high priest's questions. Speaking of the Messiah, the prophet Isaiah wrote these words that Jesus certainly fulfilled at this point: "He was oppressed and afflicted, yet he did not open his mouth; he was led like a lamb to the slaughter, and as a sheep before her shearers is silent, so he did not open his mouth" (Isaiah 53:7). At the same time, Jesus knew the high priest was not done with his questioning; he would "open his mouth" at the appropriate time.

B. Convicted by Truth (vv. 61b-65)

61b *Again the high priest asked him, "Are you the Christ, the Son of the Blessed One?"*

Caiaphas decided to try a more direct approach. He used the term *the Blessed One* as a way to refer to God without pronouncing his name, thus avoiding a possible violation of the Third Commandment against "misuse" of the Lord's name (Exodus 20:7). He would not abuse the name of God, but he had no scruples about killing his Son.

⁶² *"I am," said Jesus. "And you will see the Son of Man sitting at the right hand of the Mighty One and coming on the clouds of heaven."*

It was fitting that Jesus respond with silence to questions that were based on the confused statements of contradictory witnesses. But Caiaphas's question about his identity could not be ignored. With the utmost assurance (and knowing full well that his answer would bring a death sentence), Jesus replied *I am.* He also affirmed that he would have an exalted place at the *right hand of* God (alluding to a messianic prophecy in Psalm 110:1) and would one day come *on the clouds of heaven.* His power might not be obvious at this very moment, but it will be some day—even to Caiaphas.

⁶³ *The high priest tore his clothes. "Why do we need any more witnesses?" he asked.*

The tearing of one's *clothes* was a sign of intense grief or distress (as in Numbers 14:6-9; Ezra 9:3; Job 1:20; 2:11, 12). The *high priest* pretended to be overwhelmed with horror at a man who would be so presumptuous as to claim to be divine. For him, there was no further *need* for *witnesses* when Jesus' own words could be used against him.

⁶⁴ *"You have heard the blasphemy. What do you think?" They all condemned him as worthy of death.*

Blasphemy is deliberate disrespect for God or anything divine or sacred. To the Jews, any human claiming to be God was both a deceiver and a blasphemer and was *worthy of death,* according to the law of Moses (Leviticus 24:16). The members of the Sanhedrin, however, did not consider the possibility that Jesus might be speaking the truth. They did not ask if he had any defense concerning this charge. They did not call any of the hundreds of witnesses who could have testified that his miraculous works substantiated such a claim. They had found a pretext for condemning Jesus to death, and that was all that mattered. Both of the charges brought against Jesus (temple destroyer and messianic pretender) were later used as taunts against him when he was on the cross (Mark 15:29-32).

⁶⁵ *Then some began to spit at him; they blindfolded him, struck him with their fists, and said, "Prophesy!" And the guards took him and beat him.*

Since the *guards* are mentioned separately at the end of this verse, it appears that some members of the Sanhedrin, who had pronounced the "guilty" verdict in the previous verse, now engaged in verbal and physical abuse of Jesus. *Some began to spit at him.* Then *they blindfolded him, struck him with their fists,* and commanded that Jesus *prophesy* by identifying those who struck him.

II. Jesus Before Pilate (Mark 15:1, 2, 12-15)
A. Jesus' Courage (vv. 1, 2)

¹ Very early in the morning, the chief priests, with the elders, the teachers of the law and the whole Sanhedrin, reached a decision. They bound Jesus, led him away and handed him over to Pilate.

The members of the *Sanhedrin* had accomplished the first part of their plan by getting Jesus to "confess" to being the Son of God, which they considered blasphemy—a capital crime. The next step was to take him from the residence of Caiaphas to the Roman governor (or more exactly, "prefect"), Pontius *Pilate.* The Jewish religious leaders were not allowed to execute anyone. Thus the Sanhedrin needed Pilate's approval to carry out their plans against Jesus.

Roman officials were known to be early risers, preferring to finish their business by noon and leaving the remainder of the day for personal pursuits. Thus the Jewish leaders brought Jesus to Pilate *very early in the morning* (it was now Friday). That they had *bound* Jesus may have been an attempt on their part to influence Pilate by every possible implication of criminal guilt.

² "Are you the king of the Jews?" asked Pilate.
"Yes, it is as you say," Jesus replied.

John's Gospel gives a more detailed account of the exchange between Pilate and Jesus (John 18:28-38). Jesus affirmed that he was indeed a *king*, but that his kingdom was "not of this world" (v. 36). He desired to rule the hearts of men by his proclamation of the truth.

At some point during the proceedings of the day, Pilate sent Jesus to Herod Antipas, who was "tetrarch of Galilee" (Luke 3:1) and was in Jerusalem for the occasion of the Passover. The chief priests and teachers of the law were present to continue their accusations against Jesus, but Jesus offered no response. After Herod and the soldiers with him mocked and ridiculed Jesus, they sent him back to Pilate (Luke 23:8-12), who found himself once again in the middle of a dilemma he had hoped to avoid.

B. Pilate's Cowardice (vv. 12-15)

¹² "What shall I do, then, with the one you call the king of the Jews?" Pilate asked them.

Pilate believed Jesus to be innocent of any crime deserving death (Luke 23:4; John 18:38), but he did not want to cause any kind of disturbance among the Jews. A custom observed at every Passover involved releasing a prisoner as a kind of "Passover gift" to the people. Pilate presented Jesus to the assembled crowd alongside a murderer named Barabbas, assuming that the people would insist upon Jesus' release. And perhaps they would have, had it not been for the influence of the chief priests, who "stirred up the crowd to have Pilate release Barabbas instead" (Mark 15:11). Aware that "it was out of envy that the chief priests had handed Jesus over to him" (v. 10), Pilate attempted to persuade the crowd to reconsider their decision.

¹³ "Crucify him!" they shouted.

Less than a week earlier, the crowds gathered for the Passover had hailed Jesus' entry into Jerusalem. Now they called for his execution!

¹⁴ "Why? What crime has he committed?" asked Pilate.
But they shouted all the louder, "Crucify him!"

Pilate's question *What crime has he committed?* reflected his understanding that Jesus' accusers had been unable to prove any of their accusations against him. A death sentence was completely uncalled for. But those in the crowd ignored the question; they simply became more raucous in their demand for Jesus' execution.

¹⁵ Wanting to satisfy the crowd, Pilate released Barabbas to them. He had Jesus flogged, and handed him over to be crucified.

Here one sees the convergence of the self-interest of two parties. The Jewish leaders wanted to get rid of a troublemaker who had a knack for stepping on toes and attracting followers. Pilate wanted to keep the peace and maintain his position of power. In between those two concerns stood one expendable man—Jesus.

Of course, one should not think of Jesus as a helpless victim in all of this. He was the one figure in this entire drama who was not motivated by his own interests. Perhaps even at this point he continued to pray, "Not what I will, but what you will."

JESUS IS CRUCIFIED (MATTHEW 27:32-50)

Establishing the Groundwork

The Romans were not the inventors of crucifixion as a means of capital punishment, but by the first century AD, it had become their favorite method of execution. The Jews were no strangers to crucifixion, for thousands of their countrymen had been crucified since Rome took control of Palestine. In Jesus' day it may not have been an uncommon sight to see the body of a rebellious Jew hanging on a Roman cross alongside a road in Palestine. For the Romans, and in a sense for the Jews, Jesus' death was business as usual.

From the standpoint of God's plan for the salvation of the world, however, Jesus' death was anything but "usual." On the cross, Jesus paid a debt he did not owe on behalf of sinners who owed a debt they could not pay.

Examining the Text

I. Solemn Preparations (Matthew 27:32-34)
A. Help Given (v. 32)

³² As they were going out, they met a man from Cyrene, named Simon, and they forced him to carry the cross.

Prior to being led to the site where he was crucified, Jesus had endured a significant amount of abuse, both physical and verbal (Matthew 27:26-31), from the soldiers who had been placed in charge of him. Weakened by the severity of the earlier flogging (v. 26), Jesus apparently fell under the weight of his cross at some point on the way to the crucifixion site. Men condemned to death were usually forced to carry a beam of their own cross, often weighing thirty or forty pounds, to the place of crucifixion. John informs us that Jesus too started out carrying his cross (John 19:17).

A man from Cyrene, named Simon, was *forced* by the soldiers to help carry the cross the rest of the way. Cyrene was a city of Libya on the northern coast of Africa. Simon was most likely a Jew who had come to Jerusalem for the Passover. We do not know if he became a follower of Jesus, but his children were well known to many when Mark wrote his Gospel (Mark 15:21).

B. Help Refused (vv. 33, 34)

³³ They came to a place called Golgotha (which means The Place of the Skull).

The word *Golgotha* is an Aramaic word meaning *the Place of the Skull*. The precise location of the crucifixion has long been the subject of much discussion. Many scholars believe that the most probable location is a spot outside the northern walls of Jerusalem near the Damascus Gate. It is a hill with a number of caves that give it the appearance of eye sockets in a skull.

³⁴ There they offered Jesus wine to drink, mixed with gall; but after tasting it, he refused to drink it.

The *wine* that was *offered* to Jesus was a diluted sour wine. It was *mixed with gall*, which apparently was some kind of anesthetic drug intended to lessen the pain of crucifixion. (Tradition says that a charitable organization of women in Jerusalem usually provided this to those about to be crucified.) When Jesus tasted this, however, *he refused to drink it*. He chose to endure all of the agony of the cross and to do so with a clear mind. The cross was the reason he had come to the world, and he intended to let nothing affect in any way the fulfillment of that purpose.

II. Public Shame (Matthew 27:35-38)
A. Clothing Removed (vv. 35, 36)

35 When they had crucified him, they divided up his clothes by casting lots.

Part of the "spoils" of guard duty at a crucifixion was the right to confiscate a condemned man's *clothes*. John's account tells us that there were four soldiers in charge of the crucifixion of Jesus. (This was the usual number assigned to such a duty.) They were the ones who *divided up his clothes by casting lots*, which refers to some chance activity by which a decision could be reached, whether by throwing dice, flipping a coin, or some other way (John 19:23). Jesus' clothing was thus divided four ways, except for the seamless undergarment, a type of shirt that reached from the neck to the knees or ankles. Because of its value, it was not torn; the soldiers cast lots to see which one of them could claim it (John 19:23, 24). These actions fulfilled the prophecy found in Psalm 22:18, which is part of a messianic Psalm that foretold several of the indignities to be experienced by the Messiah at the hands of his enemies.

36 And sitting down, they kept watch over him there.

Death by crucifixion was generally a slow, torturous process. The victims often lived hours or even days in agony. To prevent friends of the victims from trying to rescue them, the soldiers assigned to the crucifixion *kept* a constant *watch* at the site. Of course, had Jesus wanted to be rescued from this ordeal, he could have brought this about long before now (Matthew 26:53, 54).

B. Treated Like a Criminal (vv. 37, 38)

37 Above his head they placed the written charge against him: THIS IS JESUS, THE KING OF THE JEWS.

In the case of prominent prisoners, a sign was affixed to the cross, indicating the crime for which the person was being crucified. It served to warn passersby not to contemplate such behavior. John 19:20 tells us that the message was *written* in three languages: Aramaic (the language of the Jews), Latin (the official language of the Roman government), and Greek (the world language of commerce and culture). Ironically, the sign above Jesus' head proclaimed, not a heinous crime but a wondrous truth about him.

To the Jewish leaders, the words on the sign sounded more like a tribute than an accusation. They tried to persuade Pilate to change the wording, but Pilate, perhaps as a demonstration of his disgust with the leaders, refused to do so (John 19:21, 22).

38 Two robbers were crucified with him, one on his right and one on his left.

It was the practice of the Romans to hold condemned criminals in prison until there were several who could be *crucified* at the same time, thereby requiring only one set of guards (rather than a set for each victim). Because the Jewish leaders insisted that Pilate execute Jesus without delay, the soldiers had to work with the number they had available at the time—in this case, only *two robbers*. The leaders would not have been unhappy with this arrangement, because it suggested that Jesus was a common criminal, no better than these robbers. This too fulfilled prophecy (Isaiah 53:12).

III. Hateful Scorn (Matthew 27:39-44)
A. From the Crowd (vv. 39, 40)

39 Those who passed by hurled insults at him, shaking their heads

The Romans designed crucifixion to be a spectator event. Crosses were placed next to major highways, often on a hill, for all to see. The intent was to draw a large crowd who would witness an excruciating and humiliating death for the worst kind of criminals. The crowd was encouraged to participate through mocking and derision.

40 . . . and saying, "You who are going to destroy the temple and build it in three days, save yourself! Come down from the cross, if you are the Son of God!"

The testimony in the trial before Caiaphas that Jesus had claimed he would *destroy the temple and build it in three days* had been so confused and contradictory that it was completely worthless. But it was good material to use at the cross as part of the public ridicule of Jesus. Ironically, those who used these words as an insult were fulfilling Jesus' original words about destroying the temple, because "the temple he had spoken of was his body" (John 2:21). In words reminiscent of Satan's language during the temptations in the desert after Jesus' baptism, the crowd chided Jesus to *come down from the cross, if you are the Son of God.*

B. From the Leaders (vv. 41-43)

⁴¹ *In the same way the chief priests, the teachers of the law and the elders mocked him.*

The chief priests, the teachers of the law and the elders had been bitter enemies of Jesus throughout his ministry. Jesus had warned his disciples that these three groups of leaders would be instrumental in putting him to death (Matthew 16:21). Finally, these leaders thought, they had their nemesis where they wanted him.

⁴² *"He saved others," they said, "but he can't save himself! He's the King of Israel! Let him come down now from the cross, and we will believe in him.*

He saved others, . . . but he can't save himself! With these words Jesus' enemies scorned his ministry of healing and his claim to be the Savior sent from Heaven. The one who promised and provided to others salvation from sickness, suffering, and even death was now unable to provide it for himself.

Another irony appears here. The religious leaders of Jesus' day claimed that they would believe in him if he would *come down now from the cross*; Christians believe in him precisely because he did not. Christians see Jesus' refusal to come down from the cross, not as a sign of weakness, but as the surest evidence of his determination to carry out the plan of God.

⁴³ *"He trusts in God. Let God rescue him now if he wants him, for he said, 'I am the Son of God.'"*

In their taunts, the religious leaders (perhaps knowingly) paraphrased Psalm 22:8. As previously noted, this Psalm is one of the great messianic Psalms. Jesus himself would soon quote from this Psalm also (Matthew 27:46). Previously the leaders had taunted Jesus because he apparently did not have the power to come down from the cross. Now they ridiculed him as a false teacher because God would not intervene miraculously to save him. The presence of irony in these words should once again be highlighted: Jesus' enemies took his death as a sign that God had rejected him; Christians know that by his death Jesus was accomplishing the will of God.

C. From the Robbers (v. 44)

44 In the same way the robbers who were crucified with him also heaped insults on him.

The robbers who were crucified with Jesus would have liked nothing better than for him to demonstrate divine power and show that he was the King of Israel by destroying the Romans. Such an act might result in their rescue as well. But Jesus was not that kind of King, and he did not come to establish that kind of kingdom. Luke's account records that one of the robbers became convinced of the truth of Jesus' claims and was promised a place in paradise (Luke 23:39-43). Perhaps he was persuaded by the divine power Jesus demonstrated in his prayer of forgiveness for those who crucified him (Luke 23:34).

IV. Jesus' Death (Matthew 27:45-50)
A. Hours of Darkness (v. 45)

45 From the sixth hour until the ninth hour darkness came over all the land.

According to Mark's account, Jesus was crucified at the "third hour" (Mark 15:25), which would have been, by the Jewish reckoning of time, at 9:00 in the morning. The *darkness* occurred *from the sixth hour until the ninth hour* (from noon until 3:00 in the afternoon)—the time when the sun should have been the brightest.

It is not clear what territory is included in the phrase *all the land.* In any case, the darkness was of a miraculous nature. Perhaps God was replying to the insults to his Son by silencing the reviling crowd.

B. Cry of Agony (vv. 46-49)

46 About the ninth hour Jesus cried out in a loud voice, "Eloi, Eloi, lama sabachthani?"—which means, "My God, my God, why have you forsaken me?"

Jesus died at *about the ninth hour* after six agonizing hours on the cross. In his final moments he cried out (in Aramaic) the lament from Psalm 22:1, *My God, my God, why have you forsaken me?* Many have wondered how Jesus could have spoken such words as these. Surely the Son of God knew that his Father would never abandon him. And yet the prophet Isaiah did foresee a tension between Father and Son at the cross, as the Messiah "carried our sorrows" and was "stricken by God, smitten by him, and afflicted" (Isaiah 53:4). Jesus' cry was a profound expression of suffering that is beyond our comprehension.

It is possible, however, that Jesus was thinking about more than just the opening verse of Psalm 22. After David (the author) described the misery he was suffering at the hands of men and voiced his despair with God for not responding quickly, he still expressed his belief that God would eventually rescue him (vv. 22-25). In the midst of his agony on the cross, Jesus still knew that God would "rescue" him on the third day.

47 When some of those standing there heard this, they said, "He's calling Elijah."

At this point in his crucifixion, Jesus would have been extremely weak. His tongue was likely swollen and his throat dry. His lungs would have been struggling for air, making it difficult for him to speak. His words *Eloi, Eloi* were probably spoken in such whispered tones that they sounded to the onlookers like the name *Elijah*. The general expectation of a return of Elijah in connection with the coming of the Messiah may have influenced the hearers' thinking.

48 Immediately one of them ran and got a sponge. He filled it with wine vinegar, put it on a stick, and offered it to Jesus to drink.

John's account notes that Jesus said at one point, "I am thirsty" (John 19:28). Apparently this occurred just prior to the humane act recorded in this verse. In this case, Jesus accepted the *wine vinegar* that was *offered* to him because it was not drugged as was the previous mixture that was offered to him (Matthew 27:34). It would ease the pain of Jesus' throat enough for him to speak clearly his final words before he died.

49 The rest said, "Now leave him alone. Let's see if Elijah comes to save him."

While one person gave Jesus what little help he could, others continued their taunting.

C. Moment of Death (v. 50)

50 And when Jesus had cried out again in a loud voice, he gave up his spirit.

Now that his throat was moistened enough for him to speak for a few moments longer, Jesus *cried out again in a loud voice*, "It is finished" (John 19:30), and then, "Father, into your hands I commit my spirit" (Luke 23:46). Jesus then *gave up his spirit*, highlighting once more the fundamental truth that men did not take the life of Jesus; he gave his life (John 10:18).

JESUS IS BURIED (MARK 15:42-47)

Establishing the Groundwork

After Jesus died, the crowd that was present most likely dispersed rather quickly. Besides the soldiers in charge of the crucifixion, "many women" who were devoted followers of Jesus remained in the vicinity, though at a distance (Matthew 27:55, 56). We are not told about the presence of any of the 12 disciples at the crucifixion except for John, to whom Jesus had entrusted the care of his mother (John 19:25-27). None of the Gospel accounts includes a complete listing of those who were present, so we do not know whether others of the disciples were there or not.

The Jewish leaders who had worked so intently to arrange for Jesus' death were just as vigilant about making sure his body was removed from the cross that same day (Friday). The next day was a Sabbath (John 19:31), and they did not want the bodies left on the crosses during the Sabbath. No doubt they were also concerned that some of Jesus' disciples might try to steal the body and create rumors of a "resurrection." Later these leaders created their own account of a stolen body as a way of explaining away the resurrection (Matthew 28:11-15).

The Gospel writers were very careful to record exactly what happened to Jesus' body after he died. It seems they wanted to establish for posterity the essential facts of the gospel message as later defined by Paul: "Christ died for our sins, . . . he was buried, . . . [and] was raised on the third day" (1 Corinthians 15:3, 4).

Examining the Text

I. Claiming Jesus' Body (Mark 15:42-45)
A. Joseph's Action (vv. 42, 43)

⁴² It was Preparation Day (that is, the day before the Sabbath). So as evening approached,

The Jewish day ran from sunset to sunset. The phrase *as evening approached* would thus refer to sunset on Friday. Jesus died at around the "ninth hour" (Mark 15:34-37), which was 3:00 in the afternoon, so it was during the three hours or so between that time and sunset that arrangements had to be made for his burial.

The day before the Sabbath was called *Preparation Day.* This term referred to the preparations that were necessary to observe properly the approaching Sabbath. Work such as cooking and shopping was not permitted on the

Sabbath; so families had to take care of those duties the day before. *Preparation* was as common a word to designate this day as "Friday" is for us. Mark paused to explain this term for his non-Jewish readers.

> **43 Joseph of Arimathea, a prominent member of the Council, who was himself waiting for the kingdom of God, went boldly to Pilate and asked for Jesus' body.**

Joseph of Arimathea displayed true courage in going *to Pilate* and asking *for Jesus' body* that he might see to his burial. Roman magistrates were not in the habit of releasing the bodies of convicted criminals, often preferring to have them simply tossed into a dump. Joseph is described as *a prominent member of the Council,* or the Sanhedrin. He was, however, quite different from the majority of the council, who had given their approval to putting Jesus to death. Luke notes that Joseph "had not consented to their decision and action" (Luke 23:51). Perhaps he chose not to attend the hastily called meeting described in Mark 14:55, at which "all" who were present condemned Jesus to death (v. 64). Or perhaps his sentiments were known by Caiaphas and he was not invited. John records that Joseph had been "a disciple of Jesus, but secretly because he feared the Jews" (John 19:38). Now, however, he came forward, risking association with the very one his colleagues had condemned to death.

It is also noted that Joseph *was himself waiting for the kingdom of God.* Perhaps he, like other followers of Jesus, had been waiting for him to make clear the nature of the kingdom he had said was near. That Jesus had suffered such a humiliating death may have left Joseph's faith in some measure of disarray, but he did not let that keep him from paying proper respect to Jesus' body.

B. Pilate's Amazement (v. 44)

44 And when Jesus had cried out again in a loud voice, he gave up his spirit.

Weakened by the rush of events and harsh mistreatment prior to being nailed to the cross, not to mention the spiritual suffering he had experienced, Jesus had died in the relatively short time of about six hours. Victims of crucifixion sometimes survived much longer than this (as much as two or three days), so Pilate's being *surprised* is understandable. Apparently not many minutes had passed since he had given the order to break the legs of the three men who had been crucified. He did not know that Jesus was *already dead* when the soldiers had been told to complete the execution (John 19:32-34). To verify what Joseph was telling him, Pilate *asked* the *centurion* (likely the one who had acknowledged Jesus to be the Son of God, according to Mark 15:39) if this were true.

C. Pilate's Agreement (v. 45)

45 When he learned from the centurion that it was so, he gave the body to Joseph.

The release of the body of someone who had been condemned for treason (John 19:12), especially to an individual who was not an immediate relative, was quite unusual. It is another indication of Pilate's awareness that Jesus was innocent. It is also part of the evidence that Jesus really did die; he did not merely "swoon" or faint as some have alleged.

II. Caring for Jesus' Body (Mark 15:46, 47)
A. Overseen by Joseph (v. 46)

46 So Joseph bought some linen cloth, took down the body, wrapped it in the linen, and placed it in a tomb cut out of rock. Then he rolled a stone against the entrance of the tomb.

It was still Friday afternoon, so there was time for Joseph to purchase some *linen cloth* in which to wrap the *body* of Jesus. Joseph was a "rich man" (Matthew 27:57), so he may have sent a servant to do this. Nicodemus, another follower of Jesus who was also a member of the Sanhedrin (John 3:1), provided spices for the burial (John 19:39, 40). Joseph also provided a *tomb*, which had recently been cut out of the rock in a garden near the site of the crucifixion (Matthew 27:60; John 19:41). They *placed* Jesus' body in the tomb, then they *rolled a* huge *stone*, shaped like a wheel, in front of the *entrance* to close the tomb and protect it from marauders or animals.

B. Observed by Women (v. 47)

47 Mary Magdalene and Mary the mother of Joses saw where he was laid.

As noted earlier, Matthew records that "many women" who had followed Jesus from Galilee observed his crucifixion "from a distance" (Matthew 27:55). Of these at least the two women named *Mary*, mentioned by Mark, remained to observe the burial. Mark earlier describes the second Mary as also "the mother of James the younger" (Mark 15:40), who was most likely the same person as "James son of Alphaeus," one of Jesus' twelve disciples (Mark 3:18). Luke notes that a larger group of these Galilean women witnessed the burial (Luke 23:55). This refutes the idea proposed by some skeptics of the resurrection that the women did not know where Jesus had been buried and thus went to the wrong tomb on the morning Jesus arose.

JESUS' RESURRECTION (MATTHEW 28:1-10)

Establishing the Groundwork

Following the burial of Jesus, those women who witnessed it and took note of the location returned to their quarters to prepare spices and other items that they would use to complete the burial process. They would do that on Sunday, after the Sabbath was over (Luke 23:55, 56). The day after the crucifixion, the chief priests and Pharisees persuaded Pilate to station Roman guards at the tomb of Jesus, in order to keep his disciples from stealing the body and then spreading news of an alleged "resurrection" (Matthew 27:62-66). The scene was being set for a most astonishing discovery.

Examining the Text

I. Good News (Matthew 28:1-7)
A. God Has Acted (vv. 1-4)

¹ After the Sabbath, at dawn on the first day of the week, Mary Magdalene and the other Mary went to look at the tomb.

Matthew names two of the women who went to the *tomb* of Jesus *on the first day of the week.* They are the same women he cited earlier as having accompanied Jesus from Galilee "to care for his needs" (Matthew 27:55) and having witnessed the burial of Jesus (Matthew 27:61). *The other Mary* would therefore be "Mary the mother of James and Joses" (Matthew 27:56). Perhaps during the Passover these women and others from Galilee had been staying at Bethany where Martha, Mary, and Lazarus lived.

Mark notes that the two Marys were accompanied by a woman named Salome (Mark 16:1), who may well have been the same woman Matthew identifies as the mother of James and John (Matthew 27:56). Luke adds the name of Joanna (Luke 24:10). All of these women and possibly others were planning to pay due respect to their Master (Mark 16:1).

These women went to the tomb expecting to care for a dead body; they were not expecting a resurrection. As they neared the tomb, they suddenly realized that they would need help rolling the large stone away from the entrance (Mark 16:3). But God had a means of entry already planned for them.

² There was a violent earthquake, for an angel of the Lord came down from heaven and, going to the tomb, rolled back the stone and sat on it.

Matthew also records how "the earth shook" after Jesus died (Matthew 27:51). Here he mentions the *violent earthquake* that accompanied Jesus' resurrection. The precise time of the resurrection is not indicated in any of the Gospel accounts, but it is generally assumed that the descent of *an angel of the Lord*, the earthquake, and the resurrection were nearly simultaneous in occurrence and that all of this happened while the women were making their way to the *tomb*. The *stone* was not moved to let Jesus out; he later demonstrated that he could pass through walls (John 20:19, 26). Instead, it was moved to let the witnesses in so that they could testify that the tomb was empty.

3 His appearance was like lightning, and his clothes were white as snow.

The angel's *appearance* confirmed his identity as a being who had come from the presence of God. Mark describes him as "a young man dressed in a white robe" (Mark 16:5). Luke's account records the presence of "two men in clothes that gleamed like lightning" (Luke 24:4). Apparently Matthew and Mark mention only the angel who spoke. One is reminded of the appearance of "an angel of the Lord" to the shepherds near Bethlehem to announce the birth of Jesus, at which time "the glory of the Lord shone around them" (Luke 2:9). The radiant glory displayed at the tomb was intended to declare, along with the earthquake, that God's power had raised Jesus to life.

4 The guards were so afraid of him that they shook and became like dead men.

The sight of the angel terrified the Roman *guards*, who for a moment *became like dead men*. However, they must have regained their composure quickly and then fled; because the other Gospel accounts indicate that the tomb was unguarded by the time the women arrived. God's power had provided, not only the removal of the heavy stone, but also unobstructed access to the tomb.

B. Christ Is Risen (vv. 5-7)

5 The angel said to the women, "Do not be afraid, for I know that you are looking for Jesus, who was crucified.

By the time *the women* arrived at the tomb, *the angel* was no longer sitting on the stone (v. 2). Luke simply states that they found the stone removed, entered the tomb, and discovered that the body of Jesus was not there (Luke 24:2, 3). It was then that the "two men in clothes that gleamed like lightning" were observed in the darkness of the tomb (Luke 24:4). One of them spoke, not to respond to anything the women had said, but to address their unspoken fears and questions. He whose appearance had terrified the Roman guards now spoke comfort to the friends of Jesus: *Do not be afraid.*

6 "He is not here; he has risen, just as he said. Come and see the place where he lay.

Jesus had predicted his resurrection on more than one occasion (Mark 8:31; 9:30, 31; 10:32-34). Even the enemies of Jesus knew about this prediction (Matthew 27:63). The angel reminded the women of Jesus' own words, then invited them to *see* some (but not yet all) of the evidence for themselves. The tomb was empty—the *place* that had never been used as a tomb before was no longer being used as one now.

7 "Then go quickly and tell his disciples: 'He has risen from the dead and is going ahead of you into Galilee. There you will see him.' Now I have told you."

Matthew 26:32 records Jesus' prediction to the *disciples* at the Last Supper that he would "go ahead of [them] into Galilee" after his resurrection. Jesus would indeed meet them there at a later time (Matthew 28:16), but some important events in and around Jerusalem would occur first (John 20:19-31)—some that very day. Mark records that Jesus specifically mentioned telling Peter (Mark 16:7), perhaps to let him know that his denials of Jesus could be forgiven. They need not separate him from fellowship with the risen Lord.

Having seen the evidence that the disciples had not yet seen, these women were commissioned as the first human witnesses of the great news of the resurrection. Their testimony, however, would be met initially with disbelief (Luke 24:10, 11).

II. Glorious Sight (Matthew 28:8-10)
A. Mixed Emotions (v. 8)

8 So the women hurried away from the tomb, afraid yet filled with joy, and ran to tell his disciples.

It requires little imagination to understand the mixture of emotions within the *women*: *afraid yet filled with joy*. Fear forbade them to tell anyone along the way about the resurrection, but joy led them to seek out the *disciples* and convey their message. The morning of Jesus' resurrection included frequent running (see also John 20:2-4), because it was filled with excitement over the most awesome demonstration of God's power since the creation.

B. Memorable Encounter (vv. 9, 10)

9 Suddenly Jesus met them. "Greetings," he said. They came to him, clasped his feet and worshiped him.

We do not know how far the women had to go until they reached the disciples, or at what point in their journey *Jesus met them*. Peter and John must have arrived at the tomb soon after they left (John 20:3-9). Mary Magdalene followed them, then remained alone at the tomb. There Jesus appeared to her (John 20:10-17). It must have been shortly afterward that he appeared to the other women. They *clasped his feet and worshiped him*. Thus the sense of touch as well as the senses of sight and hearing testified that Jesus was actually alive and present with them (note also Luke 24:36-39; John 20:24-29).

The sequence of Jesus' appearances following his resurrection, as reported in the four Gospels, can be a bit confusing. The following scenario seeks to arrange these in order, taking into consideration the geography of the area in and around Jerusalem.

After the women who came to the tomb saw that the stone was rolled away, it appears that Mary Magdalene left the group and went in search of Peter and John, who were not staying with the other disciples (John 20:1, 2). The other women, in the meantime, had entered the tomb and received instructions from the angel to take the news of Jesus' resurrection to the disciples. As they were leaving to carry out these instructions, Peter and John, alerted by Mary Magdalene, were approaching the tomb from another direction. After examining the empty tomb, they returned to their homes (John 20:10). Mary, exhausted by this time, was not able to keep up with Peter and John, and arrived at the tomb after they had left. While she tarried at the tomb, overcome by her emotions, Jesus appeared to her. This was his first appearance after his resurrection, according to Mark 16:9. After this brief encounter with Mary, Jesus then appeared to the women as they were hurrying on their way to find the disciples.

> [10] *Then Jesus said to them, "Do not be afraid. Go and tell my brothers to go to Galilee; there they will see me."*

The angel's earlier message (vv. 5, 7) was now reinforced with the highest possible authority. That Jesus referred to his disciples as *my brothers* speaks of his tenderness toward them. It also foreshadowed the special relationship that all future believers would have with him (Hebrews 2:11, 12).

It is clear from the Gospel records that the disciples were highly skeptical upon first hearing the news of Jesus' resurrection. Thomas is often faulted for his refusal to believe until he could see the evidence with his own eyes, but all of the disciples acted in a similar manner. This skepticism, coupled with the desire to see irrefutable evidence that Jesus was alive, gives us greater confidence in the reality of the resurrection. Consider that in just the few weeks between Passover and Pentecost, these disciples were transformed from cowering behind locked doors (John 20:19) to preaching fearlessly in Jerusalem (Acts 2:14, 32; 4:13; 5:41, 42). Only the reality of a risen Savior and the confidence inspired by him can explain such a dramatic turnaround.

JESUS' GREAT COMMISSION (MATTHEW 28:16-20)

Establishing the Groundwork

Jesus had told his 11 disciples, both directly (Matthew 26:32) and indirectly through the testimony of the women to whom he appeared after his resurrection (Matthew 28:10), that he would go before them into Galilee where they would see him. In some manner not recorded in the Scriptures, he had set a time and place for the meeting, though we can surmise that it would have occurred approximately ten days after the resurrection. This is because Jesus had appeared to the group of 11, minus Thomas, on the day of his resurrection, then a week later he had appeared to them when Thomas was present (John 20:19, 24-26). Only after this did the 11 make the trip to Galilee, which would have taken about three days, where Jesus appeared to 7 of them one morning on the shore of the Sea of Galilee (John 21:1-24).

Each of the four Gospels, along with Acts, gives a version of what is usually called Jesus' "Great Commission" (Matthew 28:16-20; Mark 16:15, 16; Luke 24:45-49; John 20:21-23; Acts 1:7, 8). Matthew's version is probably the most frequently quoted. Although this commission was originally addressed to the first-century followers of Jesus, it falls by implication upon every Christian to hear it and obey it.

Examining the Text

I. Christ's Authority (Matthew 28:16-18)
A. Appointment Kept (vv. 16, 17)

16 Then the eleven disciples went to Galilee, to the mountain where Jesus had told them to go.

It was really only fitting for the *eleven disciples* to go to *Galilee*. Galilee was the place where they had been called to service, trained for service, and sent forth in service. Now they were being summoned to Galilee to a new phase of service for their Master. The designated *mountain* is not identified in the Gospels.

17 When they saw him, they worshiped him; but some doubted.

The 11 disciples had come to believe in Jesus' resurrection while in Jerusalem, thus they were prepared to worship him when he appeared before them on the mountain. Apparently other disciples were permitted to join the 11 on this occasion, for Matthew notes that *some doubted.* The apostle Paul states that following his resurrection, Jesus once appeared to as many as "five hundred of the brothers" at one time (1 Corinthians 15:6). This gathering may have been that occasion. Those who doubted at this point may have included followers of Jesus from Galilee who had not seen him since his resurrection. These probably required more convincing before they were sure this was Jesus—but then so had the 11 disciples.

B. Authority Declared (v. 18)

18 Then Jesus came to them and said, "All authority in heaven and on earth has been given to me.

Jesus had given clear evidence of his *authority* again and again throughout his ministry. Yet there was something climactic about his declaration here on the mountain in Galilee. He was about to return to "the glory [he] had with [the Father] before the world began" (John 17:5). By virtue of his resurrection, Jesus' identity as "Lord and Christ" (Acts 2:36) now took on an even greater significance than when the disciples called him "Lord" (John 13:13) or when Peter confessed him as "the Christ" (Matthew 16:16).

That Jesus possesses all authority is not just a doctrinal position; it has a practical and daily application to our lives. It challenges us to look within to see if in our hearts we truly honor Jesus as the one with all authority. Saving faith is not just believing facts about Jesus, but accepting him as the supreme authority in our lives.

II. The Church's Priority (Matthew 28:19, 20)
A. The Great Commission (vv. 19, 20a)

19, 20a "Therefore go and make disciples of all nations, baptizing them in the name of the Father and of the Son and of the Holy Spirit, and teaching them to obey everything I have commanded you.

We call Jesus' instructions for evangelizing the world the "Great Commission," for these constitute the "marching orders" for the church. We are to *make disciples of all nations.* There are no national, ethnic, or racial prerequisites to becoming a follower of Jesus, only a wholehearted commitment to Christ. Those willing to make such a commitment are to be immersed in water, which is the actual meaning of the Greek word rendered *baptizing*. When applied to a repentant believer, it washes away sins (Acts 22:16) and then empowers the person for Christian living with the "gift of the Holy Spirit" (Acts 2:38; Romans 8:11-13).

That baptism is to be done *in the name of the Father and of the Son and of the Holy Spirit* implies that the act is to be carried out under their authority. It also suggests that through baptism a repentant believer is brought into a special relationship with the Father, the Son, and the Holy Spirit.

The task of evangelism is not complete when individuals rise from the waters of baptism. There remains a lifetime of *teaching them to obey everything* Jesus the Lord has *commanded*, for the Word of God has a depth that is never exhausted; and our lives are always in need of constant challenge and growth.

B. The Guiding Presence (v. 20b)

20b **"And surely I am with you always, to the very end of the age."**

When God commissioned Moses, he said he would be with him (Exodus 3:12). When God called Joshua, he gave the same promise (Joshua 1:5). When God called spokesmen such as Jeremiah, he reassured them with these same words (Jeremiah 1:8). Here Jesus gives the promise of his presence to his disciples as they faithfully carry out his marching orders *to the very end of the age*. This promise brings to a glorious climax the meaning and message of the name given to Jesus at the very beginning of Matthew's account: Immanuel, meaning "God with us" (Matthew 1:23). It is a thrilling thought indeed—that *surely* he will continue to be *with* us until we are able to be with him.

How to Say It

ALEXANDER. Al-ex-*an*-der.

ANNAS. *An*-nus.

ARAMAIC. *Air*-uh-*may*-ik (strong accent on *may*).

ARIMATHEA. *Air*-uh-muh-*thee*-uh (*th* as in *thin*; strong accent on *thee*).

BARABBAS. Buh-*rab*-us.

BLASPHEMY. *blas*-fuh-me.

CAIAPHAS. *Kay*-uh-fus or *Kye*-uh-fus.

CYRENE. Sigh-*ree*-nee.

DAMASCUS. Duh-*mass*-kus.

ELOI, ELOI, LAMA SABACHTHANI *(Aramaic).*
        Ee-*lo*-eye, Ee-*lo*-eye, *lah*-mah suh-*back*-thuh-nee.

GALILEE. *Gal*-uh-lee.

GETHSEMANE. Geth-*sem*-uh-nee (G as in *get*).

GOLGOTHA. *Gahl*-guh-thuh.

HEROD ANTIPAS. *Hair*-ud *An*-tih-pus.

ISAIAH. Eye-*zay*-uh.

ISRAEL. *Iz*-ray-el.

JERUSALEM. Juh-*roo*-suh-lem.

JOANNA. Joe-*an*-uh.

JOSES. *Jo*-sez.

MESSIAH. Meh-*sigh*-uh.

PENTECOST. *Pent*-ih-kost.

PONTIUS PILATE. *Pon*-shus or *Pon*-ti-us *Pie*-lut.

RUFUS. *Roo*-fus.

SALOME. Suh-*lo*-me.

SANHEDRIN. San-*huh*-drun or San-*heed*-run.

SIMON. *Sigh*-mun.

TETRARCH. *Teh*-trark or *Tee*-trark.